A Journey Ar[illegible]ver

Dan Santillo is a professional photographer based in Neath in South Wales specialising [illegible]
Astrophotography of Gower and the Brecon Beacons as well as further afield.

After completing a degree in Satellite Communications, Dan worked for 7 years as a so[illegible] engineer. In 2003, he spent three weeks on a road trip in Canada with friends - the scenery and the outdoor life made him realise that he couldn't spend his days working in an air-conditioned office. Back from holiday, he set himself a date 18 months in the future and on that date quit his job and began his career as a professional photographer.

He loves being on the coast first thing in the morning for sunrise; the sound of the sea, the glow of the horizon just before the sun appears and then the burst of light as the new day starts. He also adores being in the mountains after walking for a few miles, having the landscape to himself and watching the sun set.

He has been known to sit on a hillside in the Brecon Beacons all night, from dusk until dawn, to photograph the stars. He has also been on Pen y Fan in a -27 degree C wind chill for sunrise! The coast is a little easier, but 3.30am has seen him getting up for the day to get to Gower for sunrise.

Dan's photos are available to buy on his website at www.DanSantillo.com and you can follow him at www.facebook.com/DanSantilloPhotography. He also regularly attends local markets and events, details are on his website.

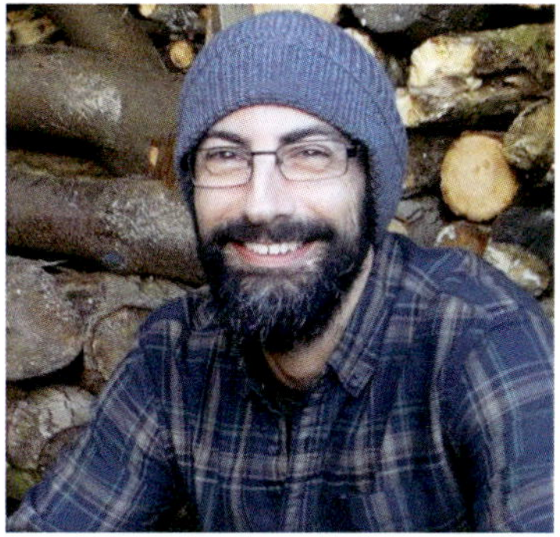

Dan Santillo

Little Book Company.org
from The Calendar Company

Swansea Bay

Long before you reach Gower, you can see the Mumbles, the gateway to Britain's first Area of Outstanding Natural Beauty (AONB). Designated in 1956, AONBs were created to protect the land to conserve and enhance its natural beauty. As of 2019, there are 46 AONBs in Britain.

Swansea Bay can give some outstanding sunsets and sunrises and when the tide is out, there are plenty of pools to reflect the beautiful skies.

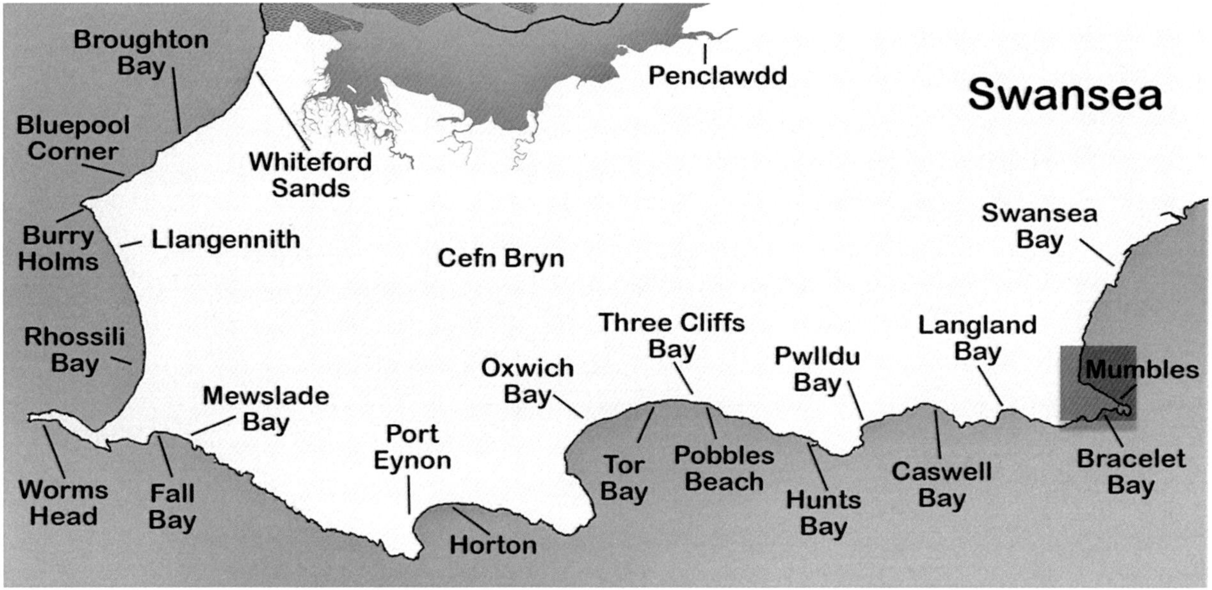

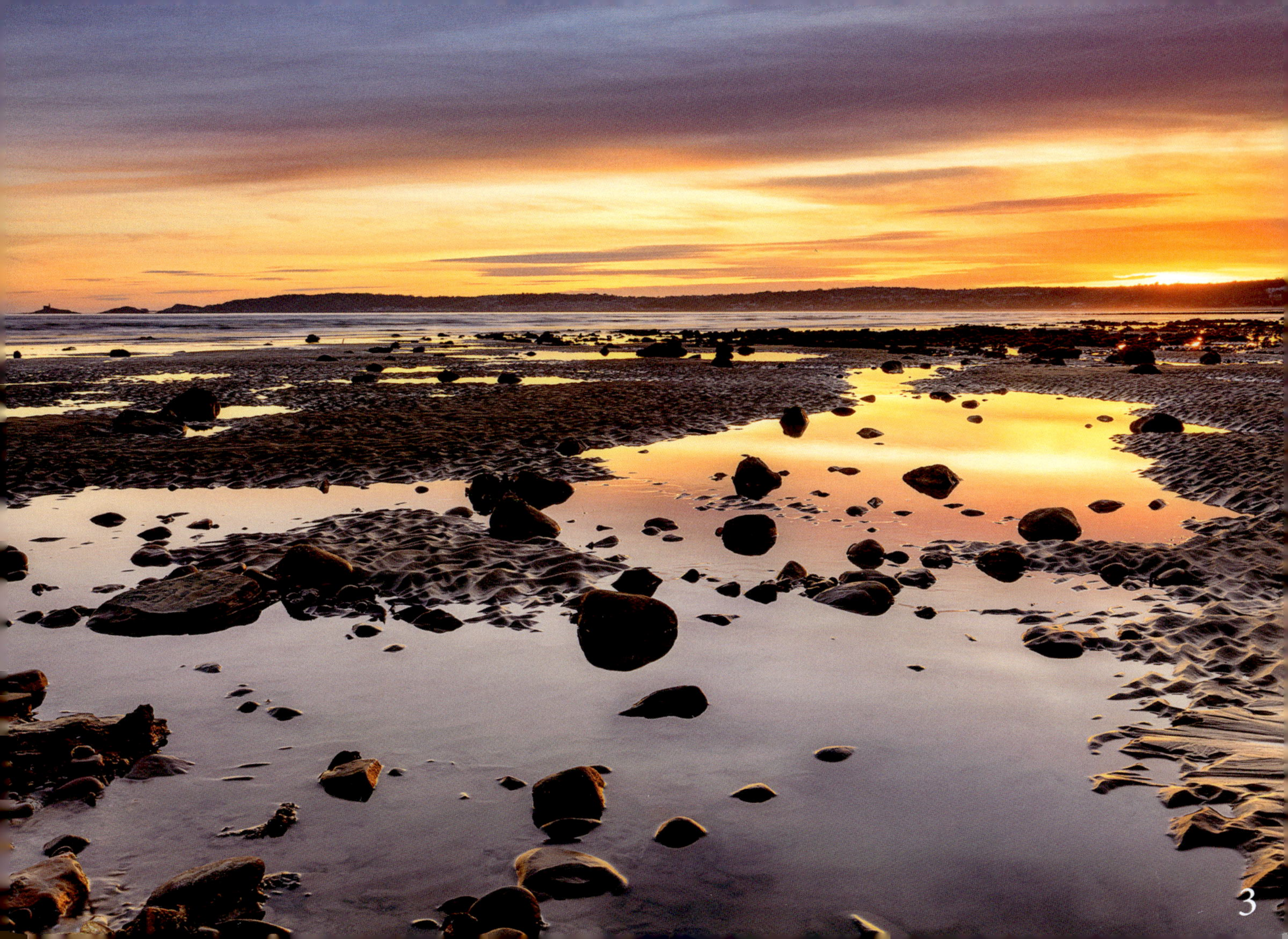

Swansea Bay

People who grew up in Swansea will remember tales about "Granny's Custard" and anyone venturing onto Swansea Bay at low tide will no doubt come across this. The "custard" is actually very sticky mud. Thousands of years ago sea levels were much lower than they are today and Swansea Bay was once a forest with lakes and ponds.

When sea levels rose, the forest was flooded which killed it off and it then became covered in sand. Sometimes ancient tree trunks are visible and also antlers from deer can occasionally make an appearance. The sticky muddy substance is actually silt from the old ponds and lakes.

This photo was taken during a rather nice lightning storm. After sheltering in the car from the rain, it finally stopped so I set the camera up and took this photo at just the right time. It was the last lightning strike of the storm!

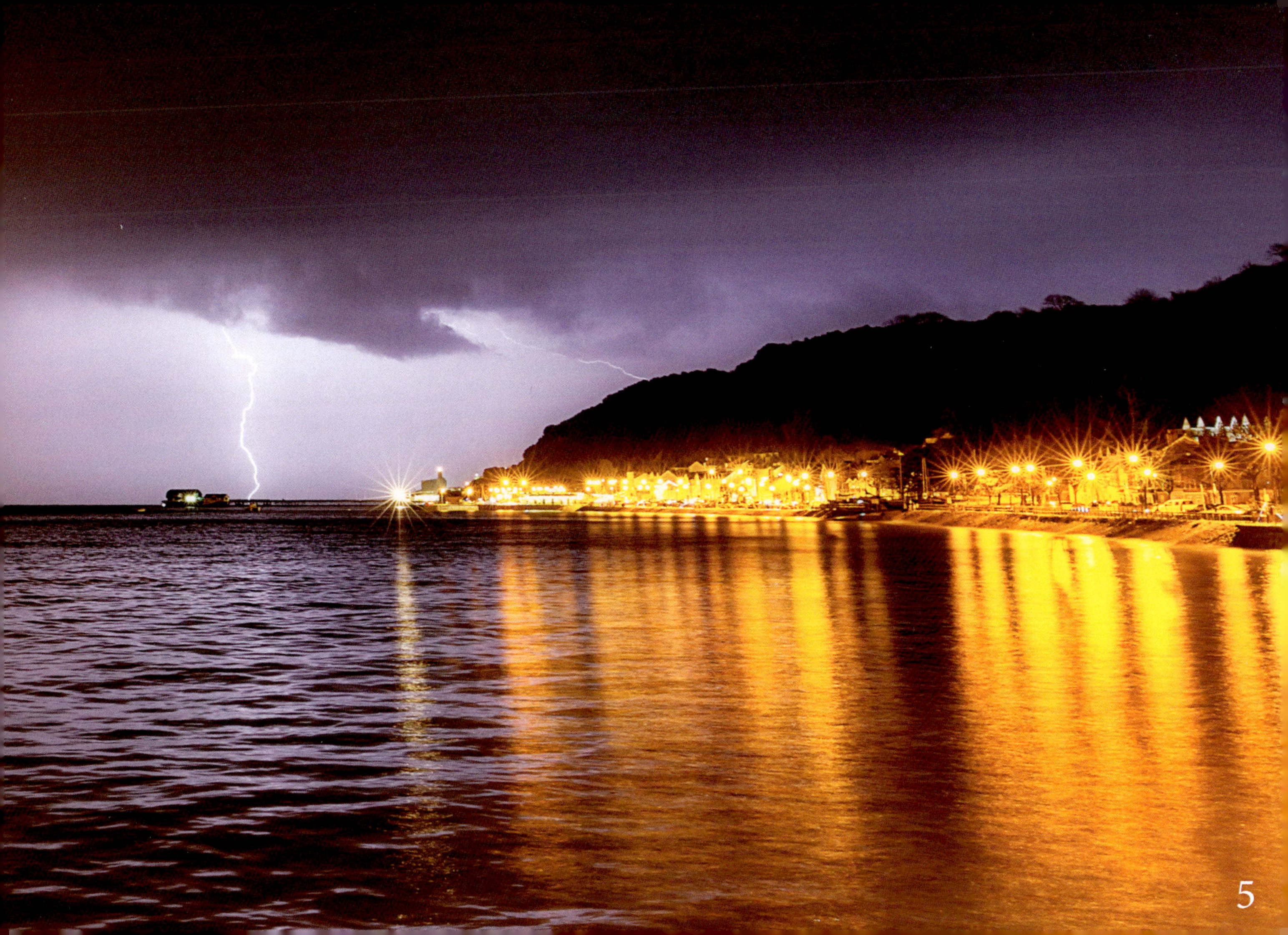

Mumbles

Mumbles Pier, built in 1898 by the Victorians, was once a very popular way to visit Swansea because the steam boats docked there. The "Mumbles Train", the first passenger railway in the world (dismantled in 1960) then transported the visitors onwards into Swansea. After the First World War, a wooden slipway was added to the pier to launch Swansea's lifeboat. It was previously launched from a stone slipway from land, but the huge tidal range of the bay made this inconvenient. A few years later, a boathouse was built.

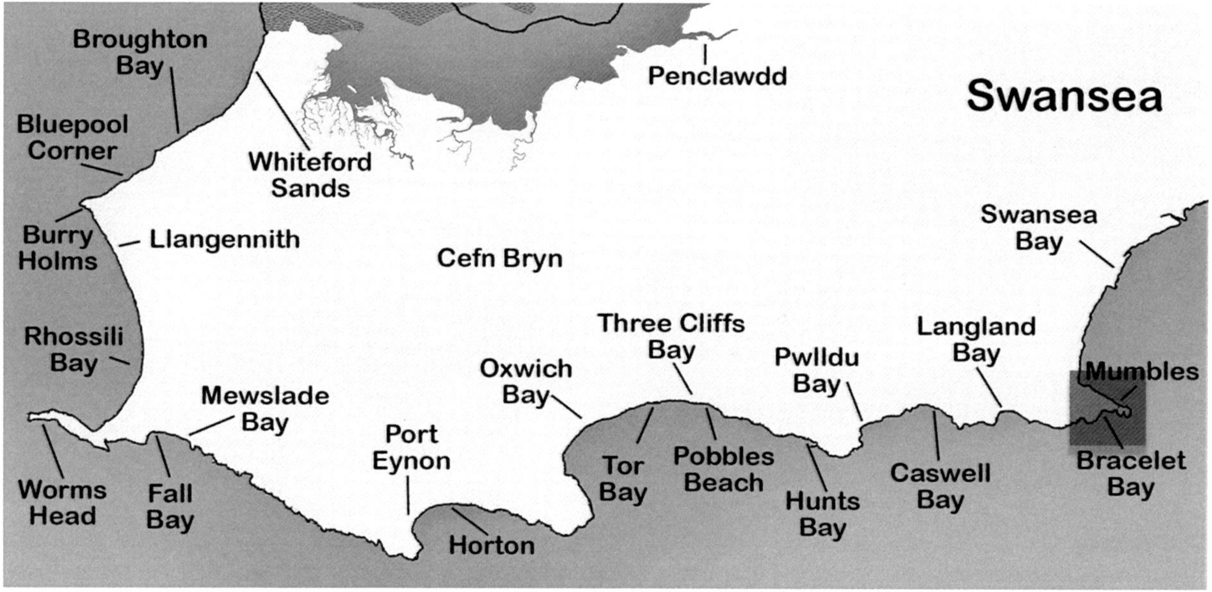

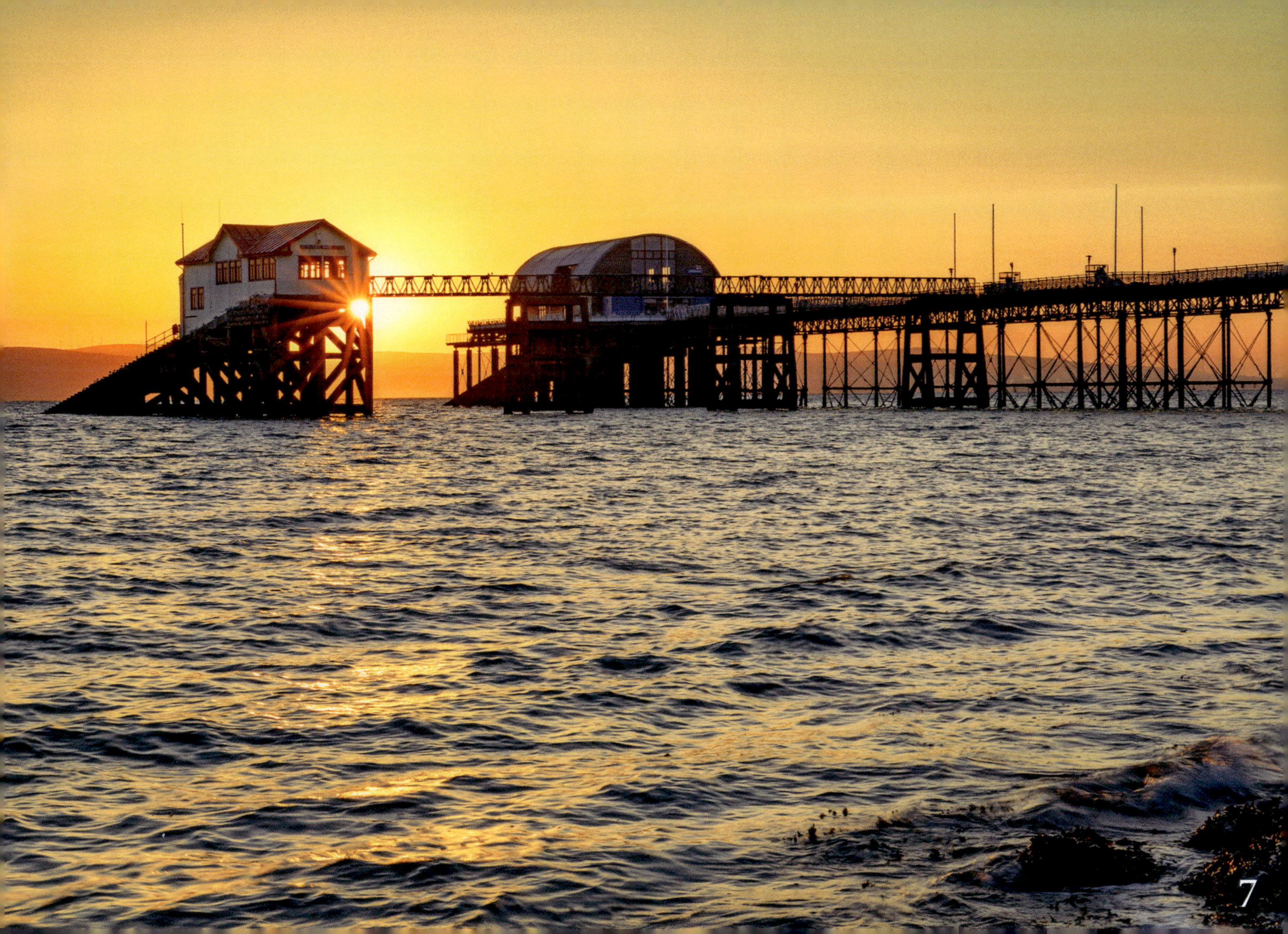

Mumbles

In 2012, a new lifeboat station and gift shop was built at the end of the pier. This was to house the new Tamar class lifeboat which improved on the lifeboat that was currently used. In 2018, the pier was closed to the public and work started to repair and restore much of the Victorian structure. The original columns from 1898 were inspected and were found to be in good condition and capable of supporting the pier! At the time of writing this book, there are further plans to change the foreshore to add a hotel and apartments as well as improve the pedestrian access from Knab Rock.

The lifeboat service for Swansea Bay was started in 1835, following the grounding of the Margaret Maltese barque and the 'Mary Ann' schooner on the Mixon Shoal within days of each other. Fortunately, there was no loss of life in either of these incidents. That wasn't always the case, however, when in January 1883 the Wolverhampton lifeboat was launched to rescue the crew of the Admiral Prinz Albert German barque. Disaster struck and heaving seas capsized the lifeboat several times causing four crew members to lose their lives while the rest were injured, some seriously.

In the bottom left of this photo, you can see the roof of what was Cinderella's nightclub. In its heyday, this was the place to go and a lot of people have fond memories of enjoying a night out there.

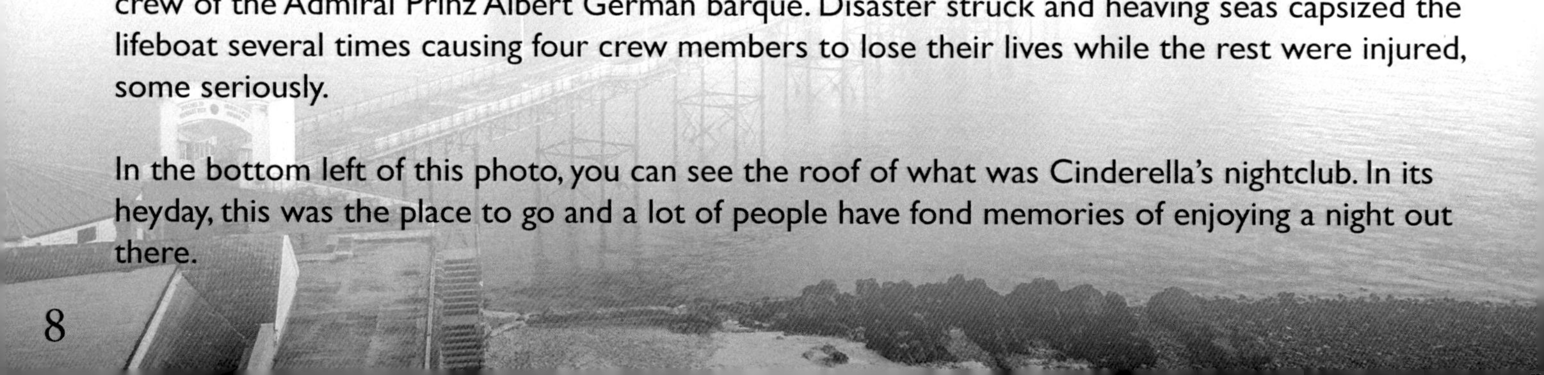

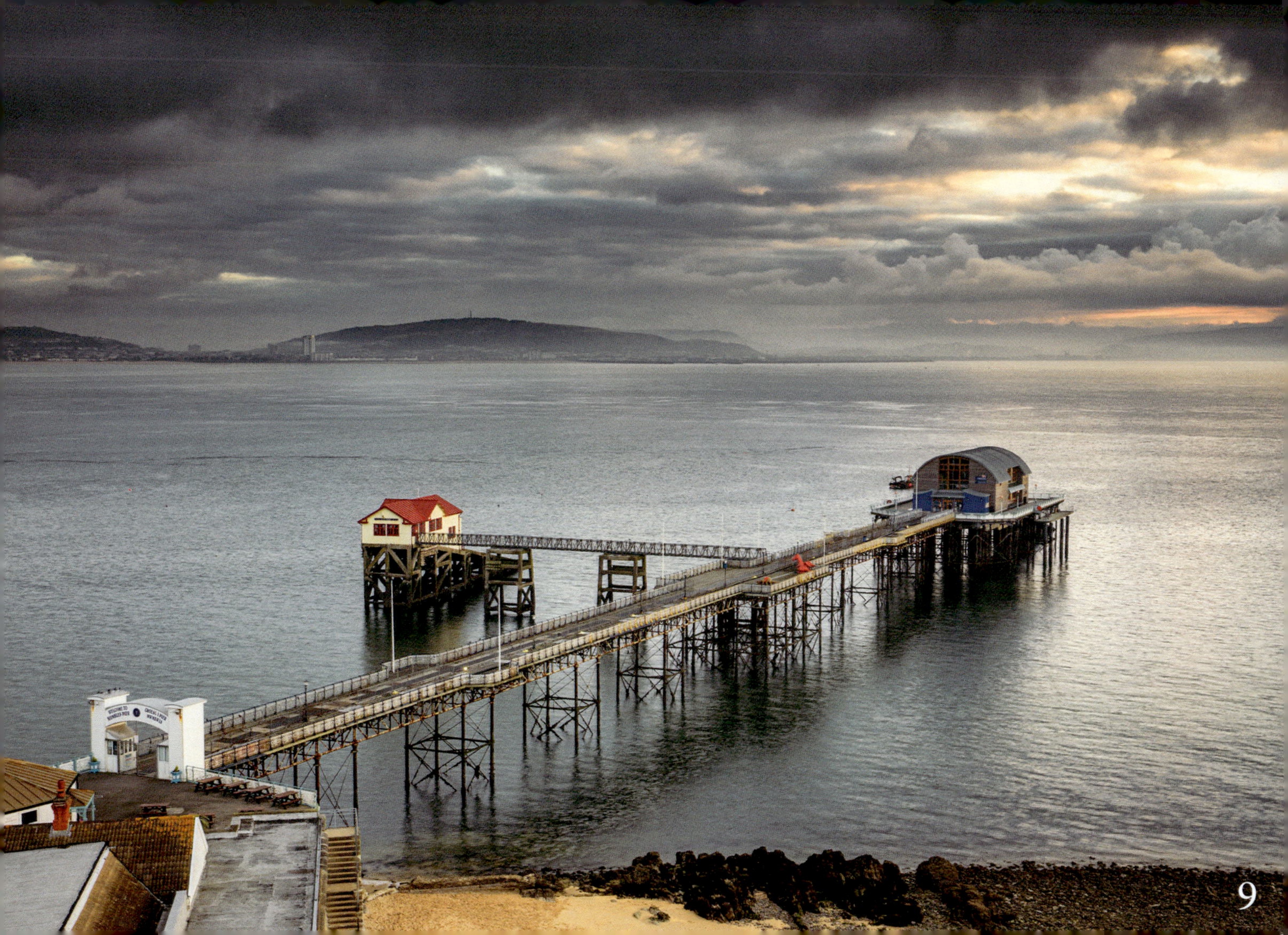

Mumbles and Bracelet Bay

The present day Mumbles lighthouse was built in 1794 from the plans of William Jernegan, a local architect, after the original lighthouse collapsed in 1792 before it was completed. It was originally lit by two coal fires, which were placed one above the other to distinguish it from nearby lighthouses. There were expensive and difficult to maintain, however, so were soon replaced in 1799 with a single oil powered light.

The lighthouse remained unchanged until 1859, when the War Office built the fort or blockhouse around it to defend Swansea and its docks. The defences were used again in the First and Second World Wars, before being decommissioned in 1957. The next upgrade to the lighthouse itself came in 1905 when the light was made to flash at regular intervals.

This photo was taken in Storm Ophelia on 16th October 2017. I always make sure I keep a safe distance when photographing storms as you never know when a wave will be bigger than the last and crash over rocks that were once safe. I was lucky with the timing of high tide and sunset when I took this photo, which gave some rather nice colour to the clouds.

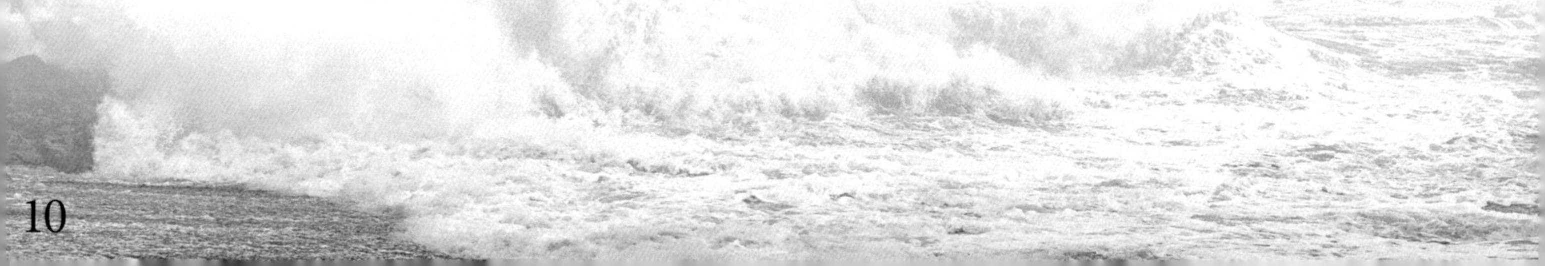

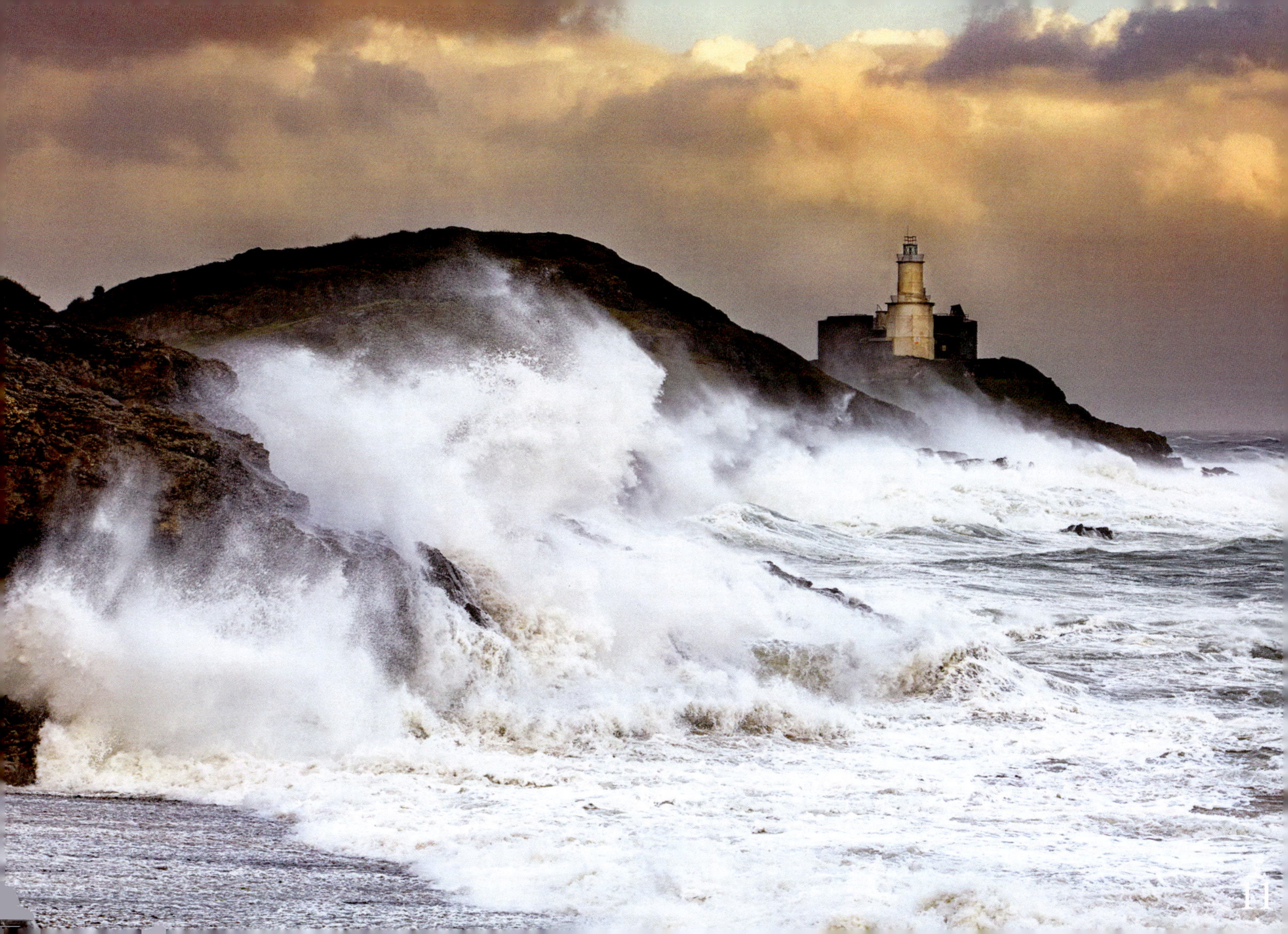

Mumbles and Bracelet Bay

In 1934, when the lighthouse keeper retired, the light was fully automated and has been unmanned ever since. Trinity House took ownership in 1975, converting it to solar power, replacing the light and adding a fog detector in 1995. The current light, at an intensity of just over 17,000 candela, can be seen for sixteen nautical miles, whilst the fog horn can be heard within a range of two nautical miles.

Approximately half a mile from the lighthouse is the Mixon Shoal (also called Mixon Sands) which is a large undersea sand bank. At low tide, waves can be seen breaking over it.

I chose this particular location for sunrise because it shows the slabs of angled rock going into the sea. I made sure it was high tide before going here as I wanted the sun reflected in the sea. The sun appeared for about 10 minutes and then went behind the cloud. A lot of photography is in the planning, but with the weather there is always an element of luck!

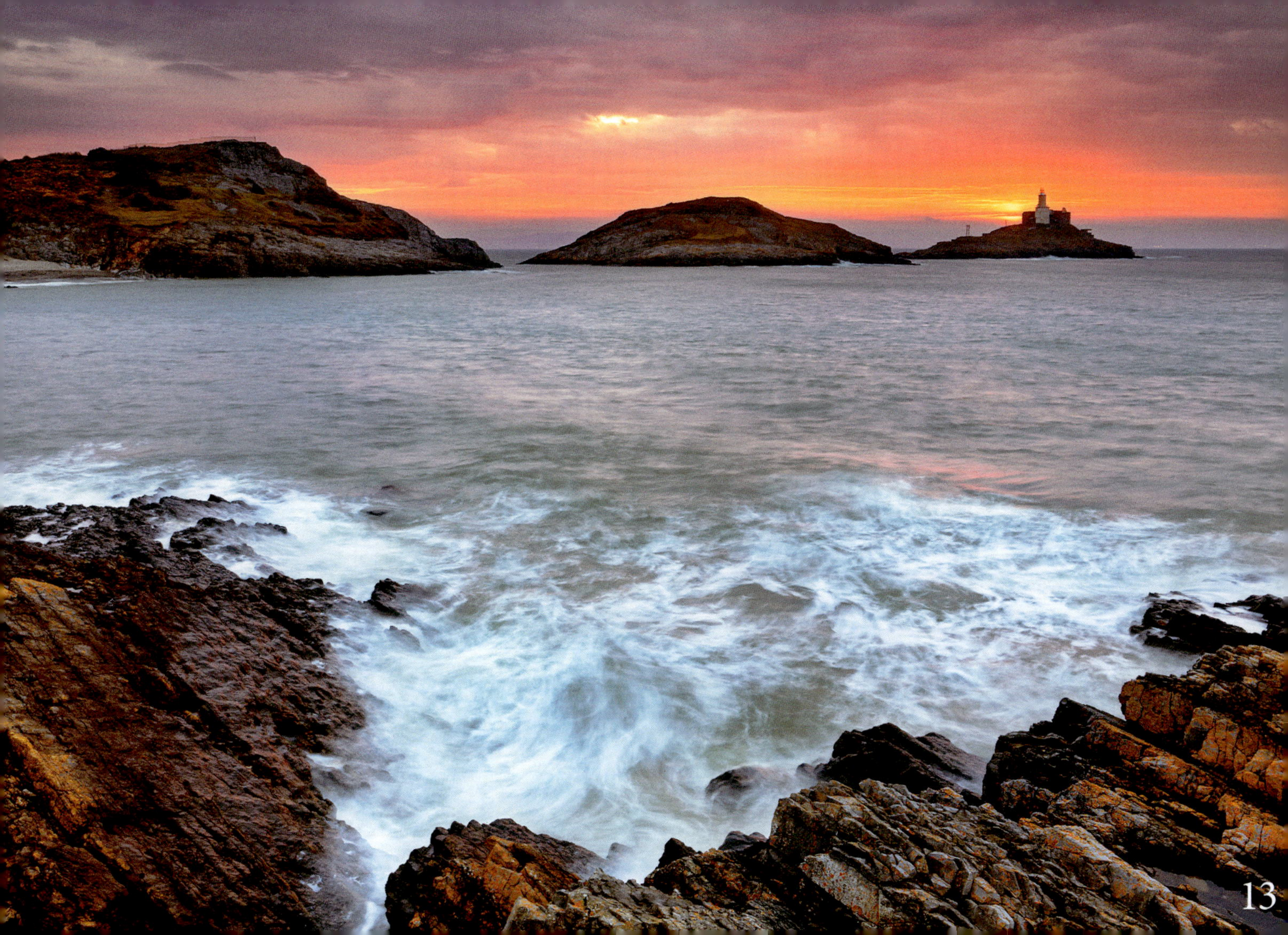

Mumbles and Bracelet Bay

This photo shows Bracelet Bay in a rare covering of snow. At the opposite end to the lighthouse is the coastguard station (just below the top of the hill) and Castellamare (an Italian restaurant).

The coastguard station was a Maritime and Coastguard Agency 999 response centre. Sadly, following a campaign to save it, the station was closed down in 2015. The Maritime and Coastguard Agency are still there but the emergency calls are now handled by the Milford Haven station. At the time of writing, alternative uses for the building were being considered.

Castellamare used to be a nightclub called Neptunes and the end point of the once legendary Mumbles Mile. In its heyday, the Mumbles Mile started at The White Rose on the corner of Newton Road and 26 pubs later ended at Cinderella's or Neptunes nightclub. However, this became so popular that crowds started to become a problem especially with rowdy hen and stag parties. Today things are very different and if you were to do the Mumbles Mile now, according to Wales Online, it would run in the other direction towards Wind Street and have just 4 pubs!

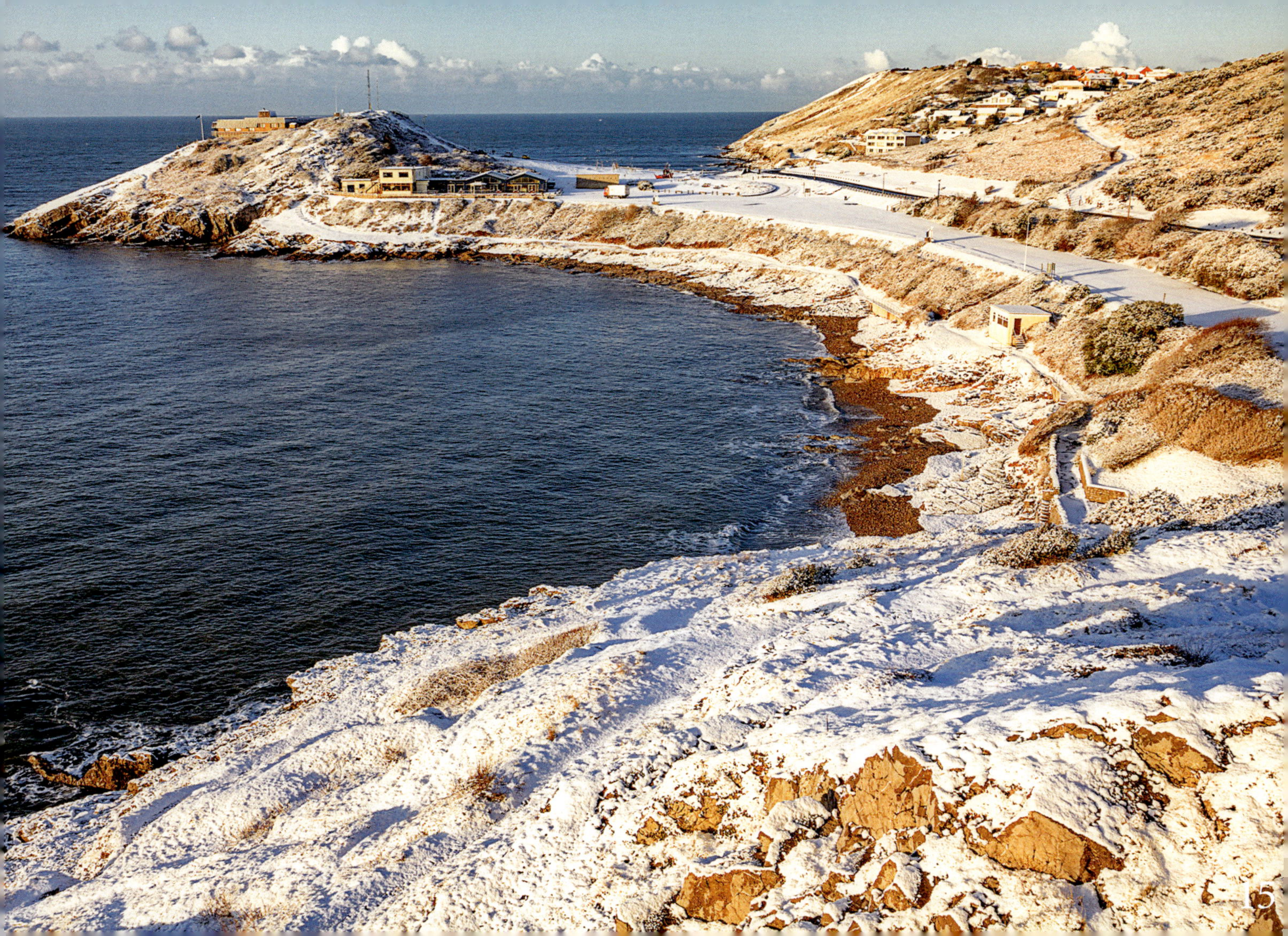

Limeslade Bay

Limeslade Bay is a small beach just to the west of Bracelet Bay comprised of mainly rocks with some sand. Near the head of the bay there is an iron mine, probably from Roman times, although it has now been sealed off. The coast path from here to Langland Bay is a highly recommended walk. According to the Oxford English Dictionary, a 'slade' is "an open space between banks or woods; a valley."

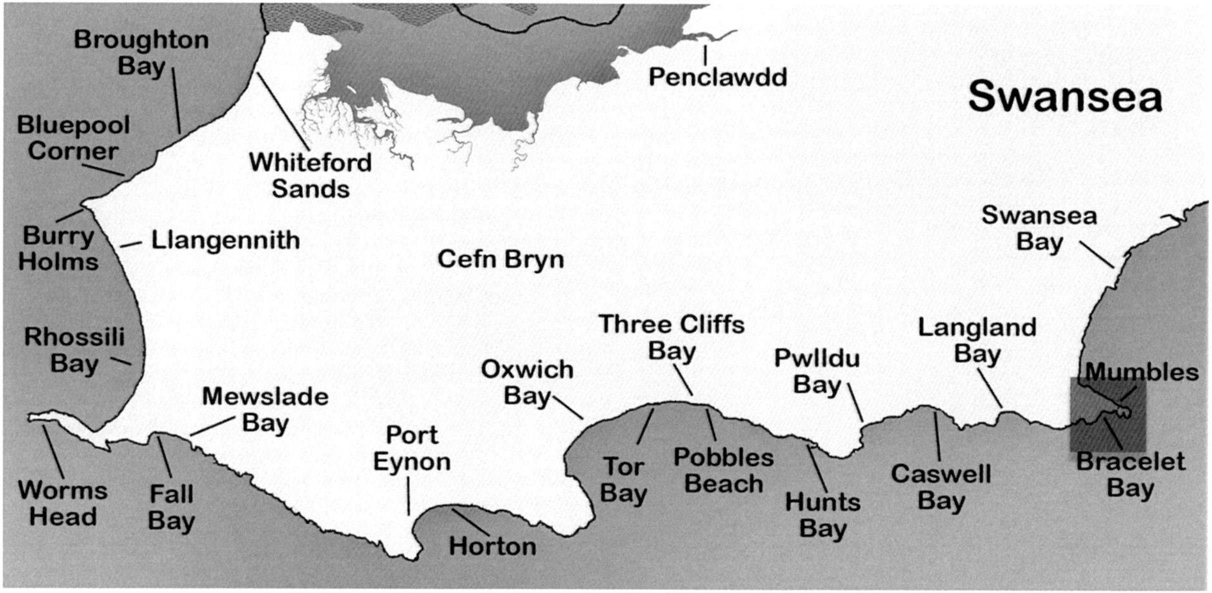

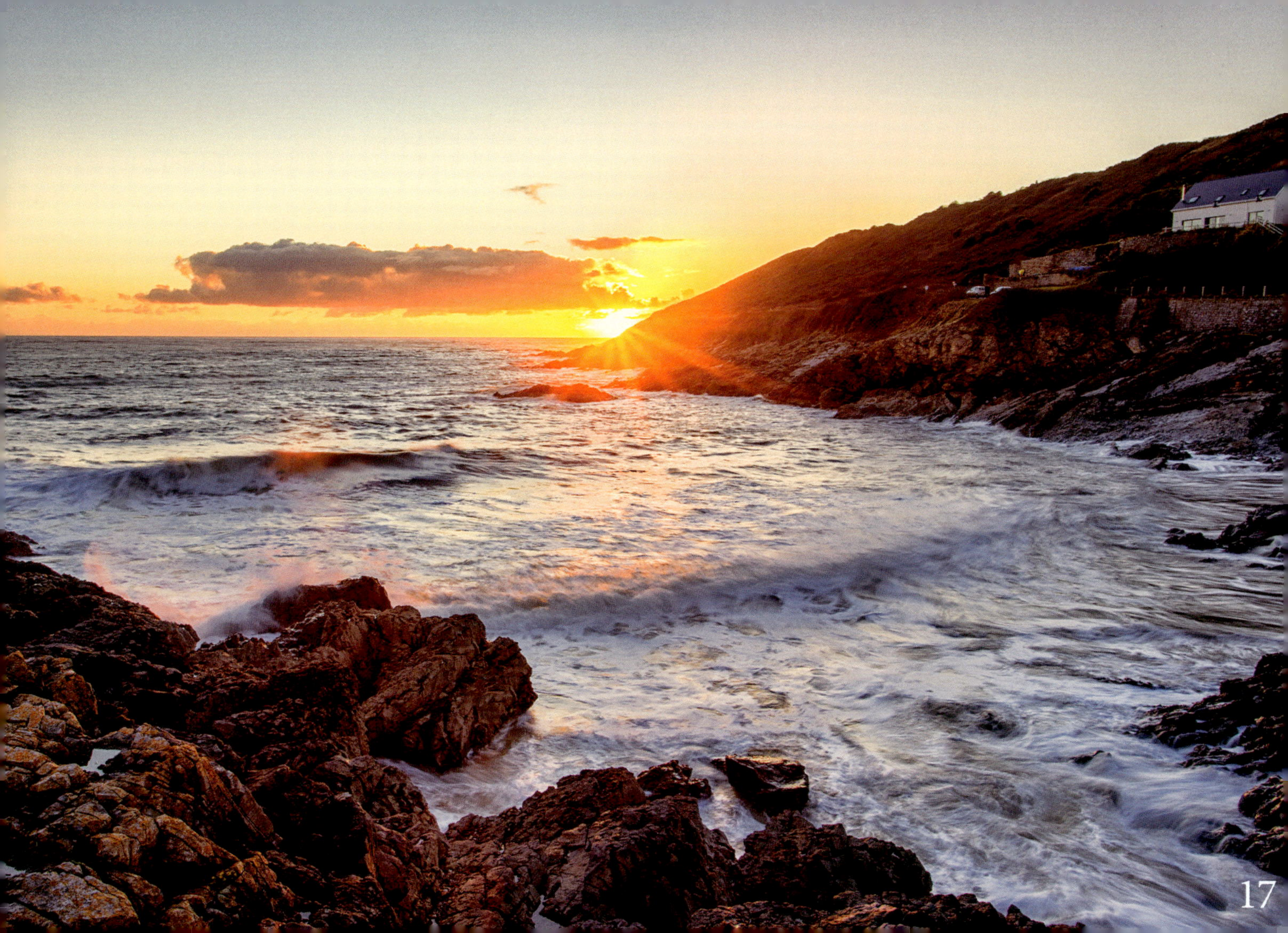

Langland Bay

Walking from Limeslade brings you to this viewpoint, just off the coast path. When I arrived at this location for sunset, I thought I wouldn't get any photos as it was so cloudy. Then, just before the sun went down, it peaked out between a gap in the clouds and I captured this photo. It was windy and by the time I left, both the camera and myself were covered in salt from the sea spray! When I got home, I had to carefully wipe down my camera equipment to remove the salt.

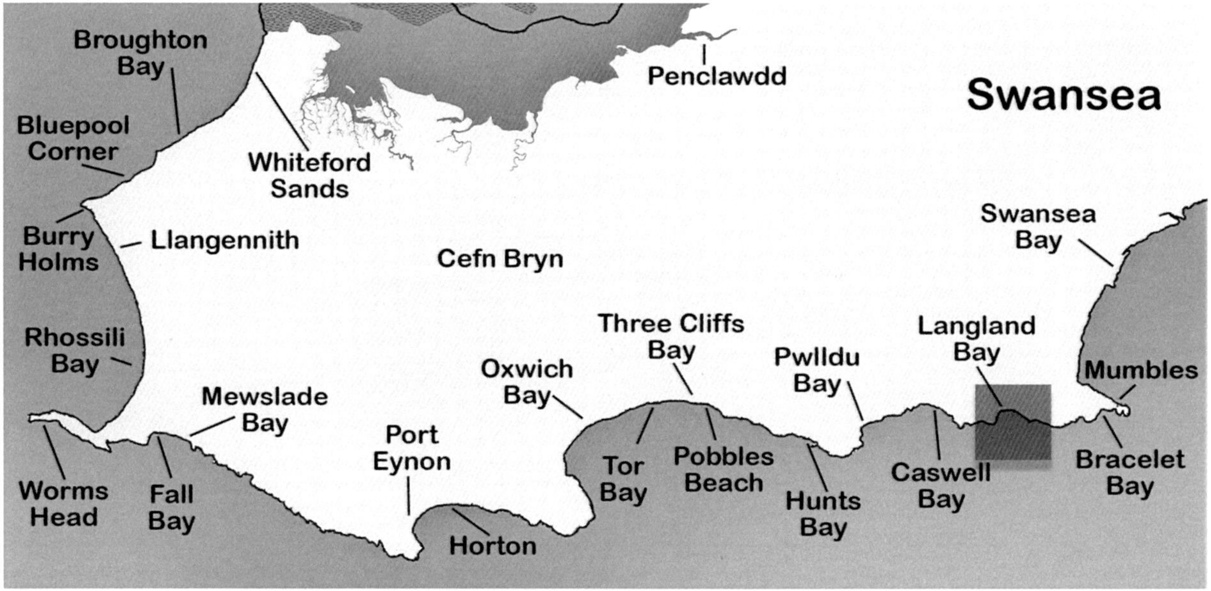

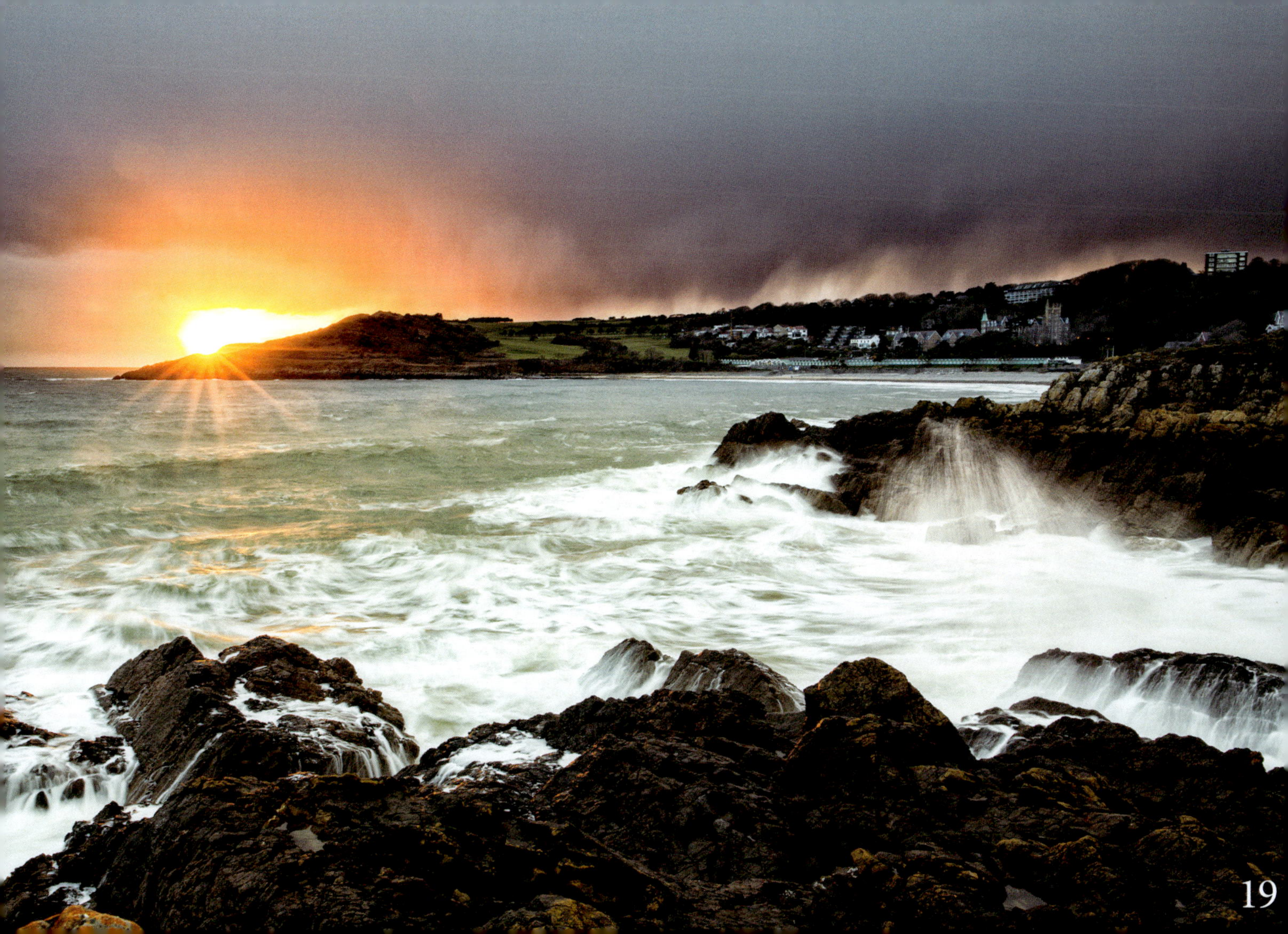

Langland Bay

Rotherslade Bay is a small beach that could be arguably thought of as part of the larger Langland Bay and, in fact, it used to be known as 'Little Langland'. Rotherslade is accessed via concrete steps that were once where a beach café and dance hall sat. After being abandoned for many years, it was demolished and the steps put in its place. Above the beach are some beach huts that, when available, attract a hefty price. In 2018, a hut was auctioned off and the reserve was set at £20,000. There is no running water or electricity and they aren't allowed to be slept in!

In 1892 when the Osborne Hotel was being built, Rother's Tor Cave was discovered and in it prehistoric finds such as a mammoth's tooth, which is on display in Swansea Museum. However, before a proper excavation was able to take place, the cave was filled in to support the foundations of the hotel.

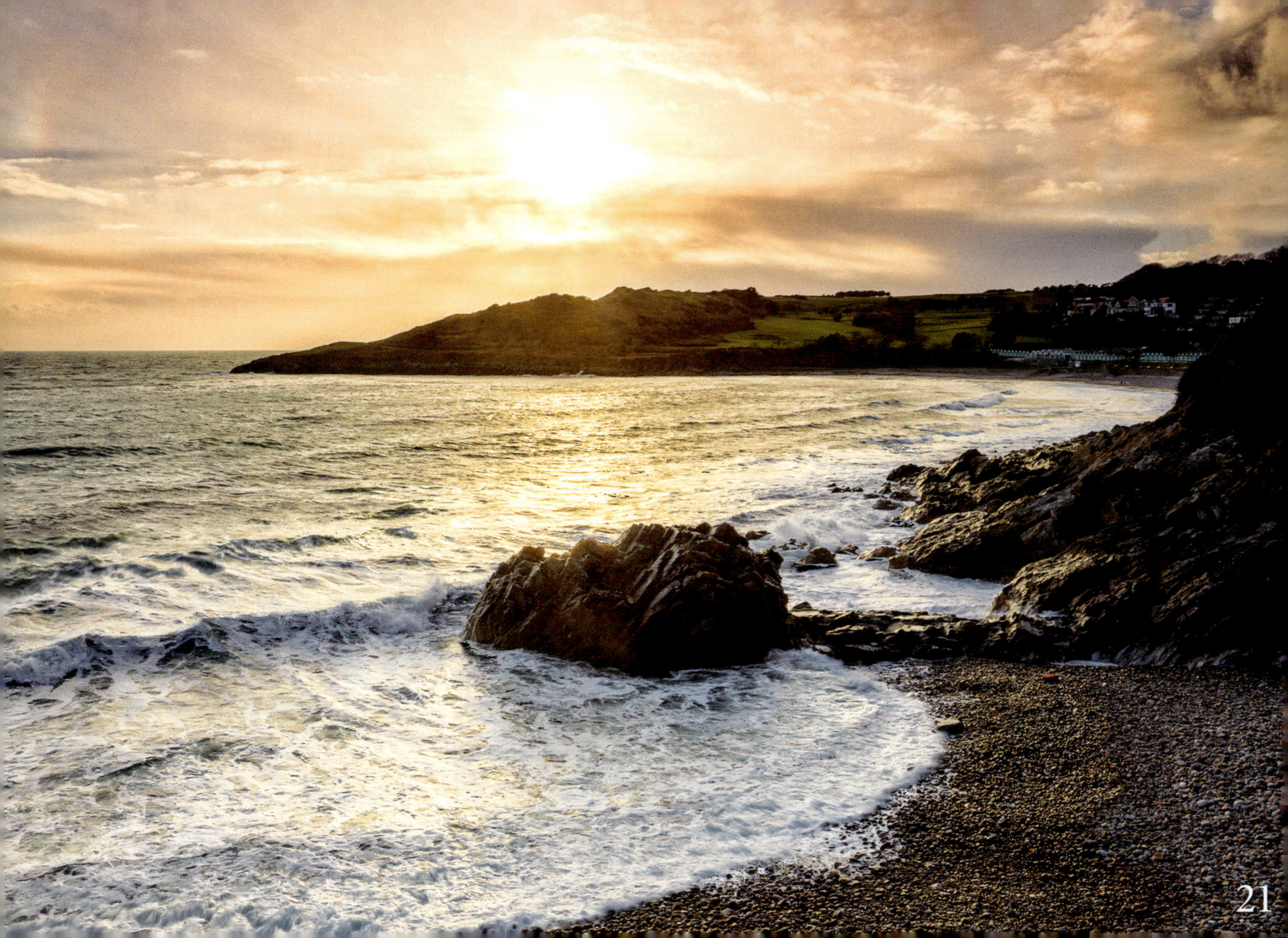

Langland Bay

If there is one thing synonymous with Langland Bay, it is the 79 beach huts. Some were originally built in the 1860s and the rest in the 1920s. They are managed by the City and County of Swansea. There also used to be green canvas tents that were put up annually at the top of the beach, some of which were occasionally claimed by high tides. There were some additional tents on the safety of the hill, but they were vandalised in the 1970s and were removed forever.

In the 2000s, the state of disrepair of the beach huts were such that they were reconstructed. To pay for this, the council put some of them up for a 10 year lease which could be purchased for £10,000. Previously they has all been allocated by ballot, which meant that people could rent them at a far more affordable price. Now, just 50 of the huts are let on a seasonal basis by ballot to make the high demand dealt with in a fair way.

In 2014, the council allowed 18 of the huts to be rented over the winter period rather than the usual spring and summer. Application is done through the council.

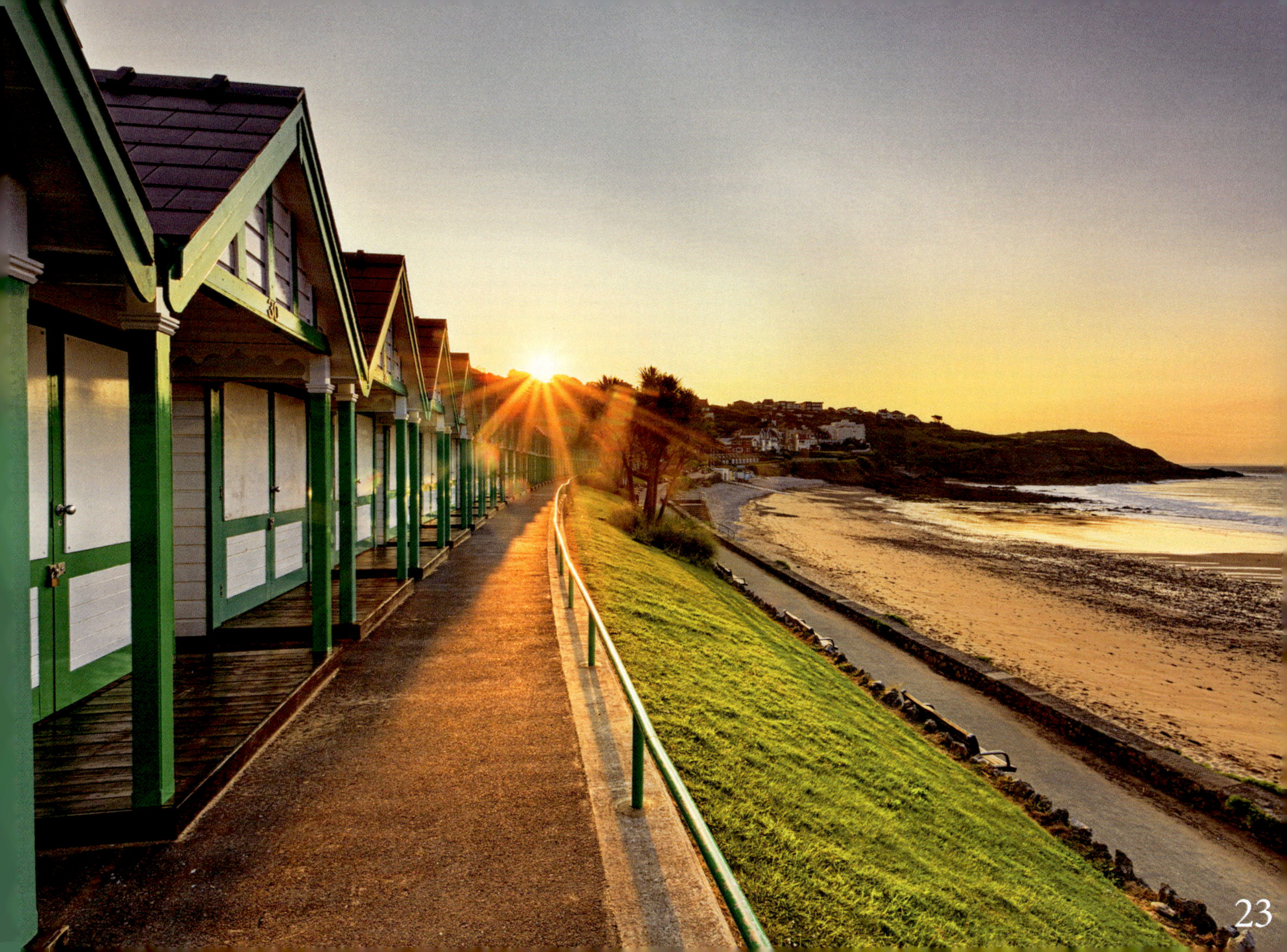

Langland Bay

When taking photos of places, I am constantly trying to take them in a way that shows them differently to other people. I had this great idea of taking photos looking back to the beach from the water with waves breaking in the foreground. The trouble is, the sea is usually very cold and is rather painful on the feet so I had another great idea of buying wellies so I could keep my feet dry. This worked well for about 5 minutes. With my feet dry, I went deeper into the water and, of course, waves soon poured over the tops of my boots… For weeks after taking this photo, each time I opened the tripod legs sand came out!

Langland Bay is one of the Gower beaches that have seasonal dog access with no dogs permitted from 1st May through to 30th September. Other beaches with seasonal dog access are Swansea Bay (parts of), Bracelet Bay, Limeslade Bay, Rotherslade Bay, Caswell Bay and Port Eynon (parts of). Dogs are allowed all year around on the rest of Gower's beaches.

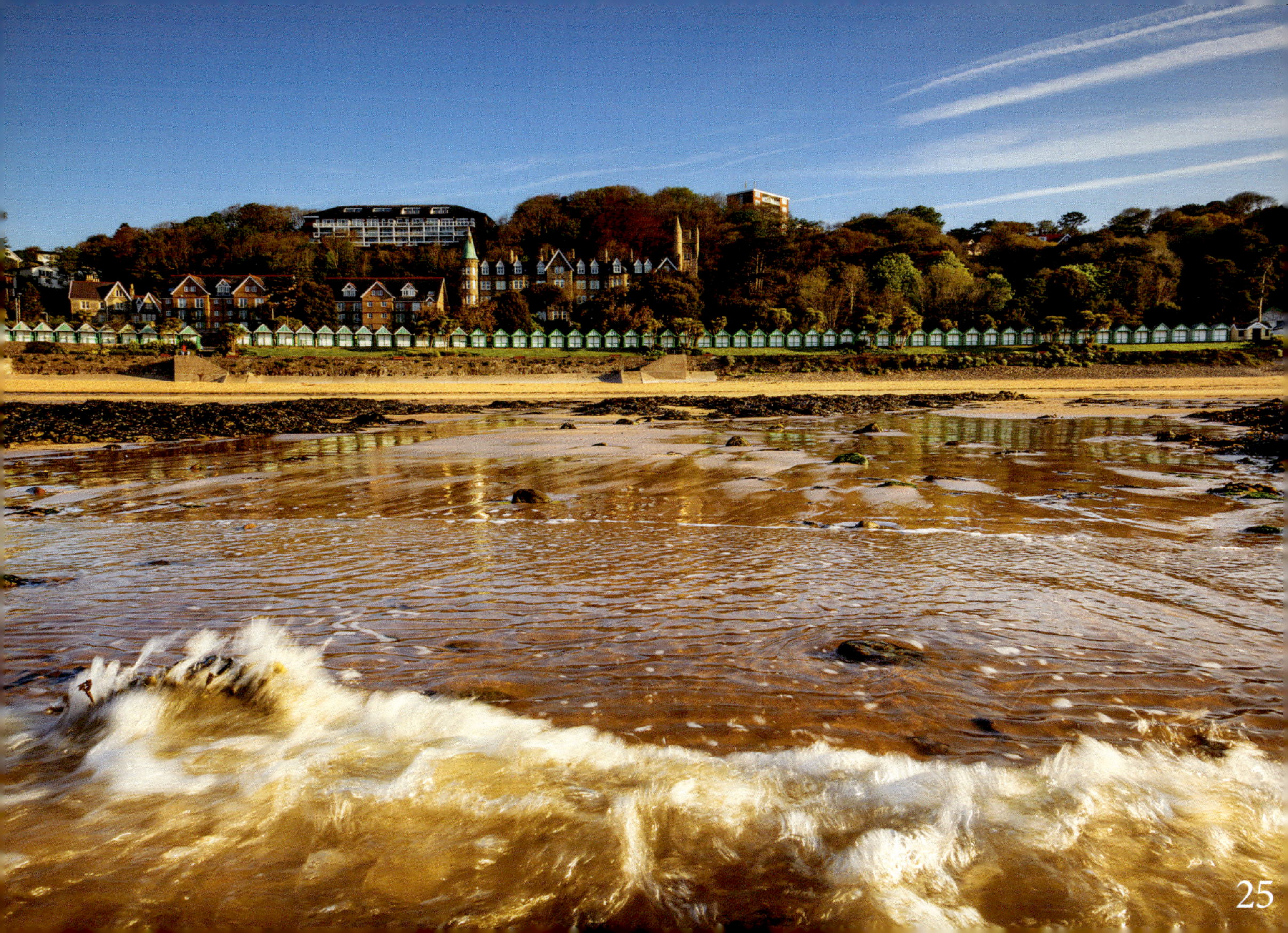

Langland Bay

Langland Bay is one of the beaches that I find a little harder to take photos of compared to, say, Three Cliffs Bay. I have very high expectations of myself and whilst you might think I've done OK, I've never actually taken a photo of Langland that I've thought "Yes, I'm happy with that one" about it. Along with the stormy one at the start of the Langland section, this photo comes close. I love the glow of orange that means the sun is literally seconds away from breaking the horizon.

It's all part of the sunrise experience, the sky becomes slightly more colourful as the time approaches. Then just before sunrise, the glow gets brighter and at that point you know exactly where the sun will rise. Seconds later with a burst of light the sun appears and a new day has started. I lose myself in photography at sunrise, the light and colours change quickly and I try to capture as much as I can. It took several goes to get the drawback of the water in this photo with the next wave coming in. How can I improve on this? I don't know, but I will keep trying until I am happy.

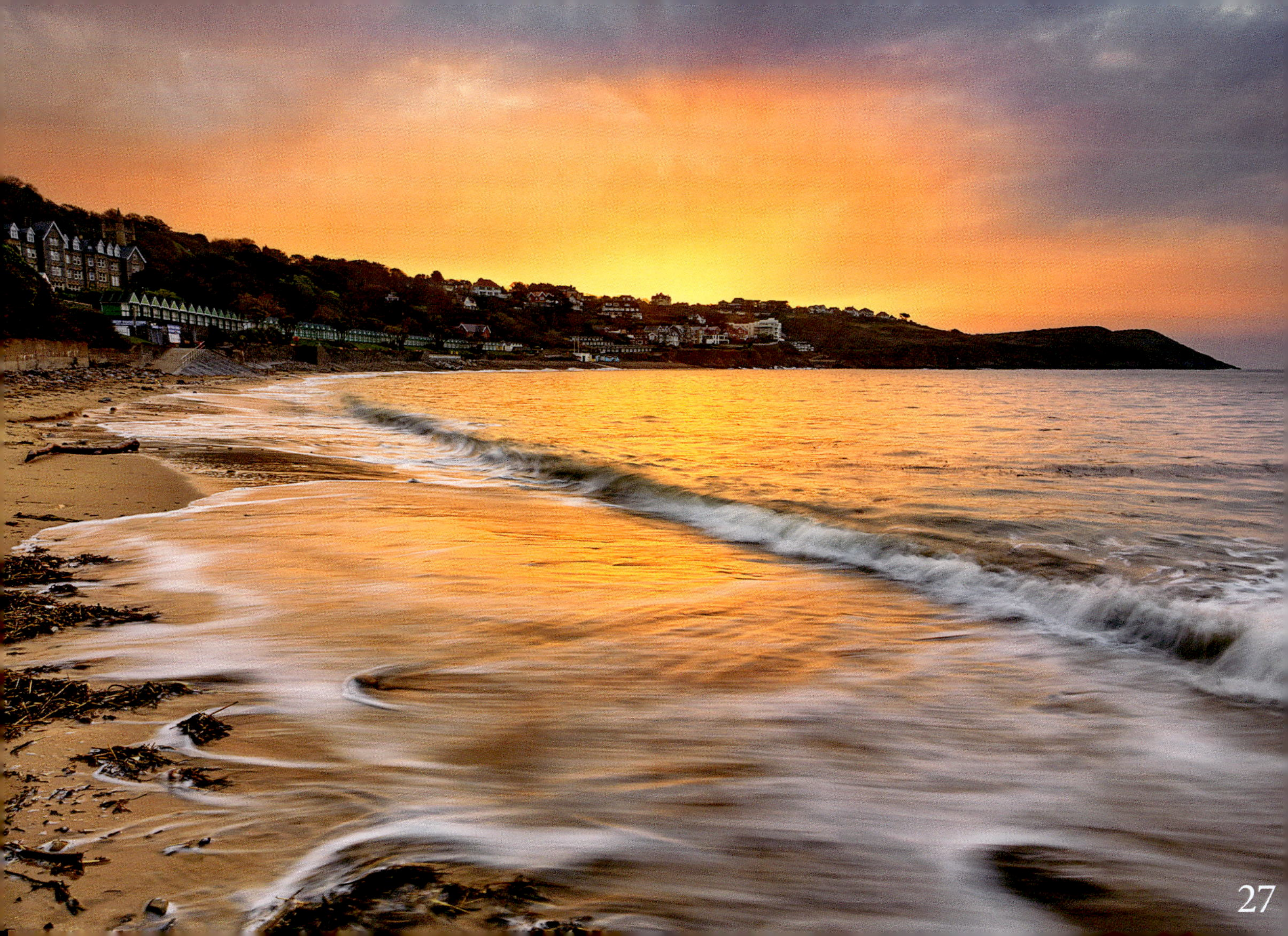

Caswell Bay

The coast path from Langland Bay to Caswell Bay is a fantastic and very popular walk. The view here is the first hint of Caswell Bay with Pwlldu Head in the distance. The railings and path have changed since this photo was taken and it is now metal and concrete. There are mixed views on this, but it is now more accessible for people with reduced mobility. The colour of the sea makes Gower look more like the Mediterranean than the Welsh coast!

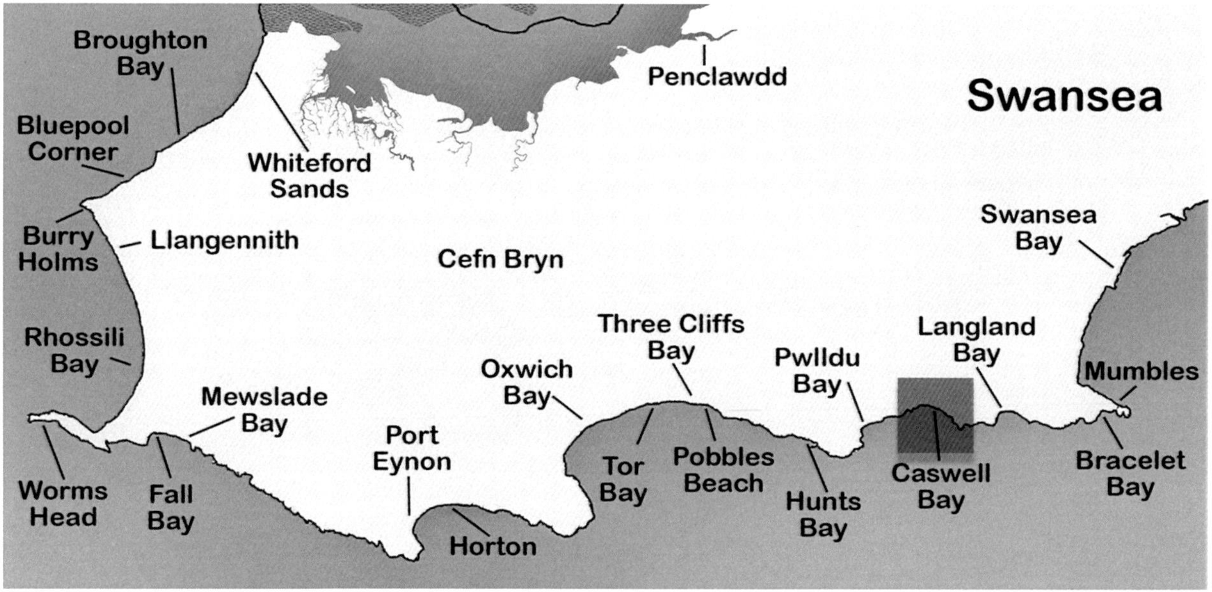

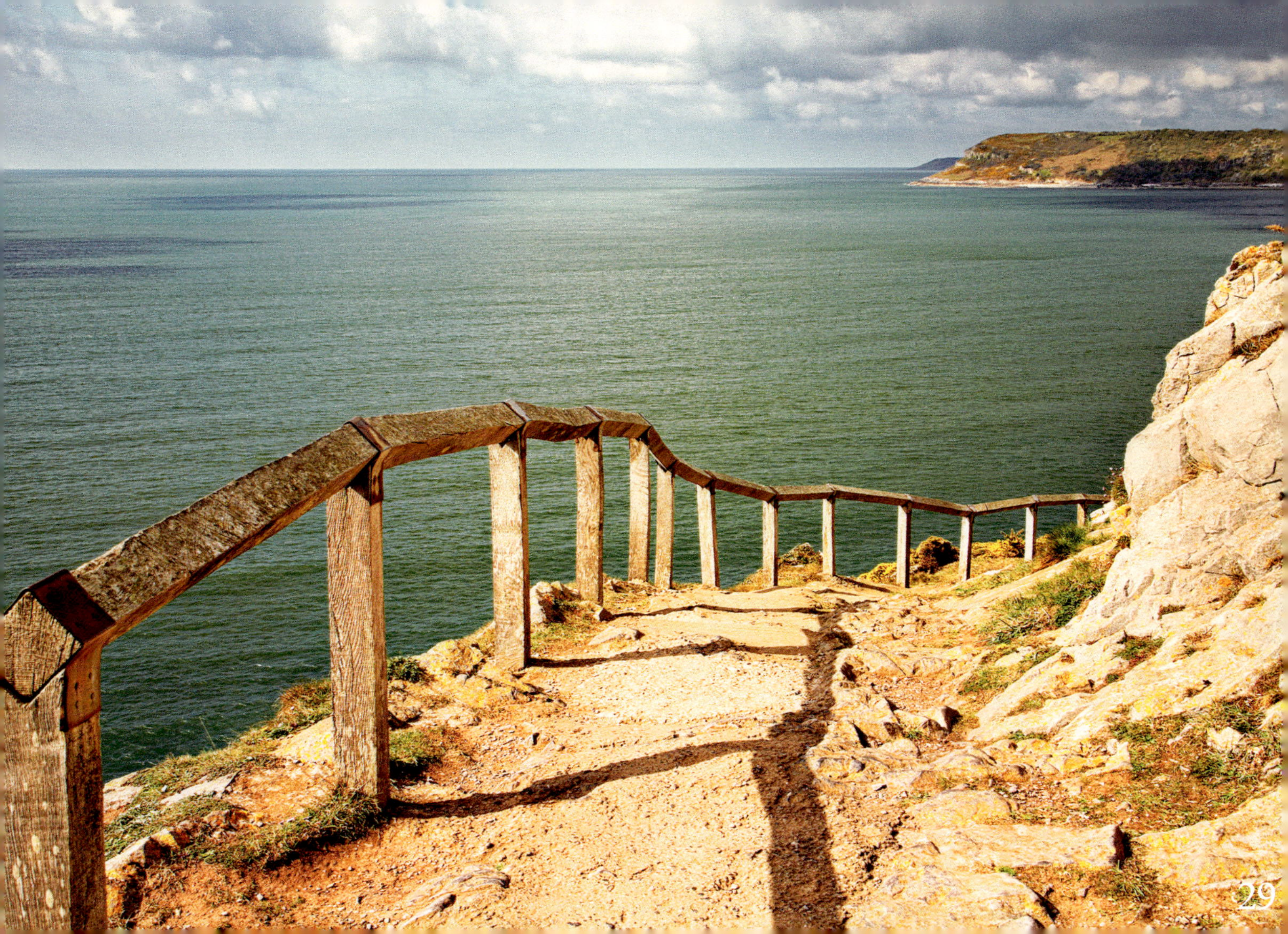

Caswell Bay

When taking photos, I have several lenses that I use for different purposes. My most used lens is a 24-70mm, which covers most scenes I like to photograph. I have a wider angle 17-40mm lens too that gives a wider perspective. These are great during the day, but when taking photos at night with the stars, I want to capture as much sky as I can so I use a 14mm lens. This gives such a wide angle that I have to be careful not to get my feet in the photo!

Sometimes, I will try this extreme wide angle lens during the day when the scene requires it. On the day I took this photo, the blue sky and white fluffy clouds contrasted beautifully with the green of the sea. To some degree the clouds mirror the waves and lead you into the middle of the photo. The 14mm lens has done well!

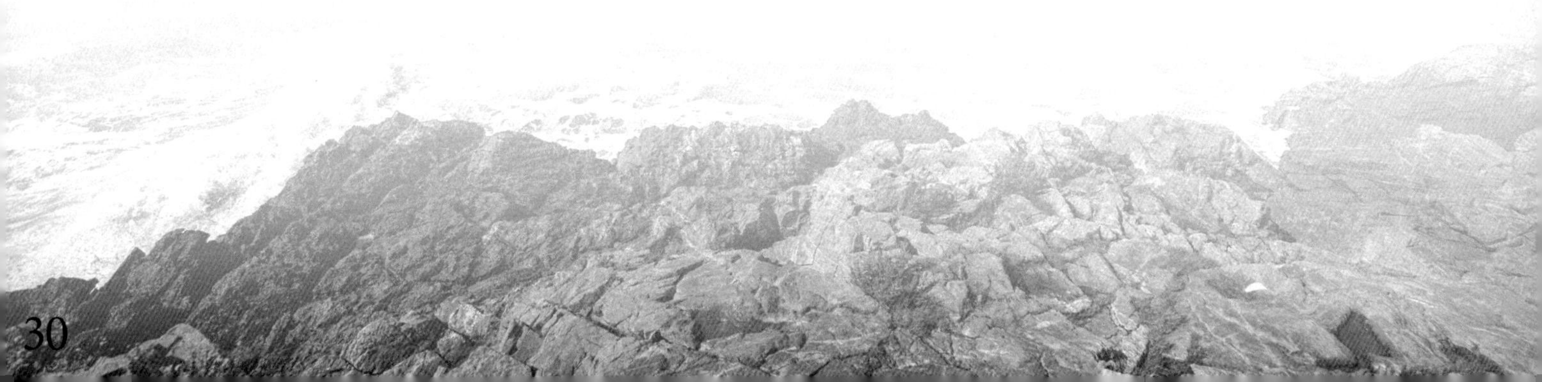

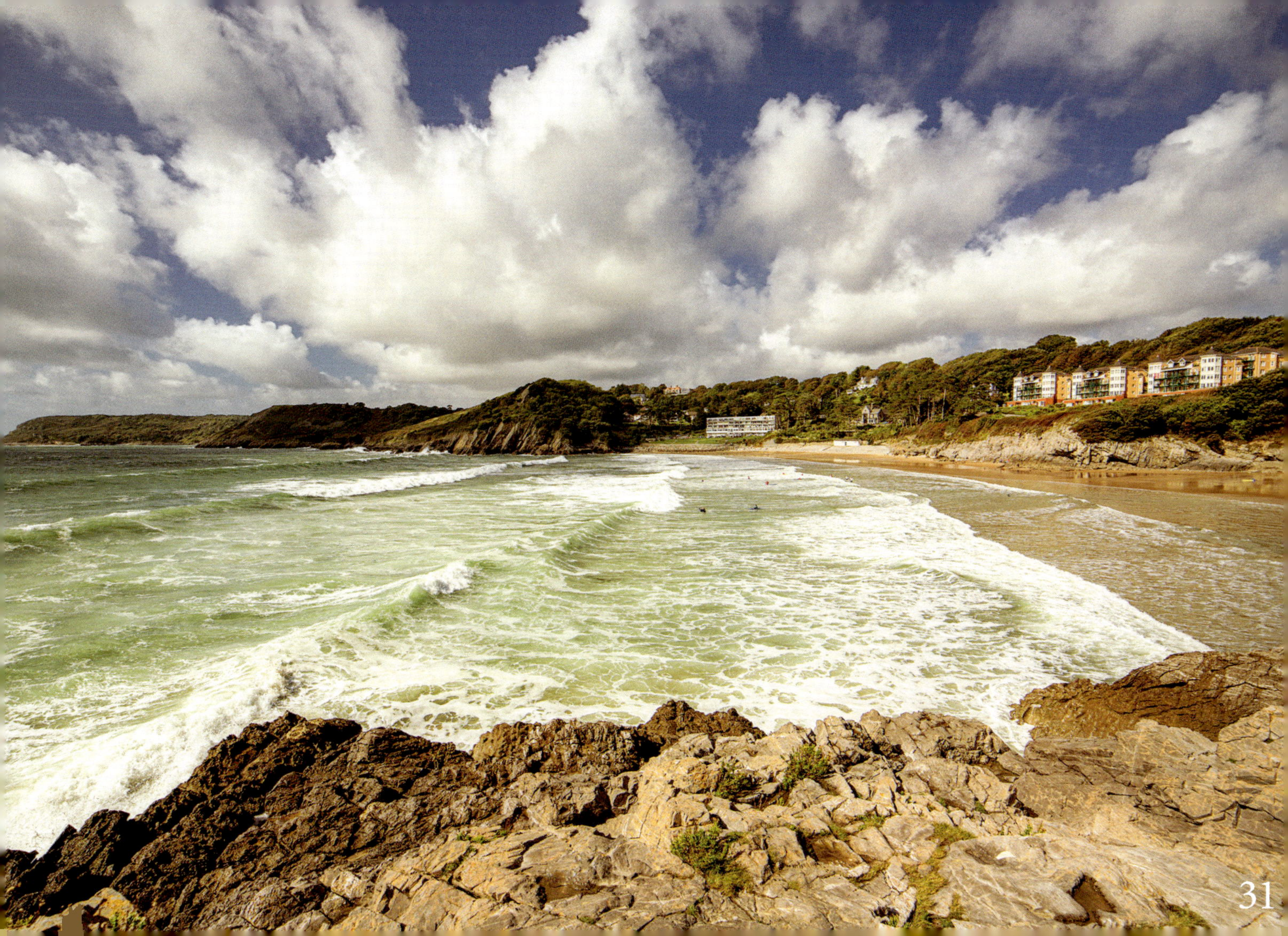

Caswell Bay

Caswell Bay, one of the beaches on Gower with seasonal lifeguard support, is very popular with both locals and tourists. Like Langland Bay, it is a popular haunt for surfers and is also regularly awarded the European Blue Flag for cleanliness, safety, facilities and so on. On the beach, there is a concrete structure built into the cliff. This is the remains on a water tank built in the late nineteenth century which was used to collect water from a spring.

In 1883 a windmill was constructed on the top of the hill above the bay to pump water from a spring below to supply a small reservoir for houses. In 1890, the Oystermouth Waterworks Company took ownership and built the water tank as well as a steam powered pump house to replace the unreliable windmill. In 1930, the windmill caught fire and was then destroyed with explosives to make it safe.

When taking this photo, I waited for the surfer to be in just the right spot.

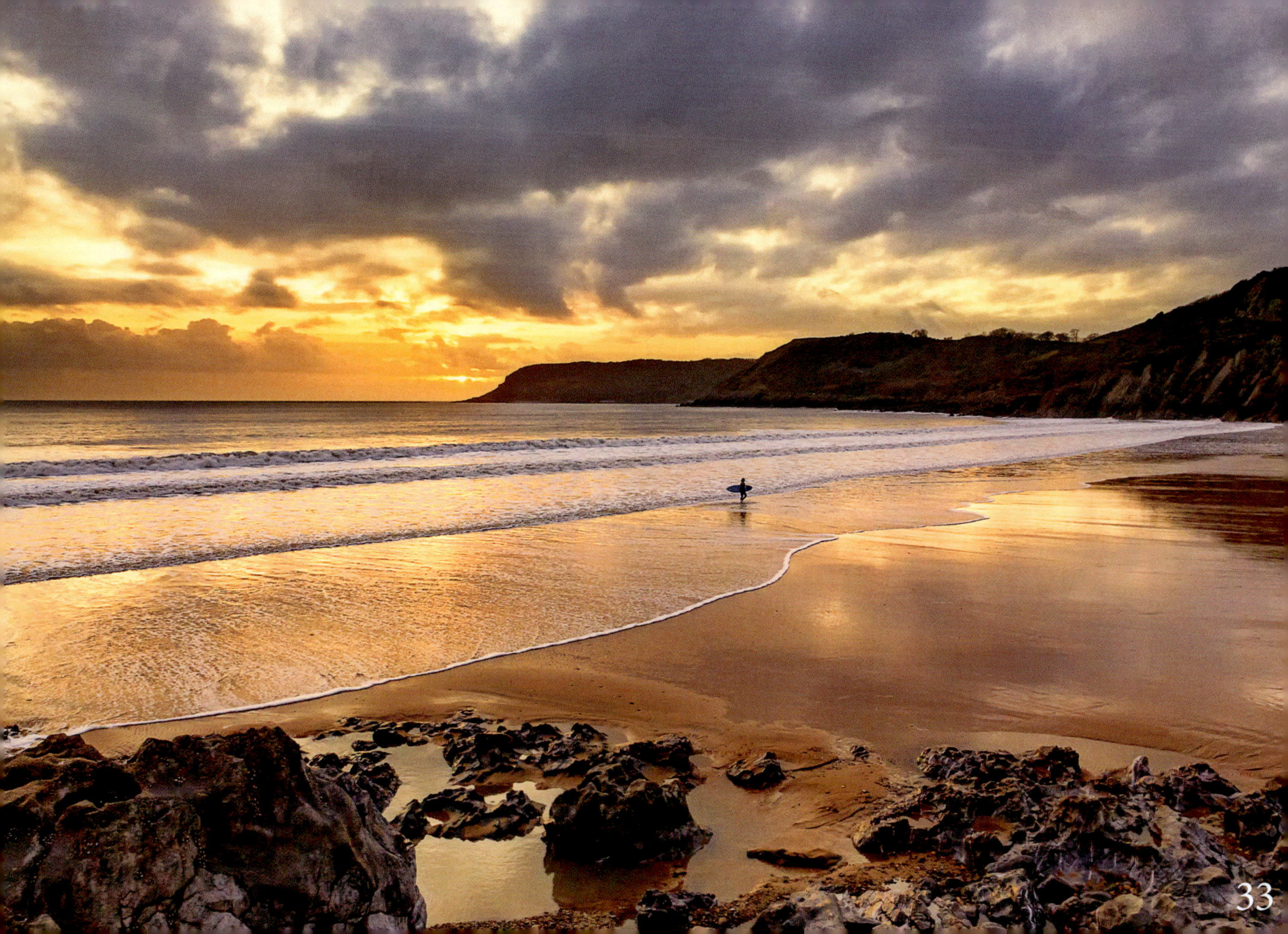

Caswell Bay

Directly behind the beach is Bishop's Wood Local Nature Reserve with 46 acres of woodland and grassland running from Murton to Caswell. It is a relatively rare limestone woodland and part of it is classified as ancient woodland, which means it has been a forest since at least the seventeenth century! It has designations as both a Site of Special Scientific Interest (SSSI) and a Special Area of Conservation (SAC) because of its rich biodiversity. It was declared a Nature Reserve in 1975 and is one of six in the City and County of Swansea.

The café in this photo might seem in a perfect location, but its closeness to the beach has led to problems. In early 2014, high tides and storms severely damaged the building. Shutters and windows were smashed and tables, chairs and other equipment was ruined. There were even fish swimming around inside!

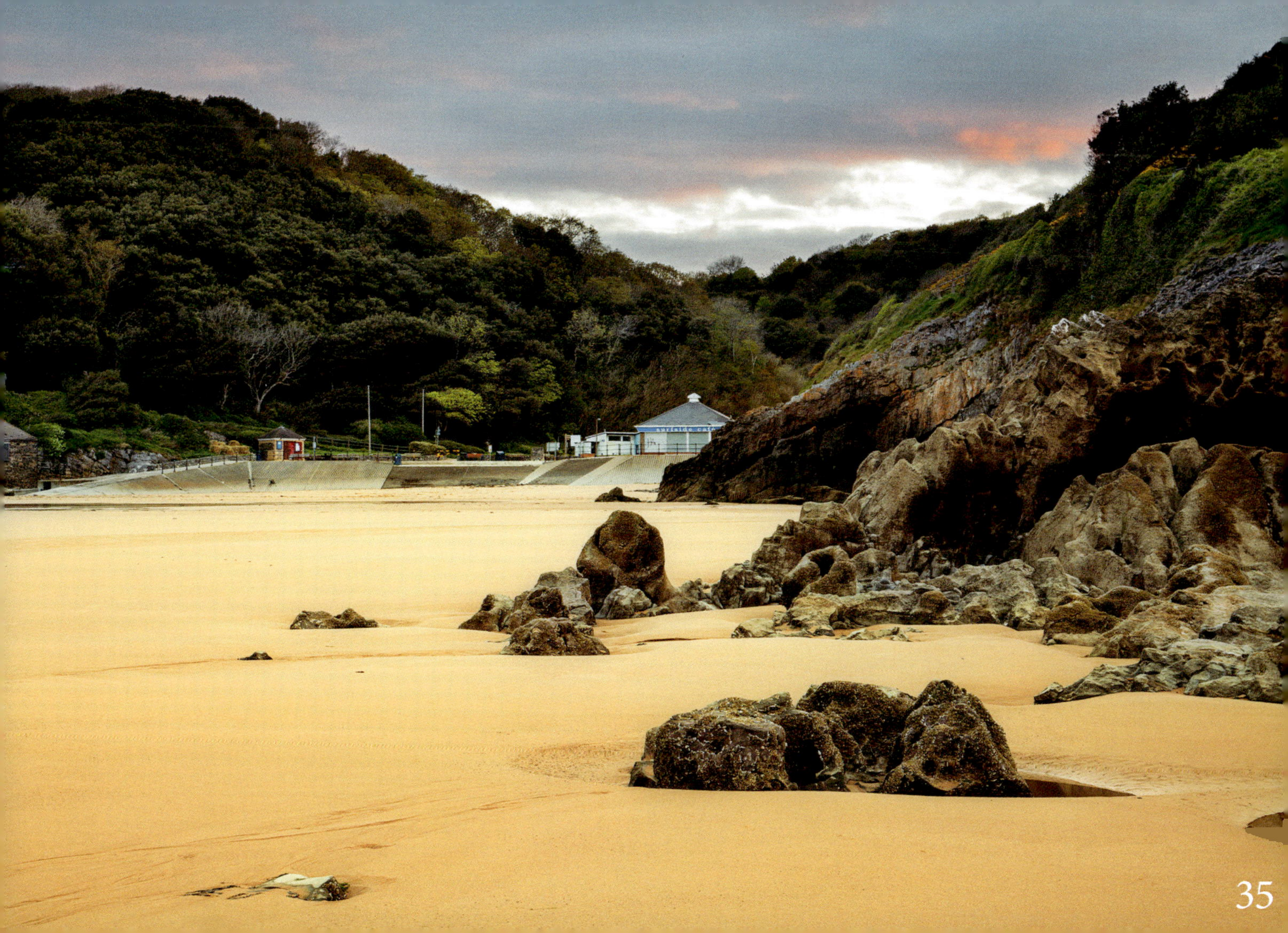

Caswell Bay

Caswell Bay is another beach that I find it hard to take a photo of that I am completely happy with. The photos here are the best I've taken of Caswell, but I still feel like I could do better. I do like this photo though and I remember the day I took it. I was recovering from a nasty chest infection and thought I was better – until I climbed the steps to the coast path. It took me a while to breath normally again and walk to this spot.

Thanks to planning the shoot, I knew exactly where the sun would rise, so I set the photo up and waited. When the sun was just above the horizon, I took this photo. I like the golden light on the trees to the left, the reflections in the sand and the sun. In fact, there is nothing wrong with it at all. I'm just left with a phrase in my mind that takes me back to my school days – "Could do better". I will definitely be going back to Caswell Bay a lot more and will be there at some rather early times of the day in summer! I'm not complaining though, the time before sunrise is the best time of the day, you feel like you have the world to yourself.

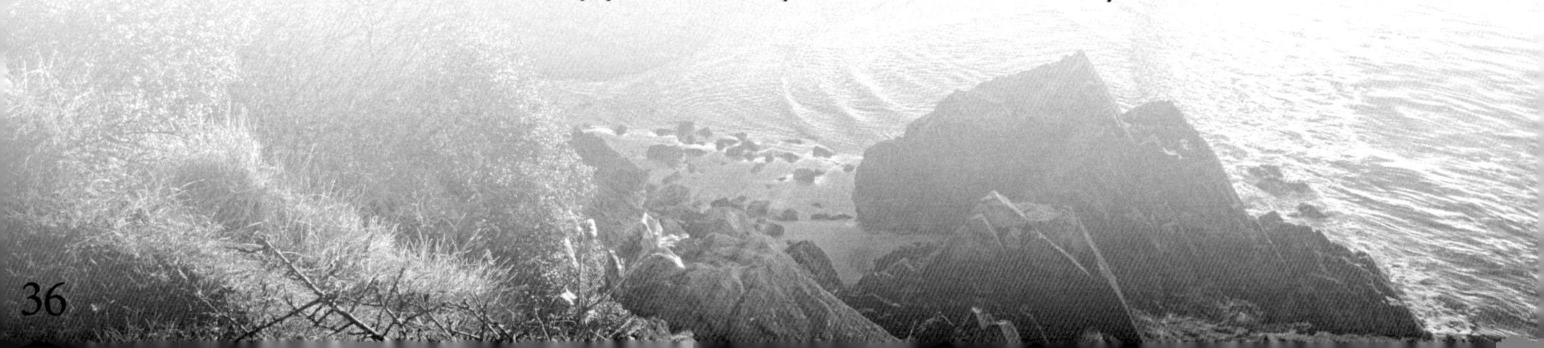

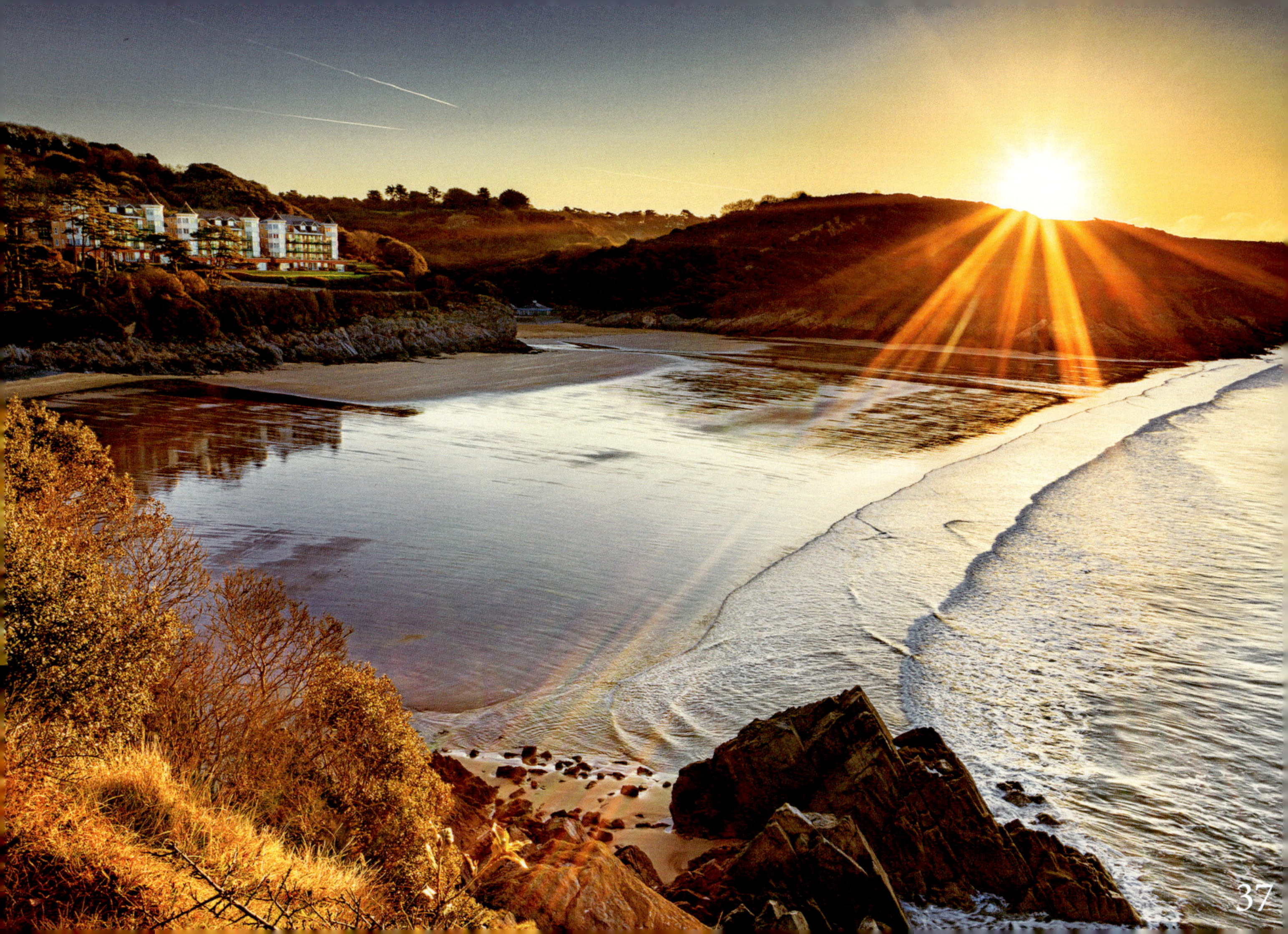

Brandy Cove

Brandy Cove is a short distance from Caswell Bay and a lot quieter than Caswell itself. If you look hard enough, you will find evidence of a raised beach which is proof that sea levels were once much higher than they are today. It is pretty rocky and not suitable for surfing. The walk is well worth it and, if you are lucky, you will have it to yourself even in summer! This photo was taken at sunrise. I love the pastel colours in this photo and find it very peaceful to look at.

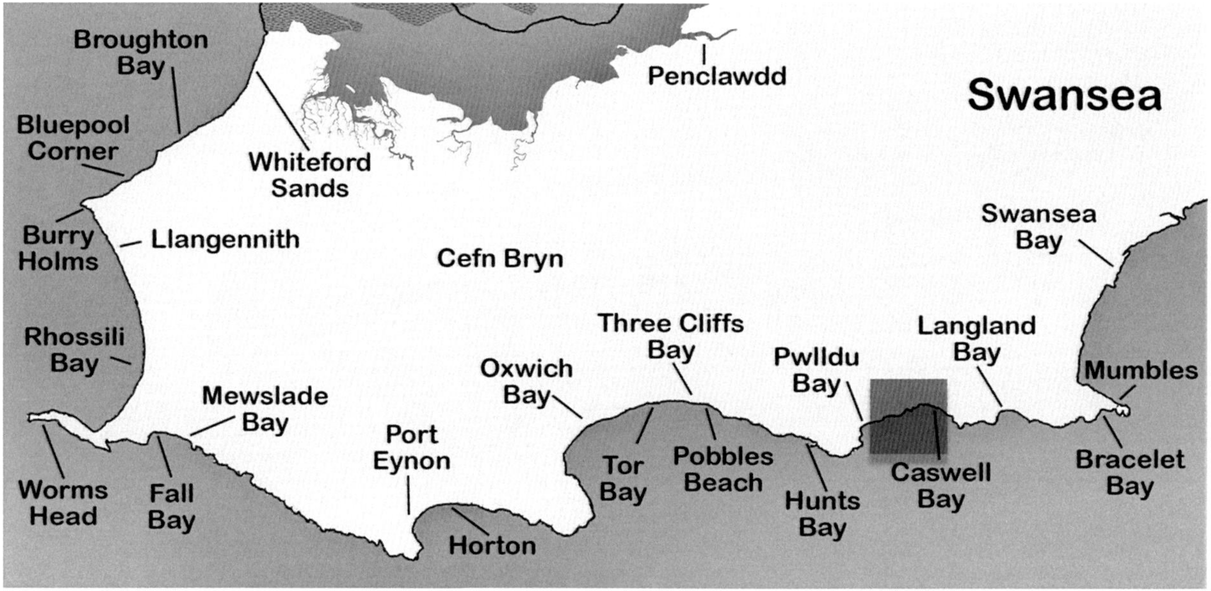

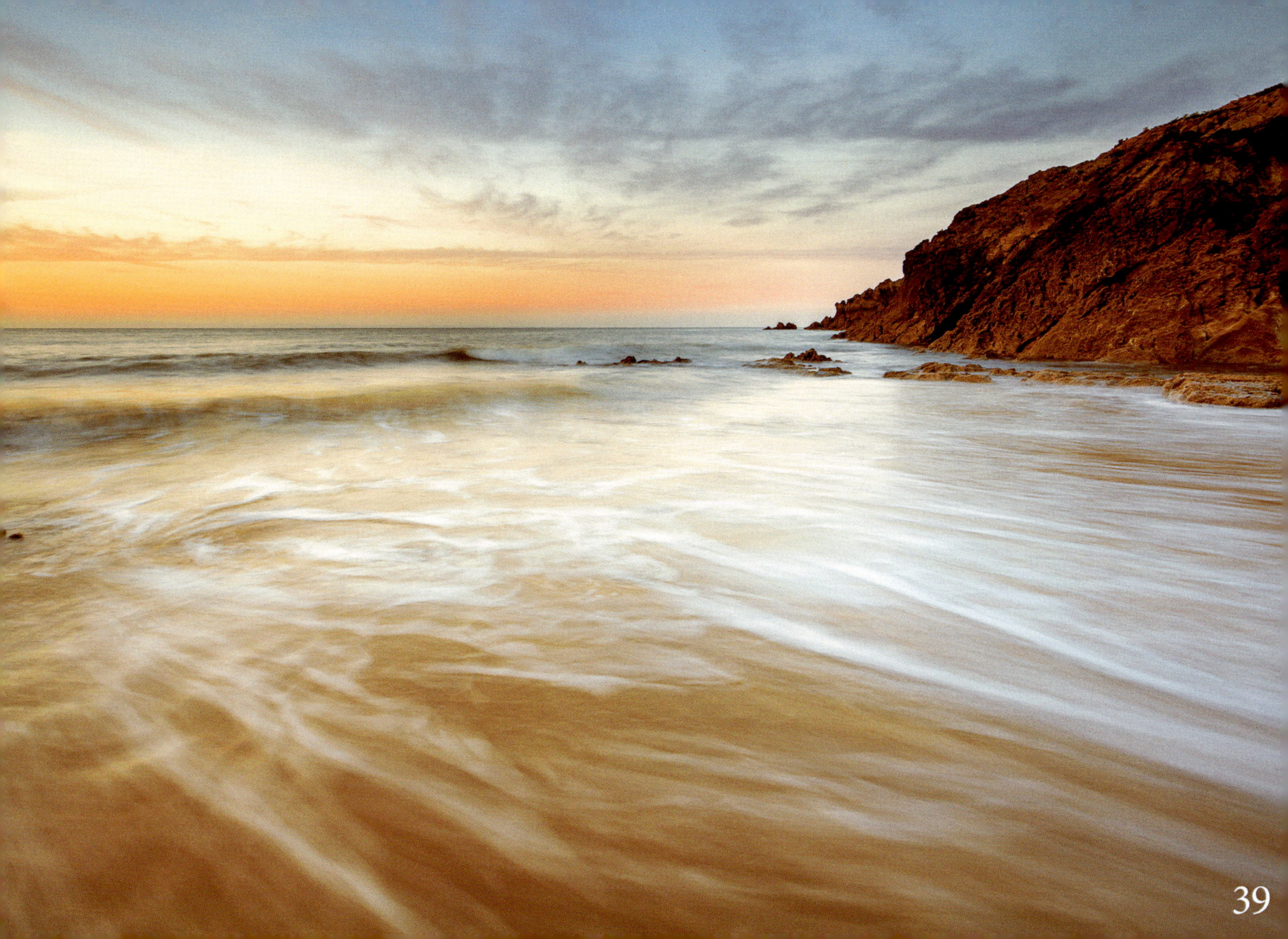

Brandy Cove

The name Brandy Cove is an unusual name for a beach and stands out from the rest of Gower beach names. It probably comes from historic links to smuggling. Pwlldu Bay is around the corner, also notorious for smuggling and in the eighteenth century smuggling was even going on in broad daylight! Brandy from France was one of the goods smuggled in and it is possible that Brandy Cove was used. In the seventeenth century, however, the beach was known as Hareslade Cove. There is logic that it became known colloquially as Brandy Cove and over time it stuck and became the official name.

At the top of Brandy Cove is an old mine adit of the Bishopstone silver/lead mine. It is gated to stop access as it is dangerous to enter without the right safety equipment and expertise. It wasn't always gated and in 1961, a sack of human bones was found in the mine entrance! Over forty years before in 1919, two people from a house overlooking Caswell Bay had disappeared and screams were reported from the Brandy Cove area. Police always suspected that George Shotton had murdered his wife Mamie Stuart but had never found any evidence – until the sack of bones was discovered. Now having enough evidence, police launched an extensive search for George, but discovered he had died himself three years previously.

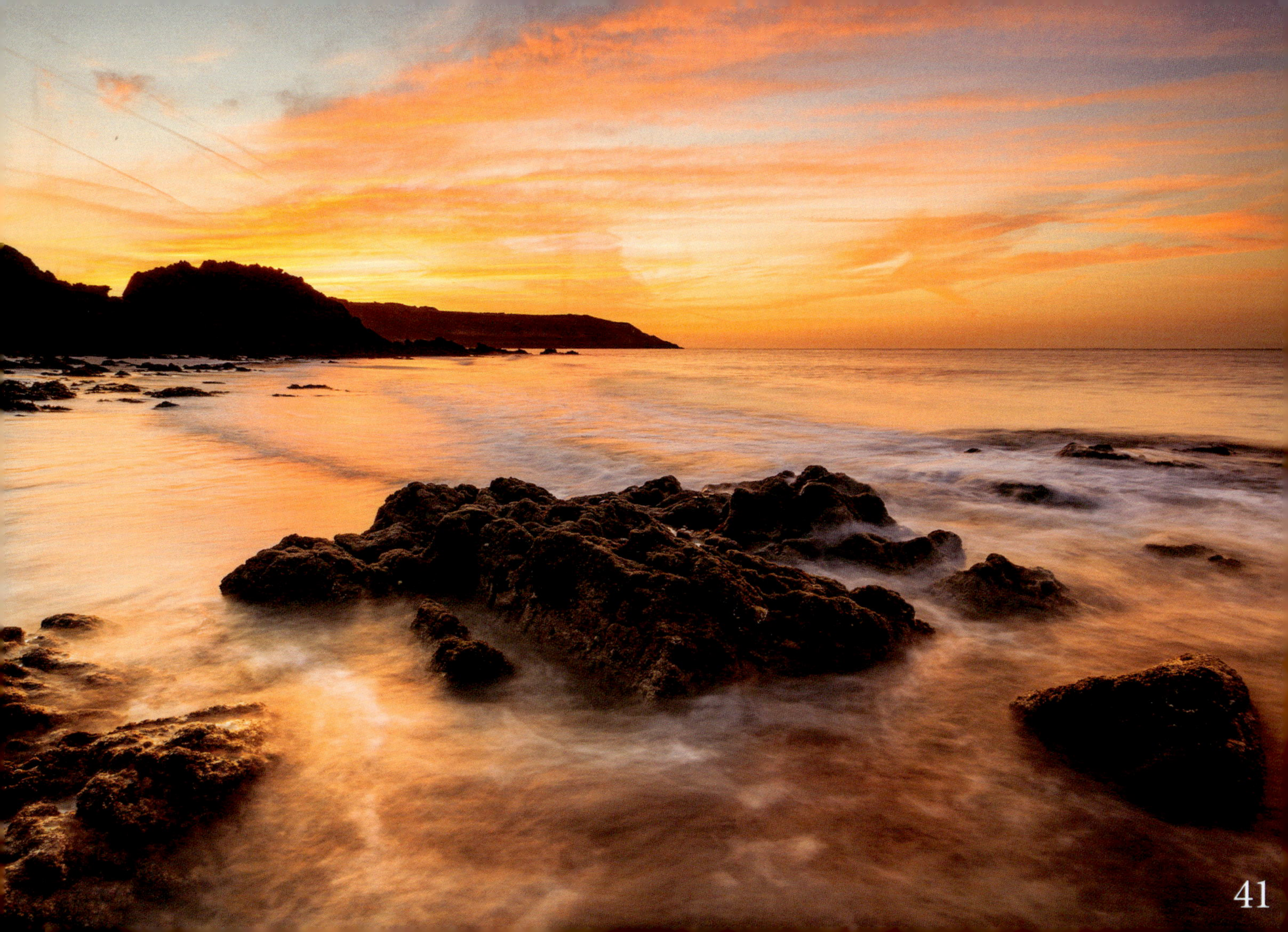

Pwlldu Bay

Pwlldu Bay is a hidden gem on Gower and only accessible via the coast path or a walk from Bishopston or Pennard. The pebble beach and shingle banks are very different from the rest of Gower and are most probably entirely from the quarrying history of the bay. They are a mixture of dumped ballast from the empty ships coming in to load the limestone and limestone that was too small to be worth loading onto the ships. The sea has washed and rolled these rocks, making them into smooth pebbles which give a distinct sound when then waves come in.

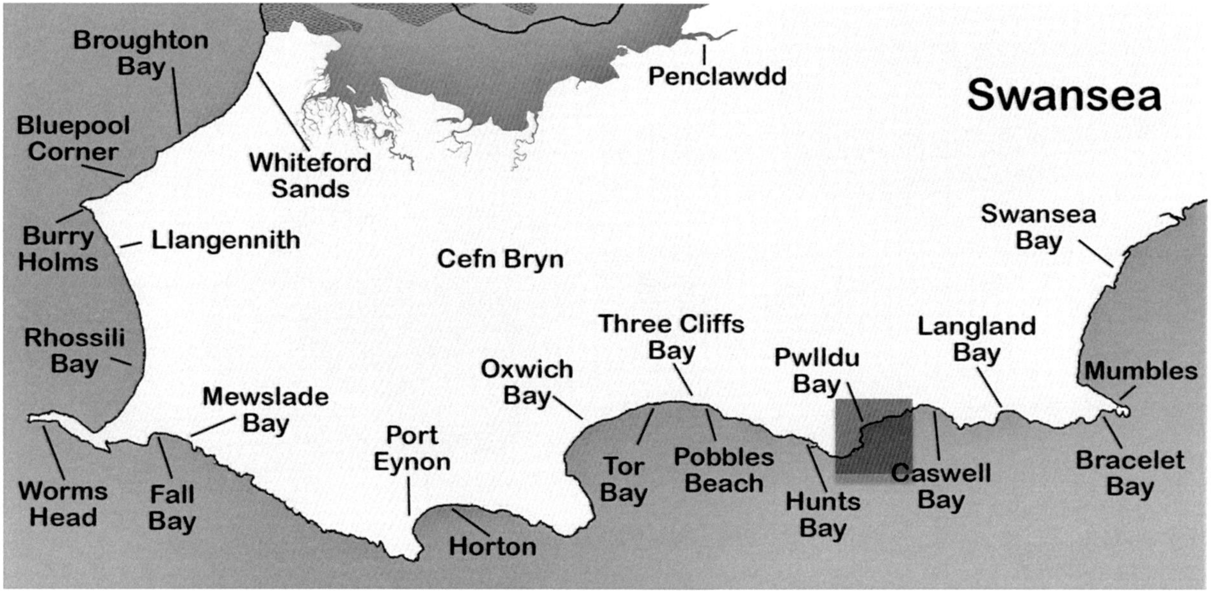

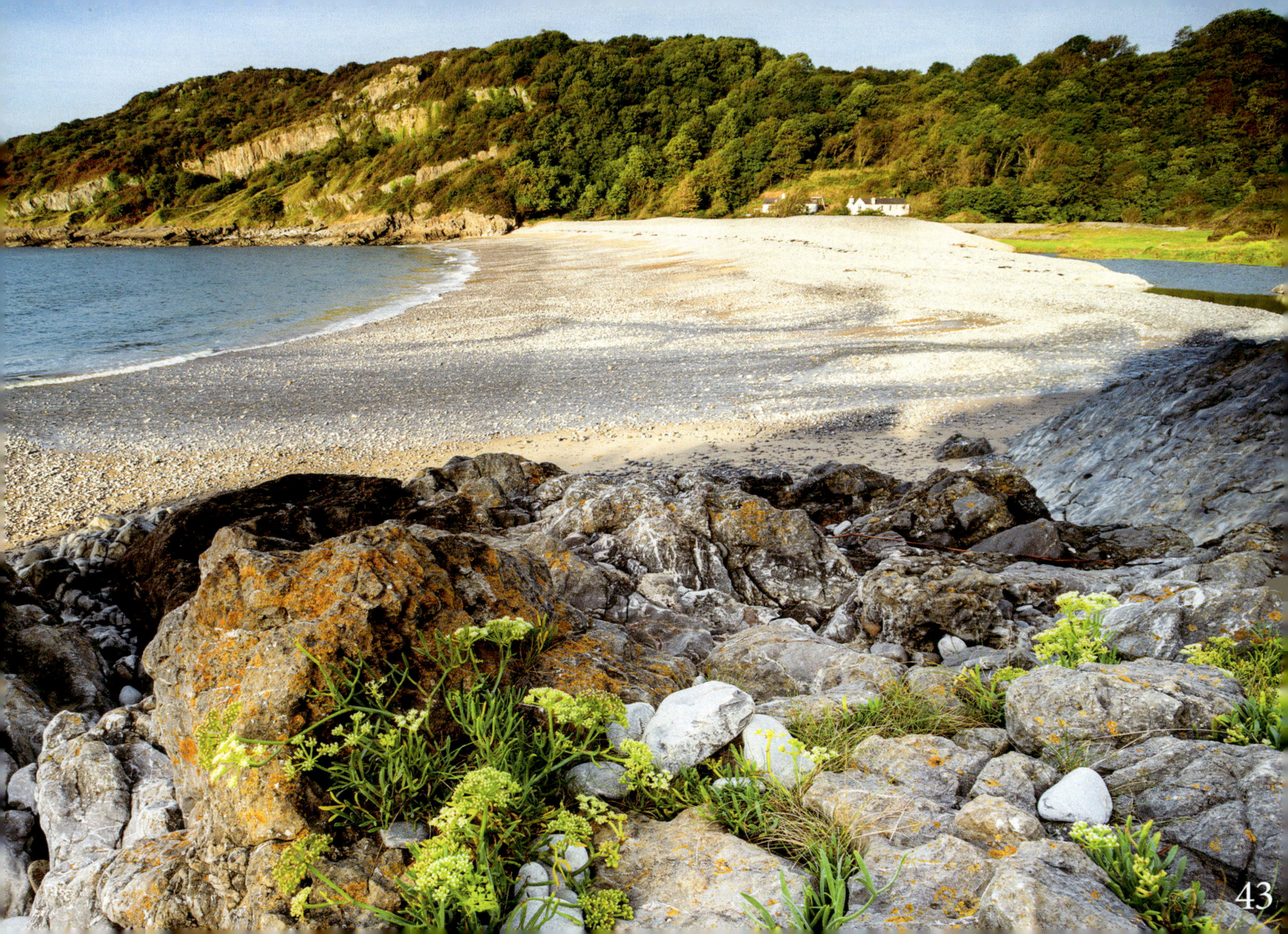

Pwlldu Bay

Quarrying is a very important part of Pwlldu's history. Limestone wasn't freely available in Devon where it was needed for farms, whilst much of Gower is made from Carboniferous Limestone of the Pembroke Limestone Group. With a demand in Devon and a supply on Gower, trade links were set up and at the time the roads weren't like they are today so sea was the obvious way to transport the limestone. The stone would be quarried by drilling holes – this might have taken a couple of days as it was all done by hand. Then explosives were detonated to break apart the cliff and the limestone assembled into piles marked with posts for collection. Some of the boulders were massive and constant movement of them to the collection points have marked the landscape.

Boats would come into Pwlldu and be deliberately scuttled to allow water to fill the hull and the seacock closed to keep the water in. Up to 60 tonnes of boulders would be loaded into the boats with the water breaking the fall and thereby protecting the ship. Then at low tide, the seacock would be opened allowing the water to drain back out. When the tide came in, the boat would refloat and sail to Devon. The whole quarrying process was hard work and the inns on the shore (seen in this photo) would have provided beer to quench the thirst of the workers.

The history of Pwlldu has been extensively researched by Heather Holt in her book Pwlldu Remembered.

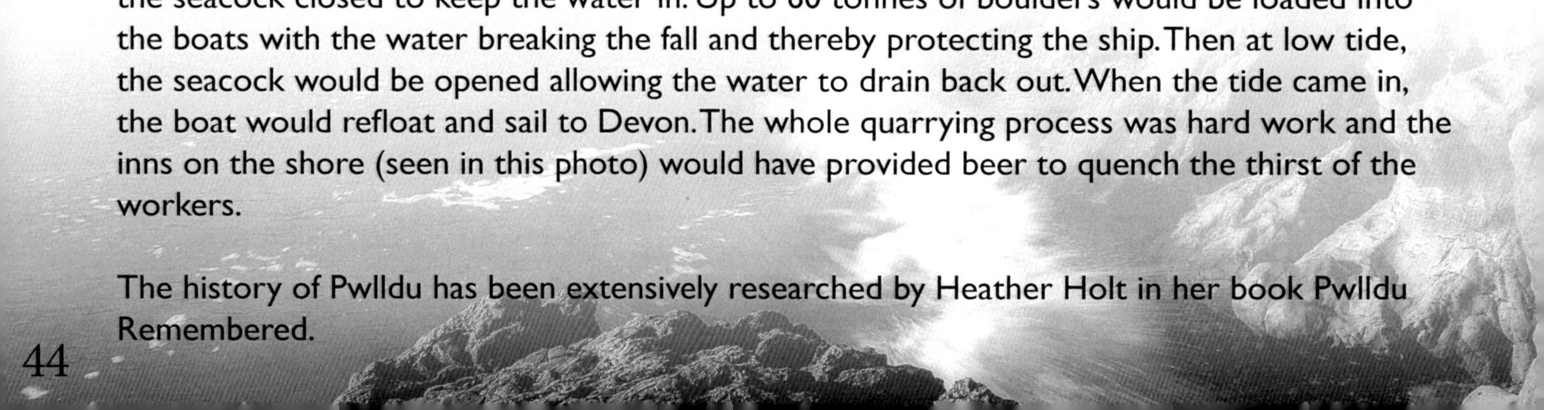

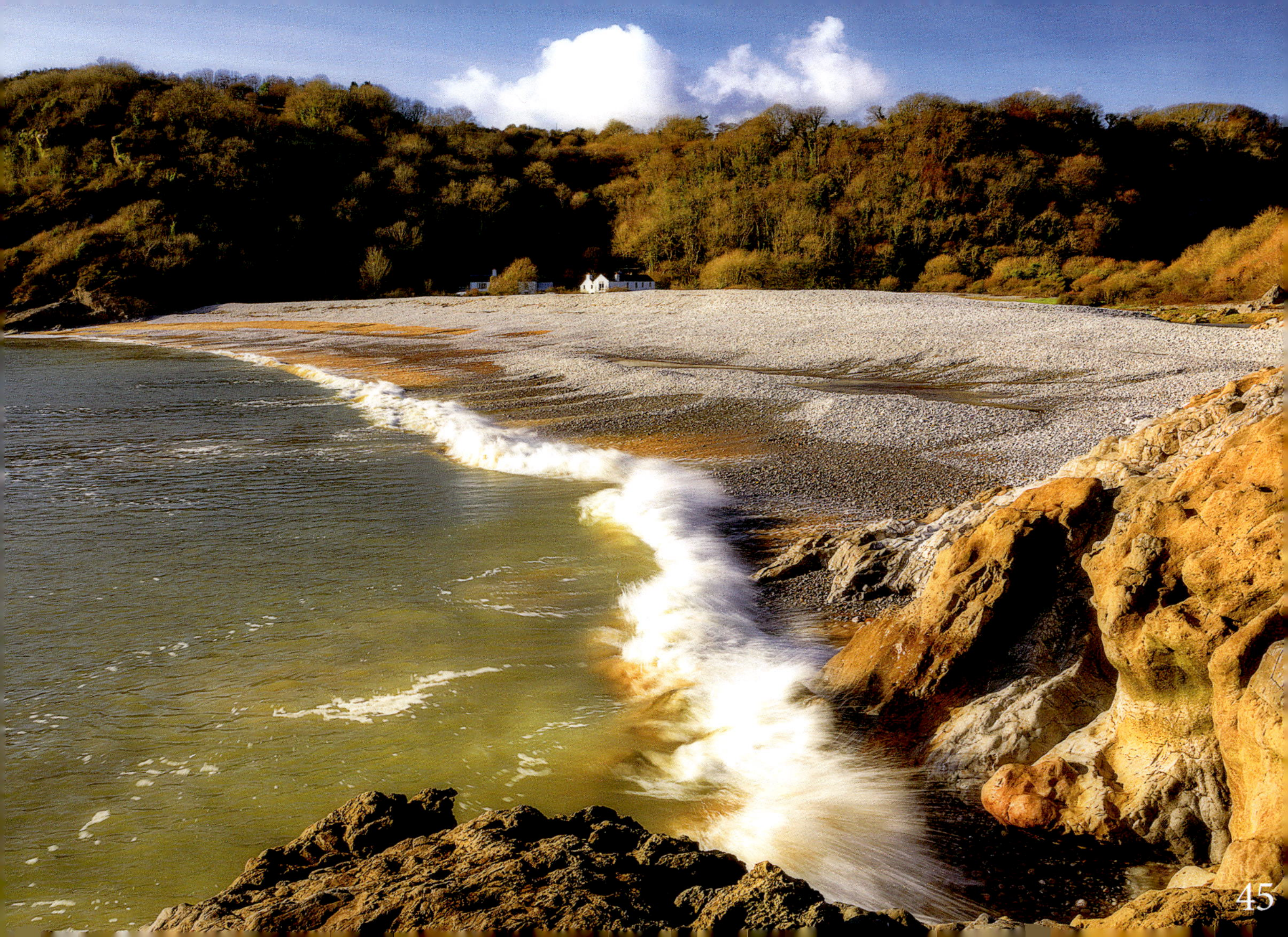

Pwlldu Bay

The pebbles on Pwlldu constantly change with the tides and when the river is in spate after heavy rain so it never looks quite the same. This river had an important role in the Second World War - for the German side! Under cover of darkness, U boats would make use of the protected bay to come and refresh their fresh water supply from the river before disappearing into the night again.

Whilst Pwlldu is a bay protected from the worst of the weather and currents, it is the location of a surprising number of shipwrecks. Perhaps the most well known one is the Admiralty ship, Caesar. In the 18th century, the Navy would sail around the coast looking for men to pressgang into the Navy to fight wars. Perfectly legal, they would be locked below deck. On 28th November 1760, rough seas forced it aground on Pwlldu Head. A few crew escaped, but the pressganged men weren't so lucky and all lost their lives.

Local villagers, hoping to salvage valuable items from the wreck, found the drowned men. They dragged them ashore and gave them a funeral, marking the place with a circle of rocks. Today the place is known as Grave's End and the circle of rocks still visible.

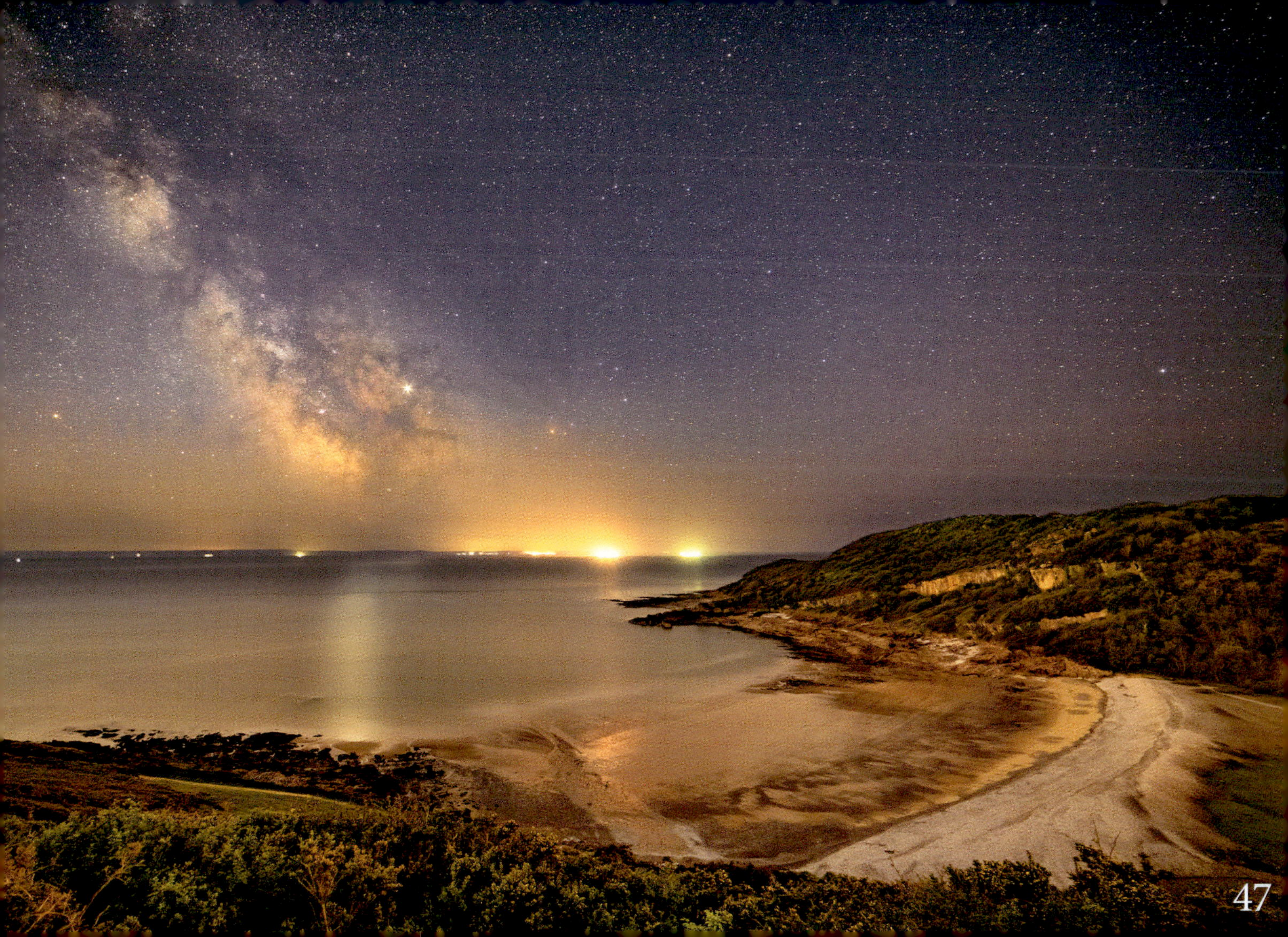

Hunts Bay

Around the corner from Pwlldu Point is Hunts Bay, also known as Deep Slade. It is a very rocky beach and has three notable caves nearby: Minchin Hole which is difficult to access and was once inhabited during the Roman times and the Dark Ages; Bacon Hole which is very easy to access and was also once inhabited during the Roman times and the Iron Ages; Bosco's Den, also known as Bacon's Eye, which is difficult to access but many ancient finds have been made such as bear, wolf and deer.

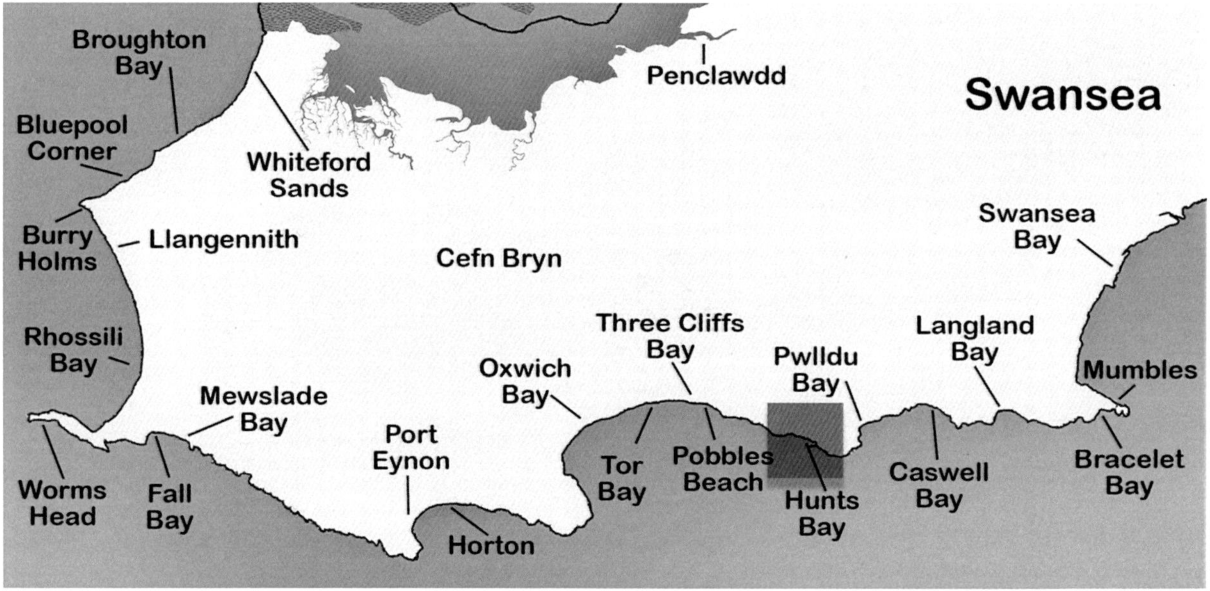

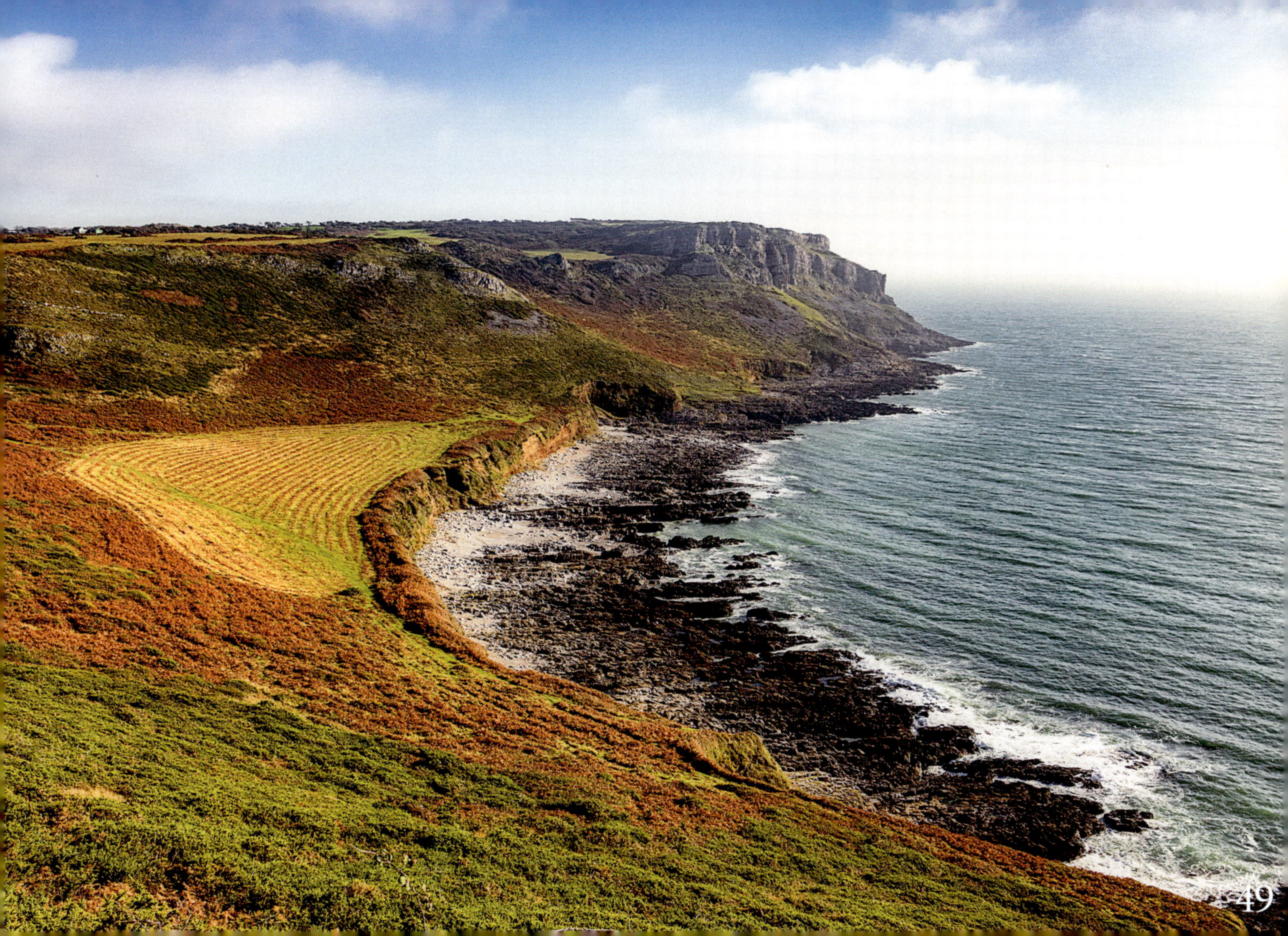

Pobbles Beach

Walking from Southgate towards Pobbles Beach, also known as Pobbles Bay, is a lovely little walk and the scenery is fascinating with the limestone cliffs and grass top which are home to an abundance of wild flowers in spring and summer. The first hint of the beach is the iconic Three Cliffs jutting out, guarding Pobbles Beach. There was apparently once a dove cote built into the cliffs here, but this has long since gone. This photo was taken on a cold and frosty winter's morning with the moon shining brightly onto the sea.

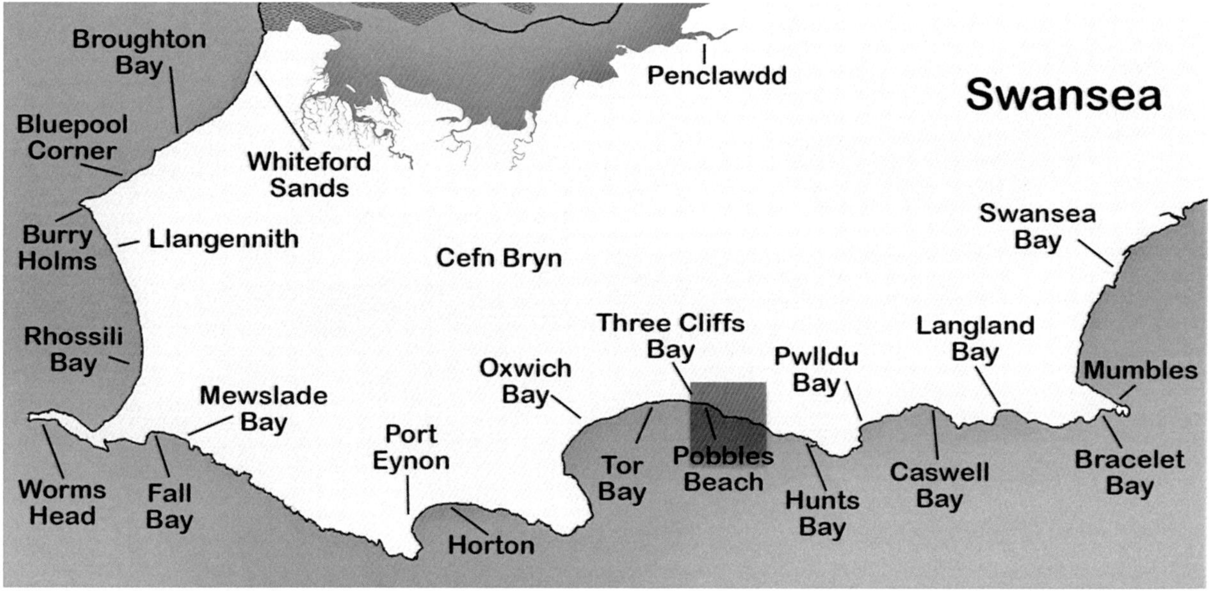

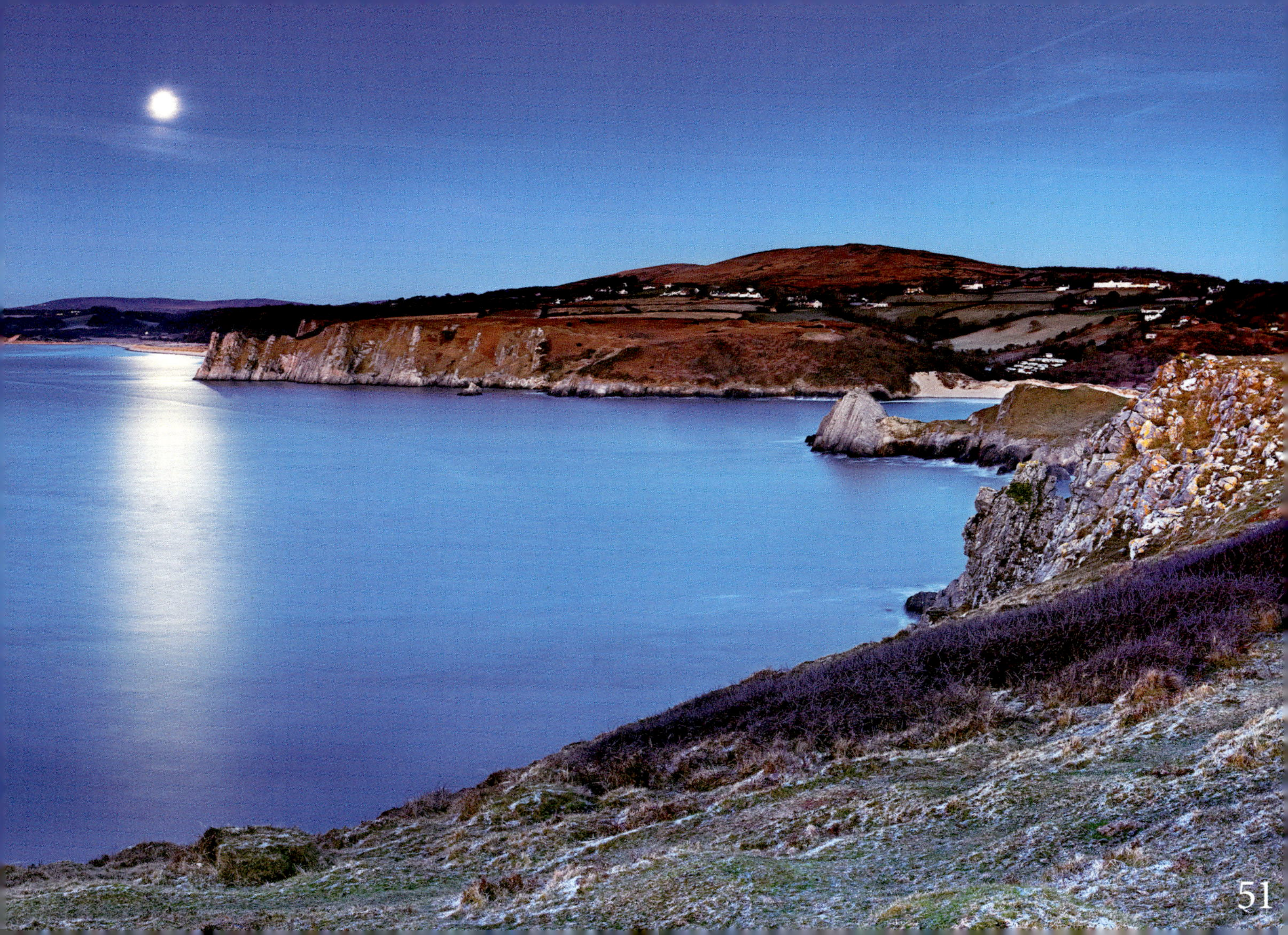

Pobbles Beach

There is a fascinating geological story in this photo - if you look at Great Tor (the cliff in the top left) and the rocks in the foreground, all the layers of rock are almost vertical when they should be horizontal.

The Carboniferous Limestone rocks you see formed some 300 to 400 million years ago. Early on in the Carboniferous period, a clear tropical sea called the Rheic Ocean flooded what would later become south Wales. It was rich with life and the animals that lived in the sea died and fell to the bottom. This went on for many years creating a thick layer. Over time this turned into rock, encasing the myriad of fossils that you can find today.

At the end of the Carboniferous period, tectonic plate action closed the Rheic Ocean. The continents either side collided and threw up mountain ranges which caused the once horizontal rocks to ripple and warp. This was known as the Variscan Deformation, which created a massive supercontinent called Pangea. After the collisions, over a long period of time, many of the rocks were eroded creating the beaches and bays you see today on Gower.

To summarise, you are looking at an ancient sea bed that was then rippled when two continents collided!

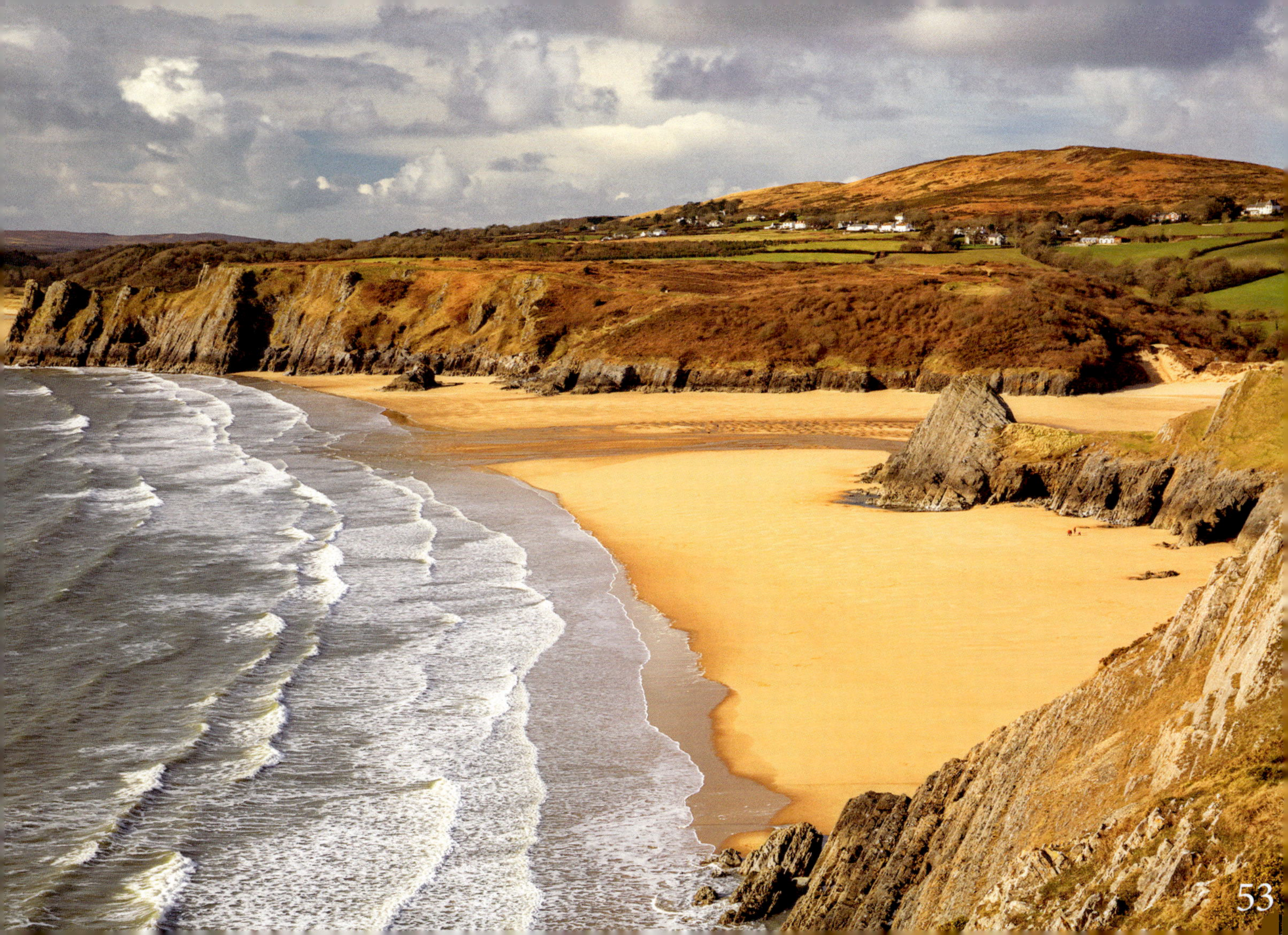

Pobbles Beach

After walking along the cliffs, you can get to Pobbles by carefully walking down the steep path and then turning left to go over the pebbles and then you are on Pobbles. At high tide you are very restricted, but as soon as the tide recedes, you can walk out onto the sand and even around the Three Cliffs themselves.

The photo here shows Pobbles at low tide. This is another time that I used my astrophotography 14mm lens during the day as it was the only way to get the whole beach in.

If you are feeling energetic after the walk from Southgate or Pennard, you can climb up the path on the other side to find the best viewpoint on Gower. Looking to your left, you will see Pobbles in its entirety (as in this photo). Looking straight ahead and to your right, however, you will see the majestic Three Cliffs Bay and this will most certainly take your breath away...

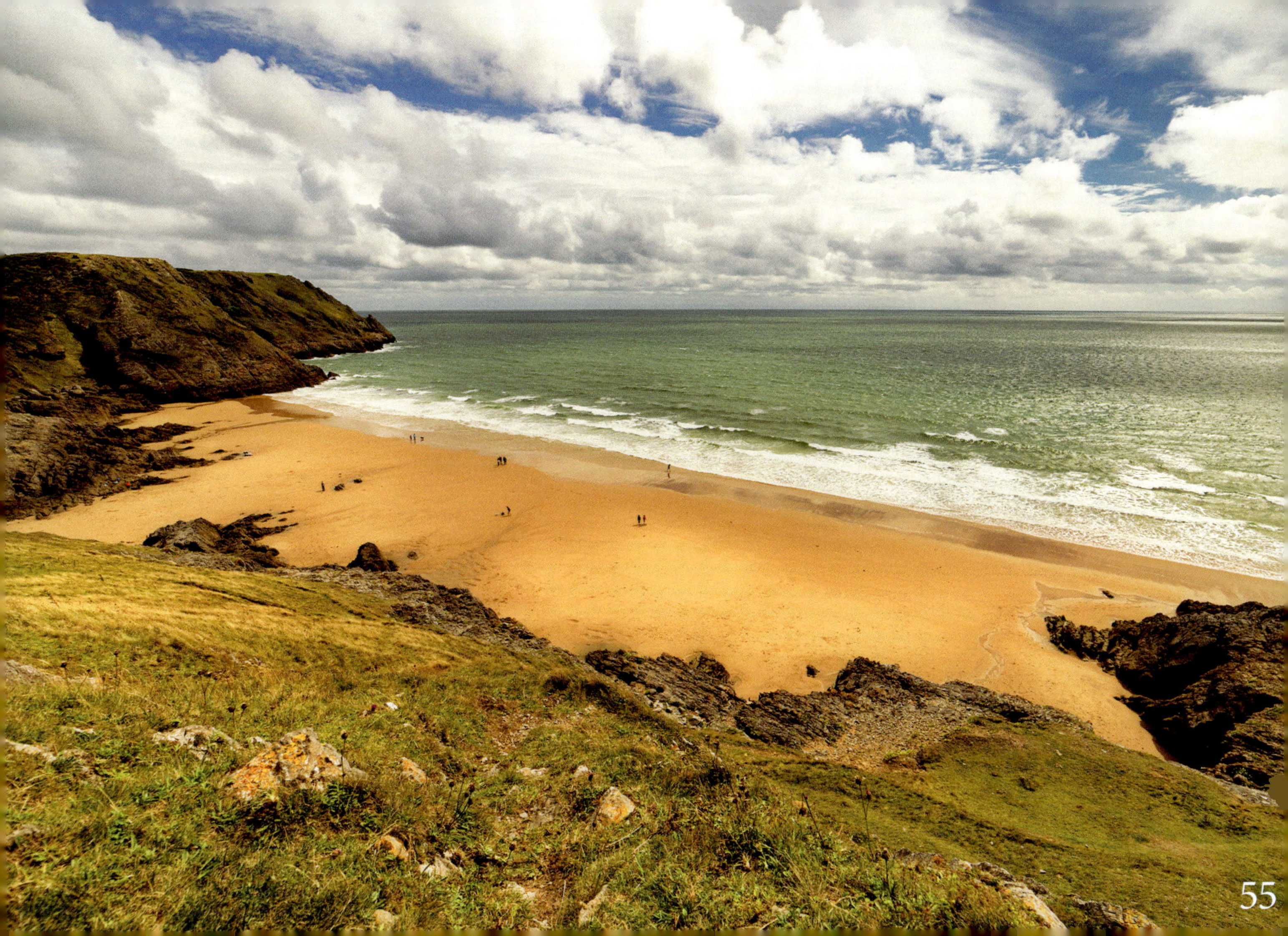

Three Cliffs Bay

Three Cliffs Bay is, in my opinion, one of the best places on Gower. It has won several awards, including in 2018 when it was voted to be in the top 10 beaches in Britain by TripAdvisor and also in the top 20 beaches in Europe during the same year. Where else can you see a sight like this in Wales or even the world? It is one of the Gower beaches that you have to walk to get to, but that doesn't make it any less popular. This photo was taken at sunset when the tide was very high on Easter Day.

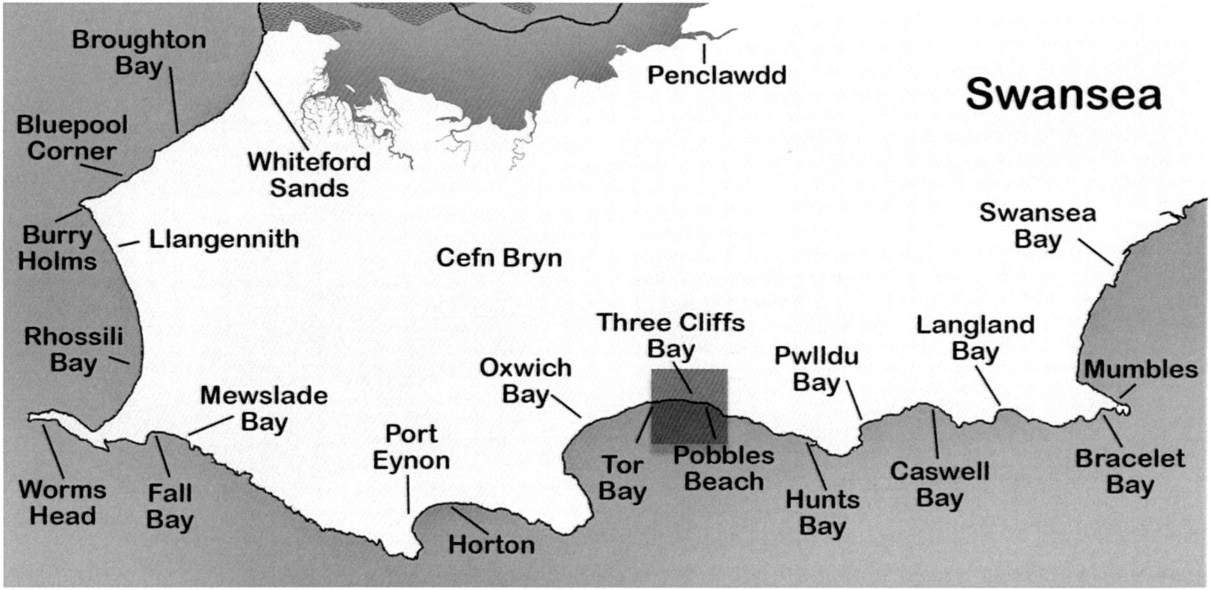

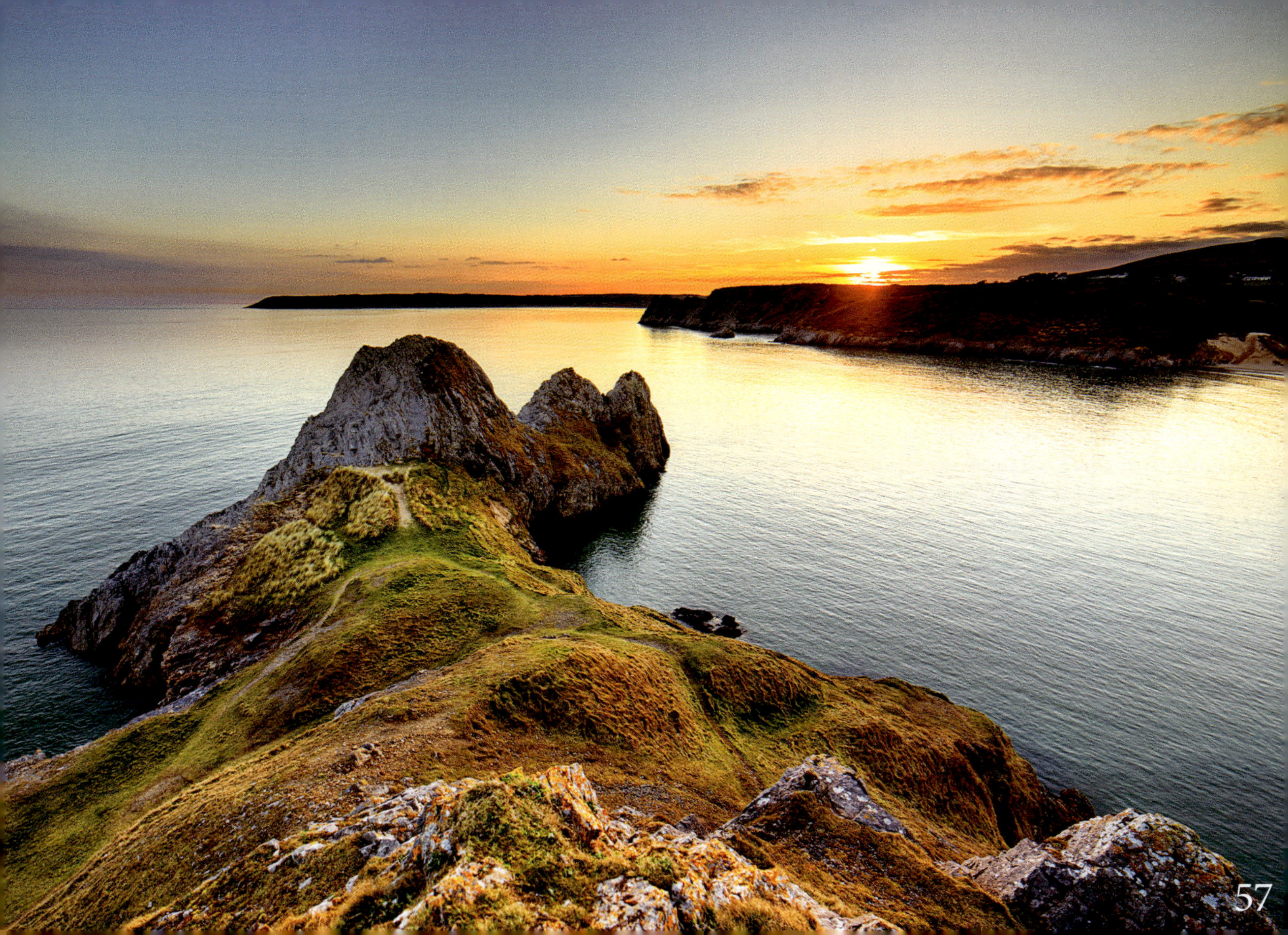

Three Cliffs Bay

This is a photo taken at night from the same spot. The green in the sky is called 'airglow' and is a natural phenomenon that occurs frequently, although you won't see it with your eyes. The camera is far more sensitive to light than our eyes are so 'sees' more than we do. I had no idea it was there until I had taken the photo!

Airglow is caused by a process called "chemiluminescence". High in the atmosphere at around 100Km, during the day the sun gives extra energy to oxygen molecules which causes then to split apart into oxygen atoms. The atomic oxygen isn't able to easily disperse the excess energy and eventually recombines to create molecular oxygen. When it does, the oxygen molecules release the excess energy in the form of light which gives the green light you can see here. Other colours are sometimes produced too. Whilst it does look a bit like the Aurora Borealis, it is caused by a different process.

The brightest star in this photo is Sirius. Sirius is 8.611 light years away, which is approximately 51 trillion miles. It would take a space ship roughly 160,000 years to get there (assuming conventional travel with no space folding or worm holes). Funnily enough, Sirius is really close to us! The light from Sirius takes just 9 years to get to us. In comparison, our nearest galaxy neighbour is the Andromeda Galaxy - it takes light 2.5 million years to reach us from there!!

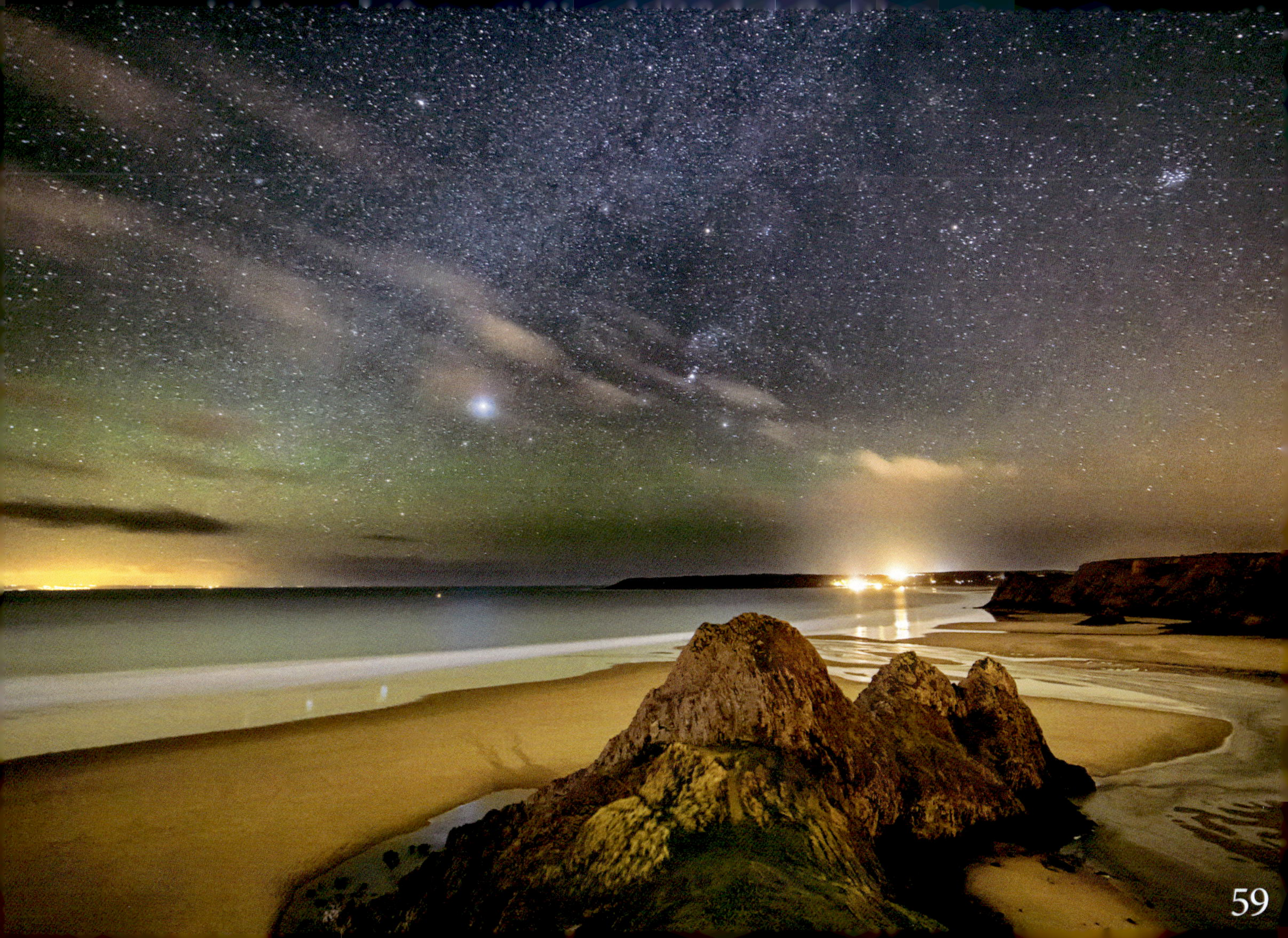

Three Cliffs Bay

When I'm at these sorts of places, I often find myself wondering how and why they look like they do. The sand mostly comes from glaciers as there is too much sand to be created by sea erosion alone – as the glaciers moved, they ground the rock to dust, sand, grit, etc. The river runs down the valley because there is a minor geological fault that the water has taken advantage of – water always takes the easiest path. Over many years, the river has helped carve the valley. And the cliffs themselves, how did they end up looking like that? It is due to the way the uplifted rocks dip into the sea. All these things have come together and created the Three Cliffs Bay we see today.

This photo was taken just before the sun disappeared for the day. I love the way the clouds are reflected perfectly in the calm part of the river.

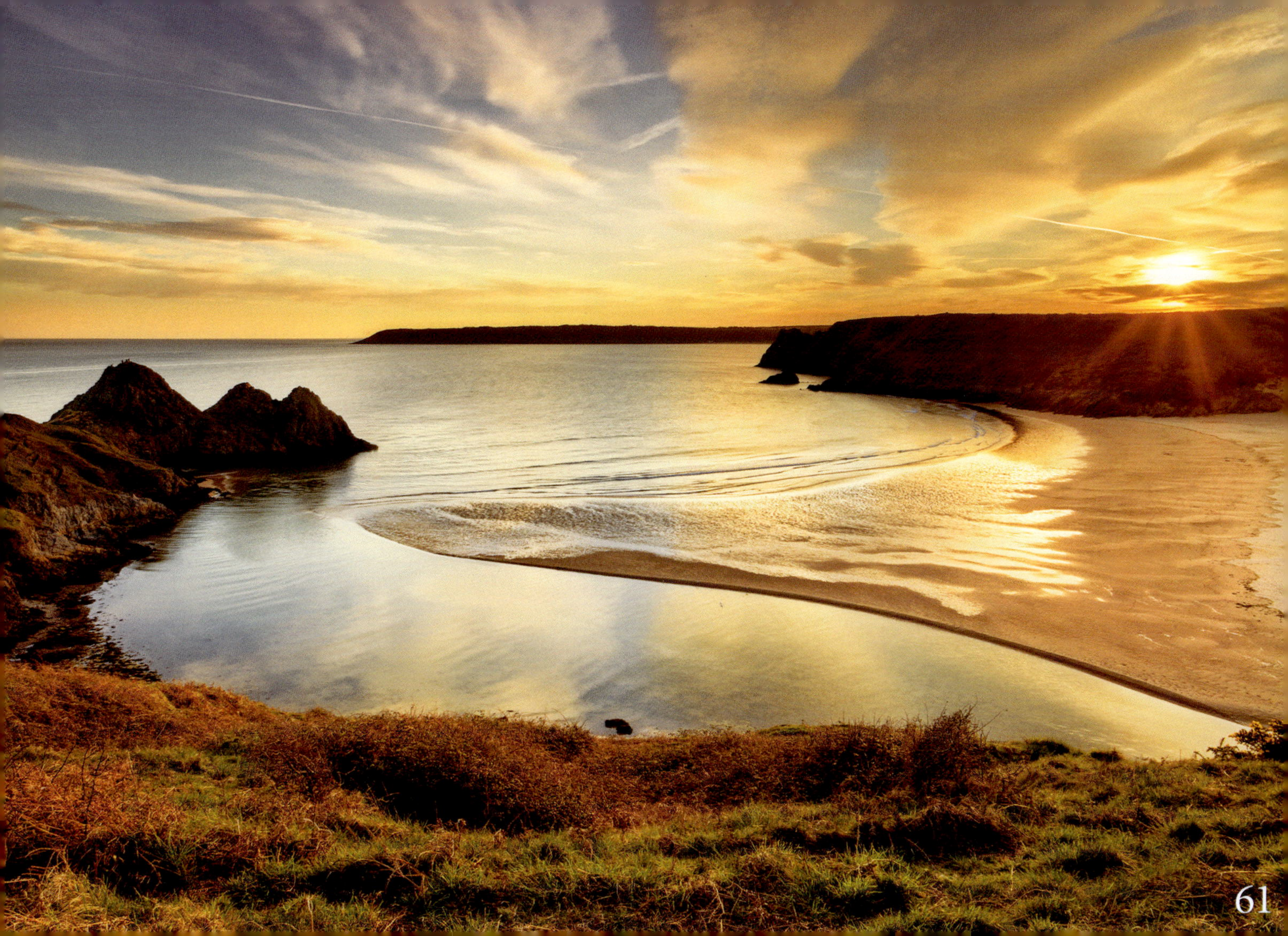

Three Cliffs Bay

Pennard Pill starts its life at Kithen Well spring in Park Wood, or Parc-le-Breos, and the marshes on Fairwood Common near Swansea Airport. They meet near the Gower Heritage Centre at Parkmill before meandering between the steep cliffs of Northill Wood and Pennard Burrows. Further springs join the river near Pennard Castle before it finally flows into the sea at Three Cliffs Bay.

Pennard Pill is a classic example of an 'old aged river' with the flood plain and meandering path taking a very non-direct route to the sea. There are three stages of rivers – Youthful, Mature and Old Age. The terms have nothing to do with actual age, however. Youthful is the upper course that is often fast flowing and active; Mature is the middle course when the river starts to slow down and meander; Old Age is the lower course with flood plains, oxbow lakes, meandering, etc.

You can walk down to Three Cliffs Bay via the path just in front of you here, but it is all sand. Going down isn't too bad, but coming back up is hard work!

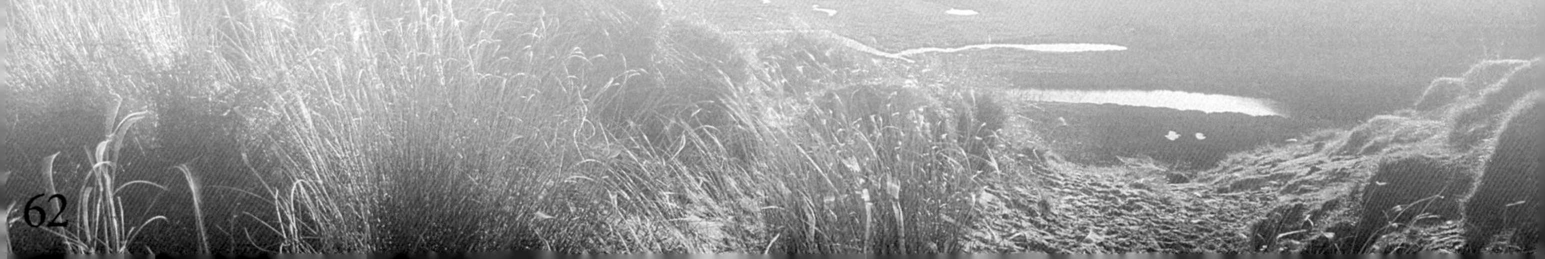

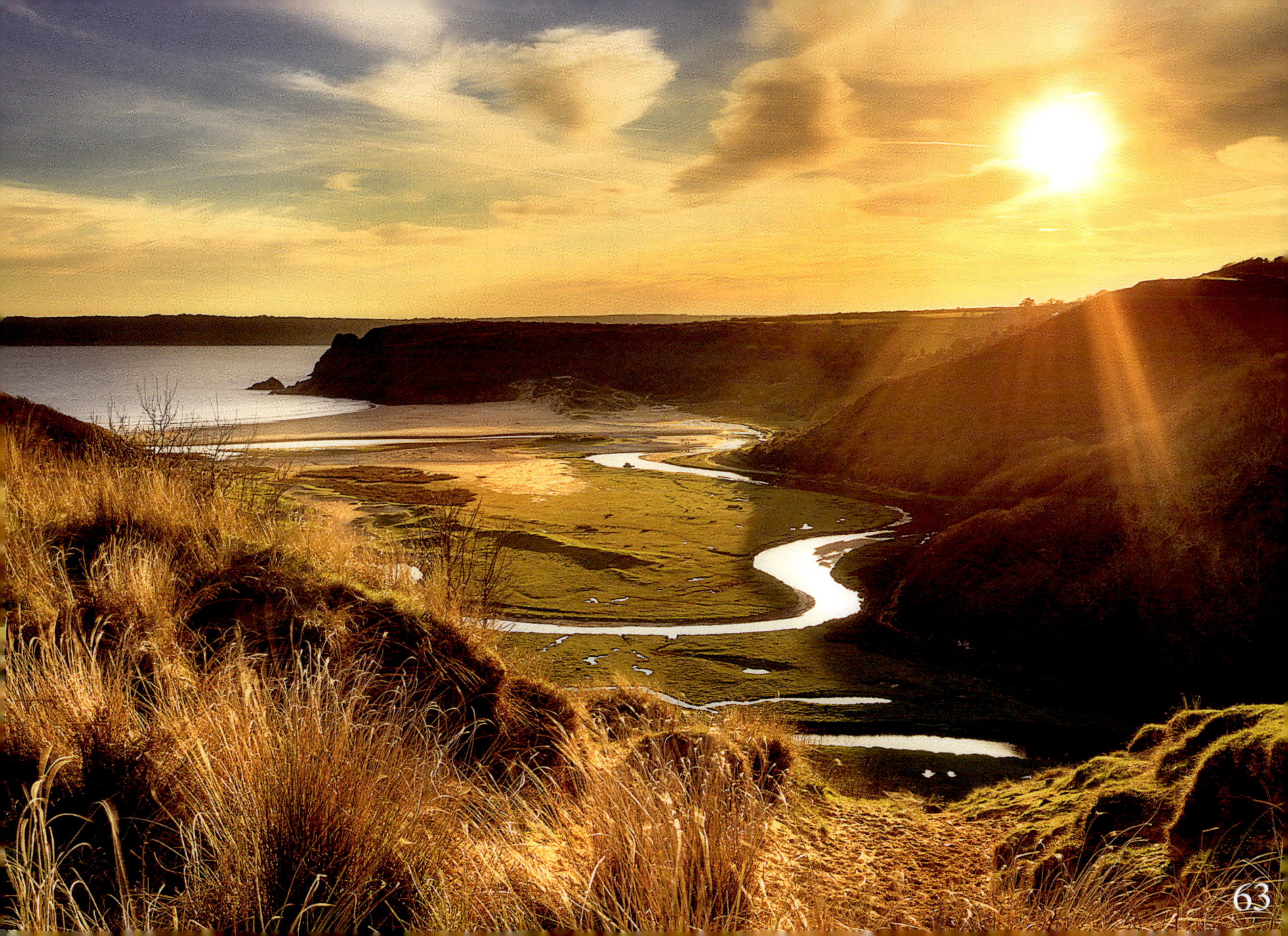

Three Cliffs Bay

This is Pennard Castle, which was originally built in the 12th century using wood but was later rebuilt with stone in the 13th century and 14th century. Shortly after that, storms started to blow sand inland which overcame the castle and also the church, the ruins of which can still be seen near to the castle on the golf course. This would lead one to naturally assume that if there is a church there, then there is also be an abandoned village beneath the sands on the golf course.

There is a story that the sand encroachment was caused by a group of fairies on their way to the castle to join in wedding celebrations, but the baron mistook them for an invading army and attacked them. As he lay on the ground exhausted, he realised it wasn't an invading army but the fairies. A wind came in blowing the fairies away and a violent storm started to batter the castle. That night, sand engulfed the castle.

Through the archway is the Pennard water tower. Now disused, it is an iconic part of Pennard. There was some discussion about demolishing it, but that was met with local resistance so it still stands today.

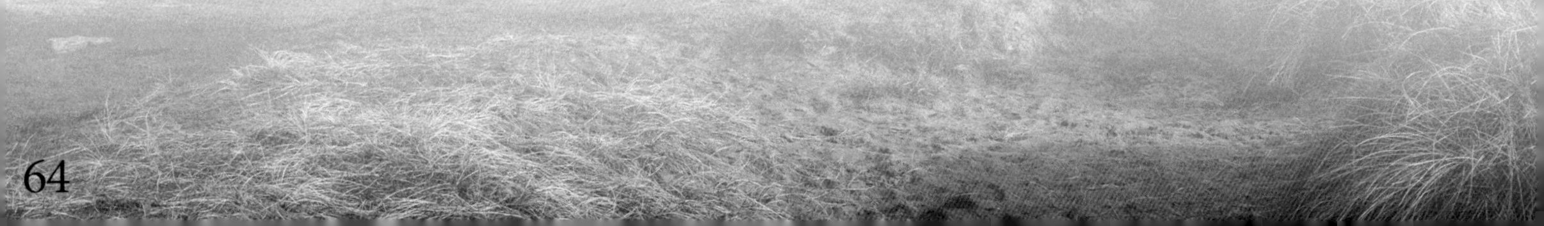

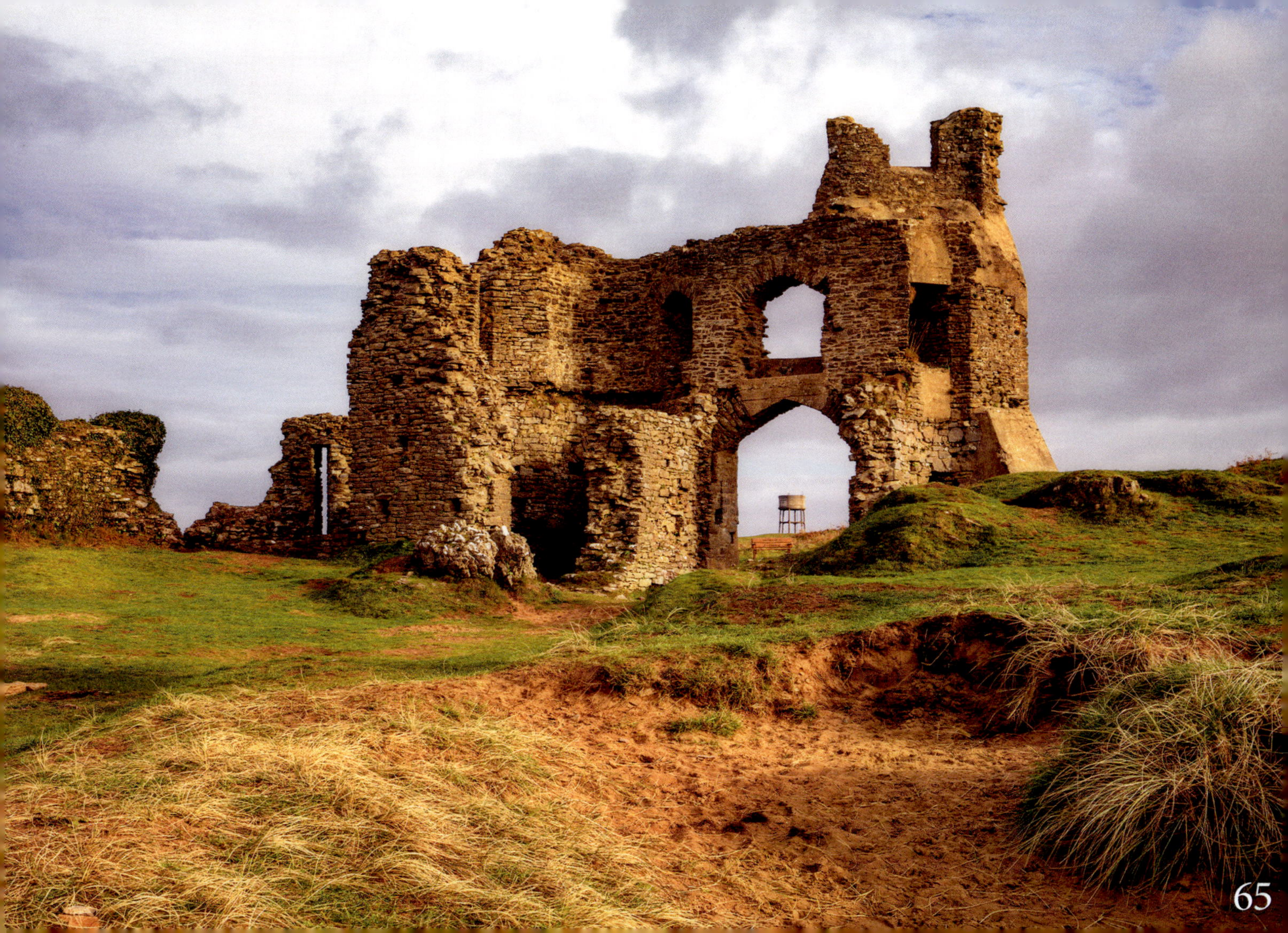

Three Cliffs Bay

Three Cliffs Bay is one of my favourite places to go at night, and this time I went onto the beach to capture the meteor shower. I didn't even see a single meteor, but I did capture this photo. After sunset, it takes approximately two hours to get completely dark. The camera is very sensitive to light so even though it appears dark to our eyes, the camera can capture a photo that looks like daylight as well as having stars in it.

Three Cliffs Bay is managed by the National Trust, who own and look after around three quarters of Gower's coastline. Mewslade Bay was the first area to be given to the Trust in 1933, but the 1960s saw most of the acquisition.

The river at the bottom of the photo, Pennard Pill, flows into the sea at Three Cliffs and is notorious for causing rip tides. Following three fatalities over two years, lifeguard support has been added to the beach during the summer months as well as some school holidays.

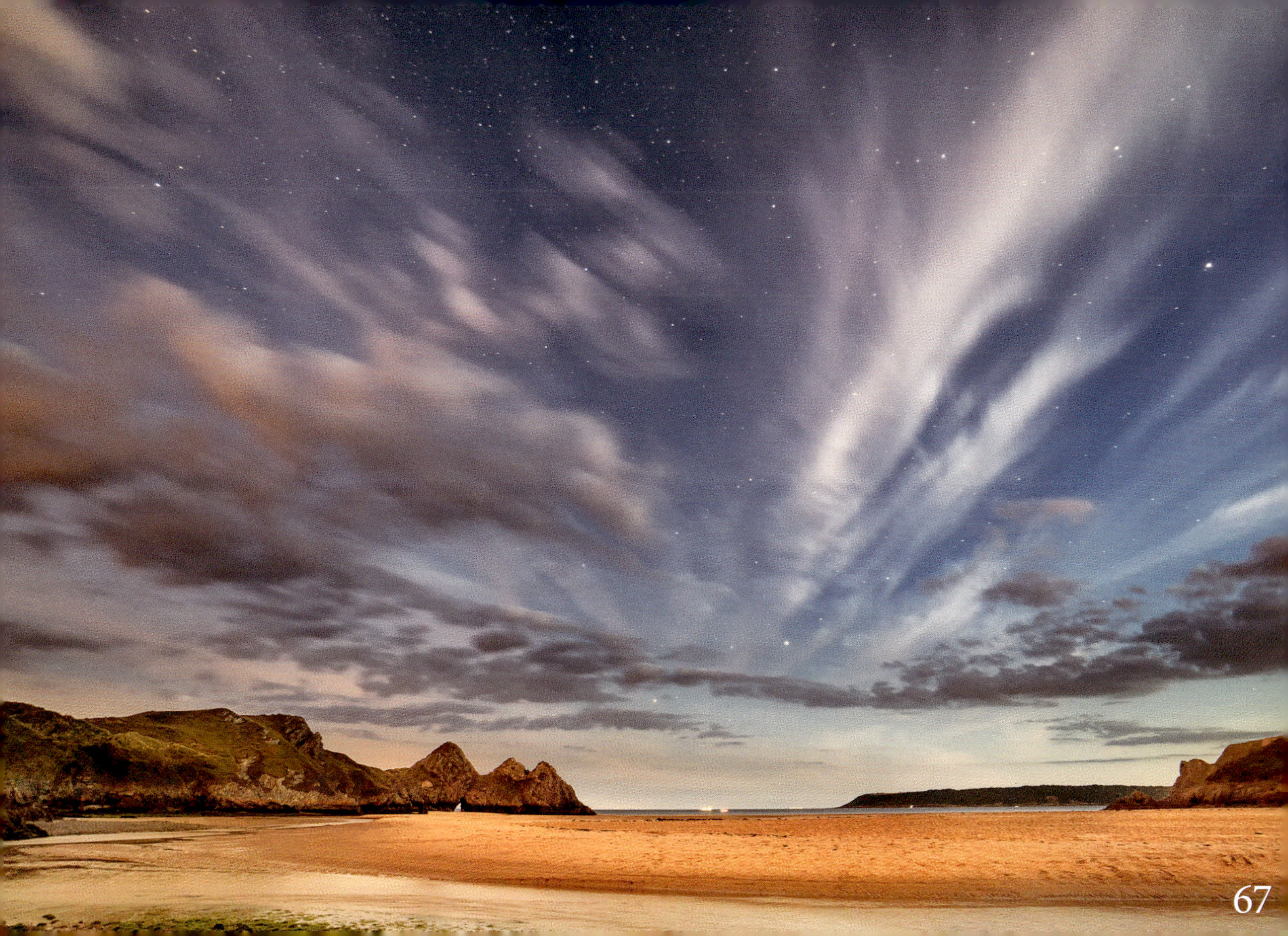

Three Cliffs Bay

During the summer of 2018, beaches around Swansea became a hive of activity at night and there were people walking around at midnight and even 2am! A natural phenomenon called bioluminescent plankton was the culprit. With the power of social media, a sighting at Aberavon meant people were there at night for weeks along with Three Cliffs Bay, Oxwich Bay and further east to Dunraven Bay on the Glamorgan Heritage Coast.

It is an incredible sight and one I am hoping to see again. After spending sunset on the edge of the beach at high tide, the water receded a lot faster than I had planned. By the time it was dark enough, the tide was too far out to photograph the plankton with the cliffs. We did see it on this occasion and were able to make the sand and pools of water sparkle bright blue, but we didn't manage to take any photos of it unfortunately.

We stayed on and walked around the beach with plenty of other people still there after midnight. There was no moon and the Milky Way was strong, so we walked to this viewpoint to capture it rising from the cliffs. It took a while to get this photo because there were so many people with head torches on. People have said this photo makes the Three Cliffs look a bit like a volcano. I now refer to this photo as the 'Three Cliffs Volcano'!

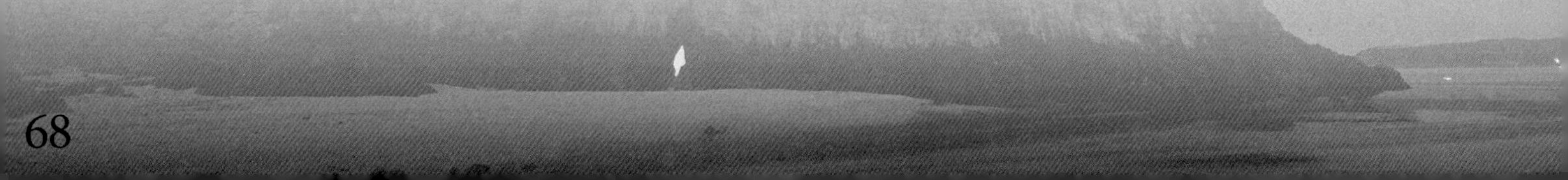

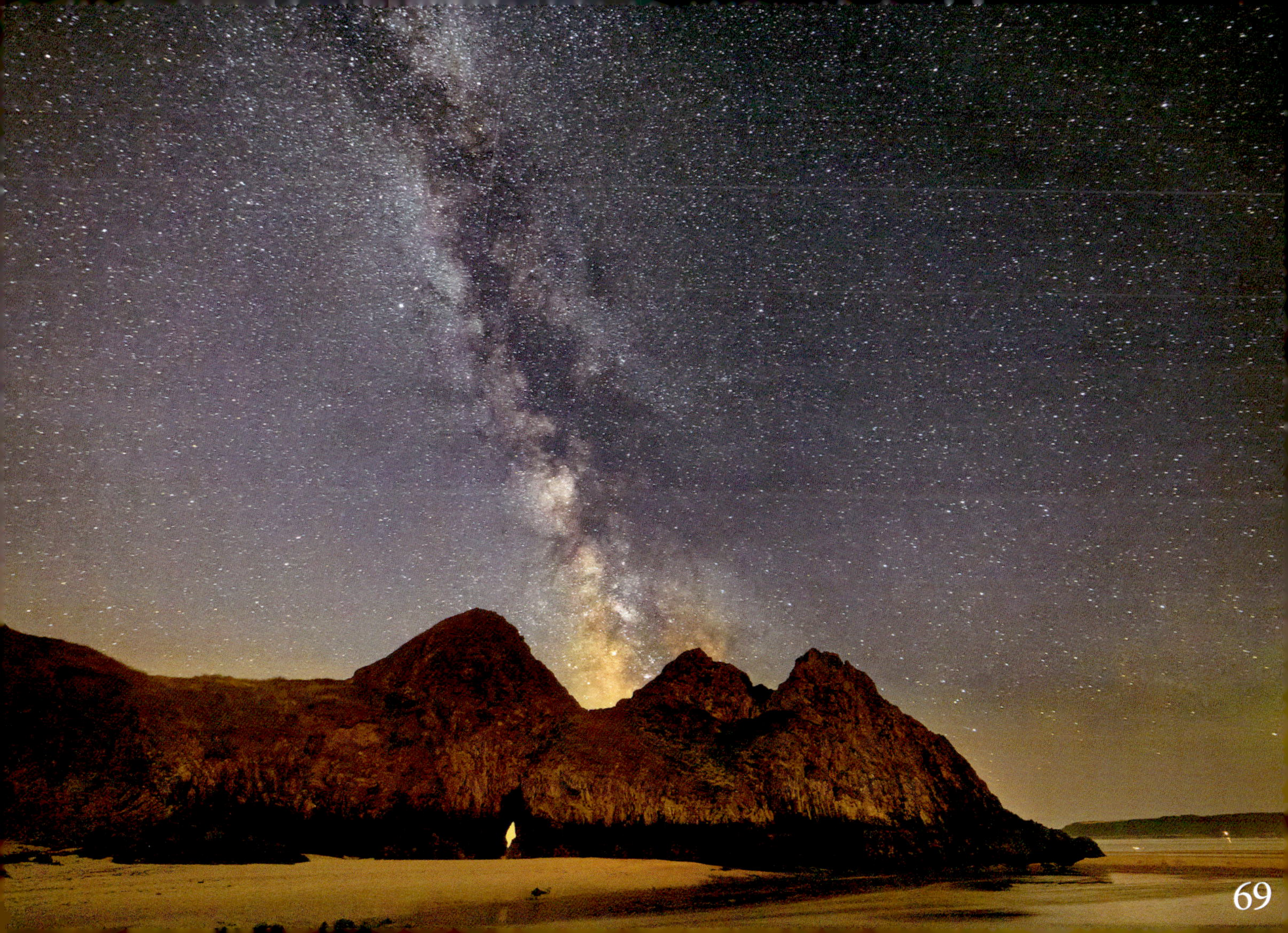

Three Cliffs Bay

The opposite side to Pennard Burrows is Penmaen Burrows. If you walk up from Three Cliffs Bay to the top of the cliffs (not easy in the sand!) and turn right, you may well walk right past this. Before you get to the gate that leads to the car park, there is a path to the left. Follow that for a few seconds and you'll find this Neolithic Burial Chamber, Pen-y-Crug! Most of it is missing or buried in the sand. The stones seen today are part of the entrance to the tomb, which was excavated in 1893. The top of Cefn Bryn is visible from the tomb, which may have had some relevance to the placement of the chamber.

The hidden history doesn't stop there. Just across the main path from the entrance to the burial chamber path, there is a depression in the ground. If you look closely, you will see it was actually once a building! The OS map says it is a chapel.

Going back to the main path, returning to the top of the path you came up from Three Cliffs and carrying on further takes you to another piece of history, earthworks for a castle. The OS map says it is a motte, "a mound forming the site of a castle or camp." It was a Norman timber castle and excavations have shown it is from around the 12th century. The earth and timber were eventually replaced with stone. At some point, the timber gate was destroyed by fire, although whether this was from attack or mishap we will never know.

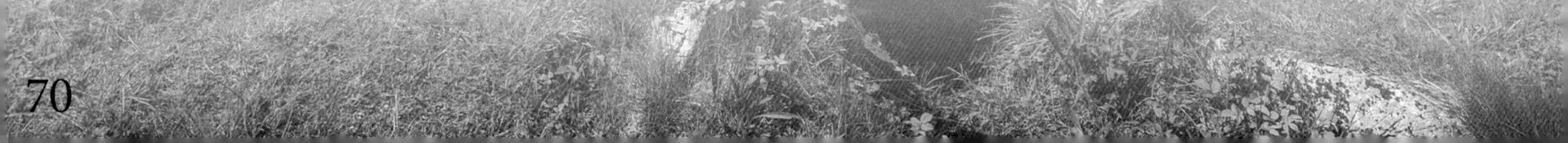

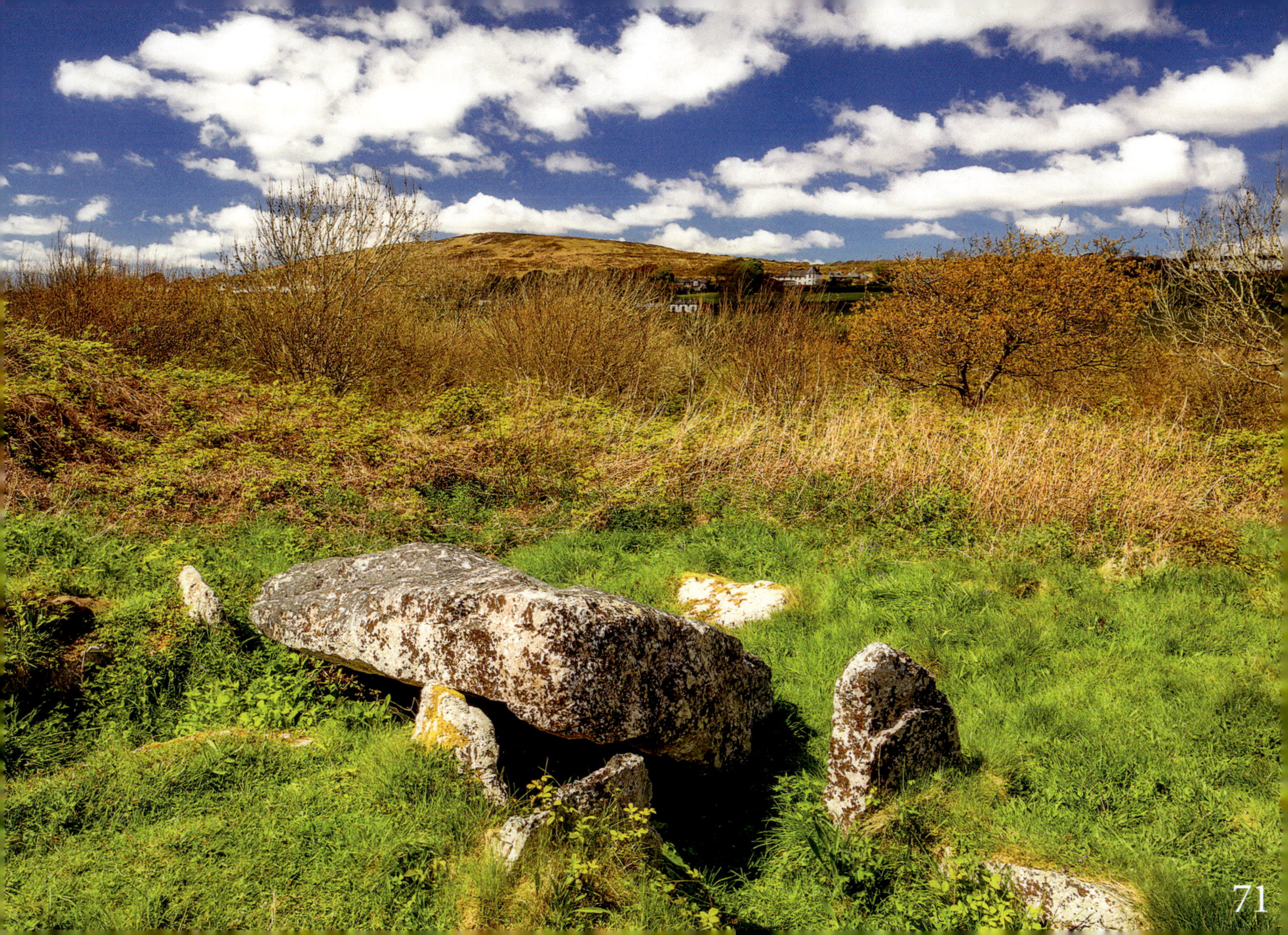

Three Cliffs Bay

Following the coast path around takes you to another of my favourite places to be on Gower. Taking this photo did involve a little bit of effort, notably the 3:30am alarm call to get here in time for sunrise! I still remember how it felt to be at this location at that time. The air was warm even at 5:30am, the wind was still and the sounds of wildlife waking up were all over. I took this photo at 5:42am after the sun had risen.

I love being on the cliffs at this time of morning as I almost always have the place to myself before the busyness of the day starts. As I drive back through Swansea through all the traffic on their daily commute, I feel very contented with my life and know I am so lucky to be able to do what I do for a living. When I get home, I creep in and download my photos to the PC with a coffee before the rest of my family stirs and wakes for the day.

The large rock on the beach is called Bendrick Rock. Who Bendrick is or was is a mystery, but there is a Bendrick Drive next to Pennard Golf Club. There is a suggestion that it is purely a geologically descriptive name as there is a promontory of Carboniferous Limestone known as Bendrick Rock in the Vale of Glamorgan near Barry, where dinosaur footprints have been found.

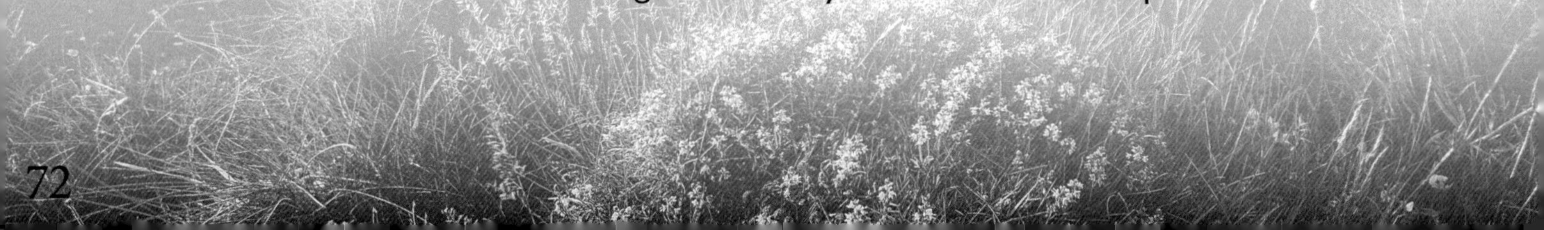

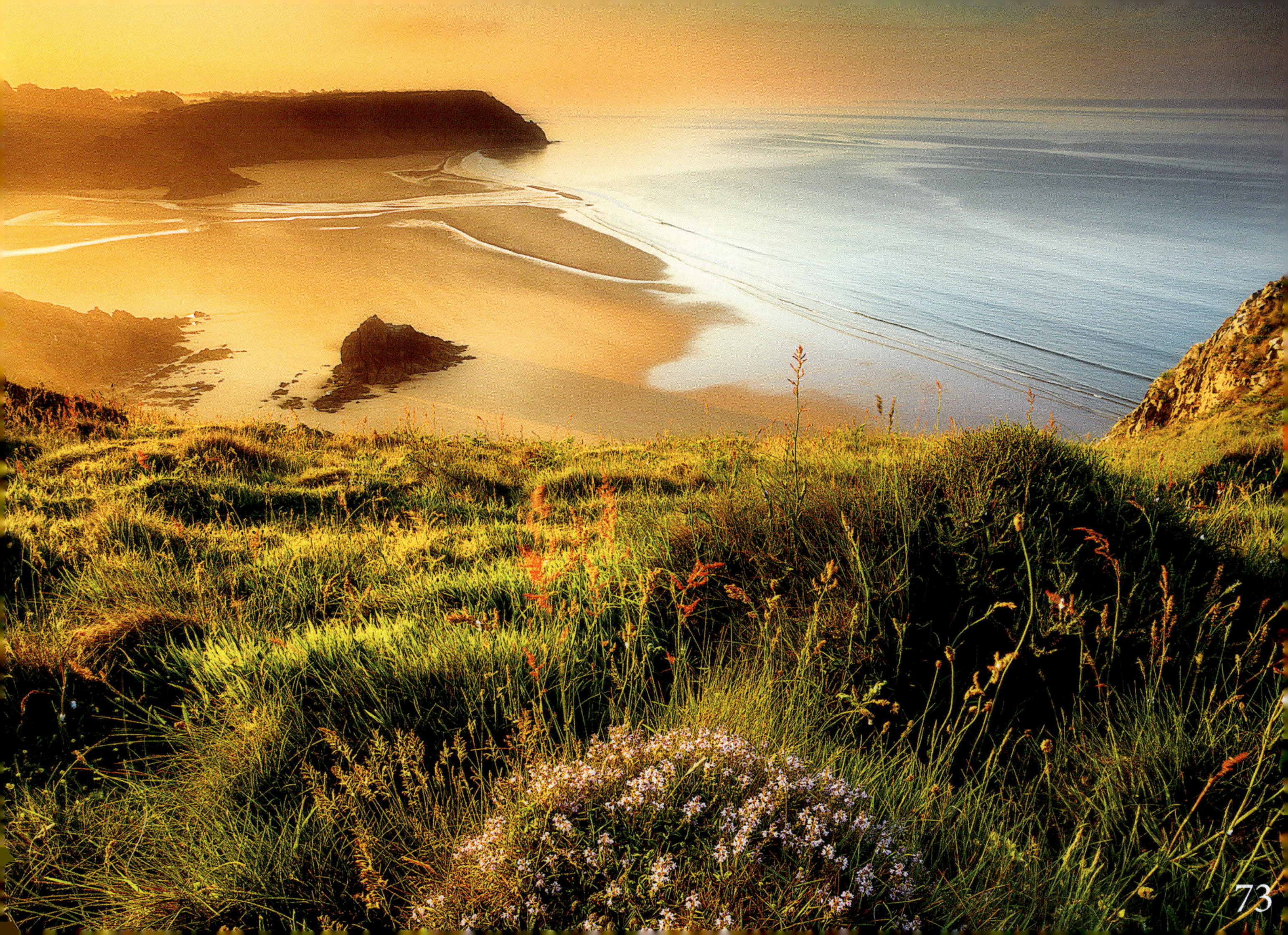

Tor Bay

Following the coast path around to Great Tor give you fantastic views over Tor Bay, Crawley Beach and Oxwich Bay. Tor Bay is a small sandy beach nestled between the Carboniferous Limestone outcrops of Great Tor and Little Tor. There is some beach left even at high tide and it is popular with bathers because it is so sheltered. At low tide, you can easily walk around Little Tor to Oxwich Bay and on very low tides, you can walk around Great Tor to Three Cliffs Bay.

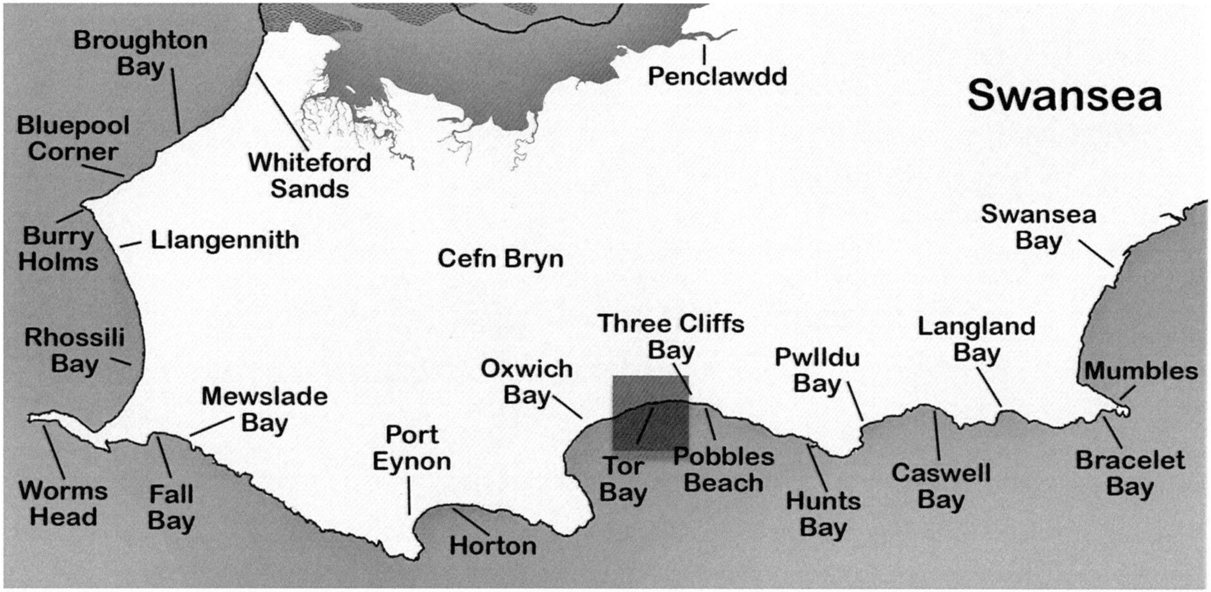

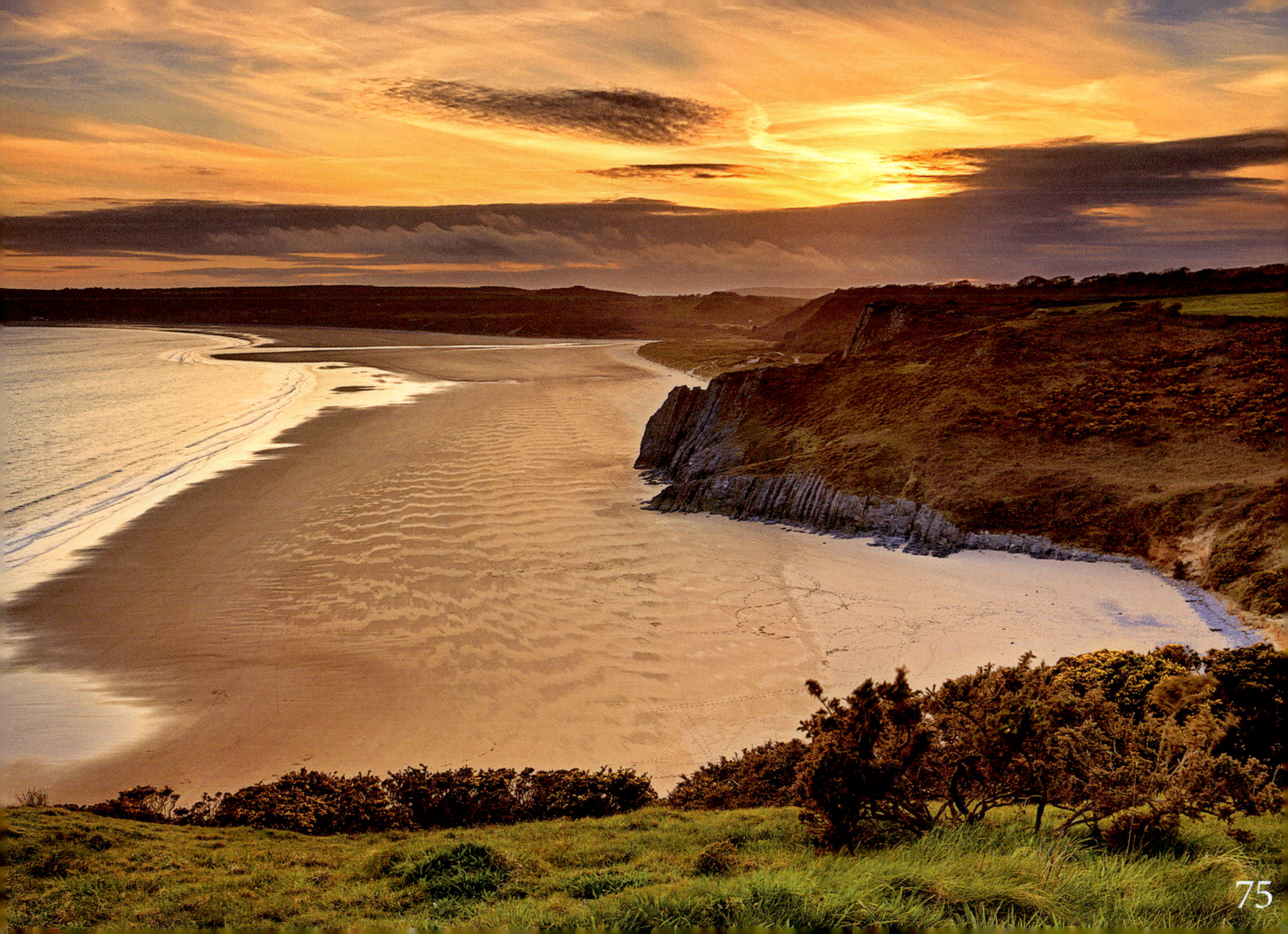

Tor Bay

This is Great Tor, one my of favourite landmarks on Gower as it clearly shows the uplifted rocks - the parallel lines of rock that once lay flat until they were buckled by movement. The tor is hugely popular with climbers and many a time I've been sat on the cliff when a head has suddenly appeared from the seemingly vertical cliff! High on the face of Great Tor is one of Gower's bone caves called Leather's Hole, which only climbers can access. Excavations in the cave have found bones from mammoths, woolly rhinocerous, wolf and hyena! It is thought that the larger animals were dragged in by smaller predators. The cave would have been far more accessible when these animals were in Wales.

Leather's Hole is a large cave with the entrance being 3 metres high and 2.3 metres wide. The passageway leads to the main chamber which is a large 4 metres high! Beyond the main chamber there is a narrow passage leading to the end chamber. Another passage leads to a second, higher entrance.

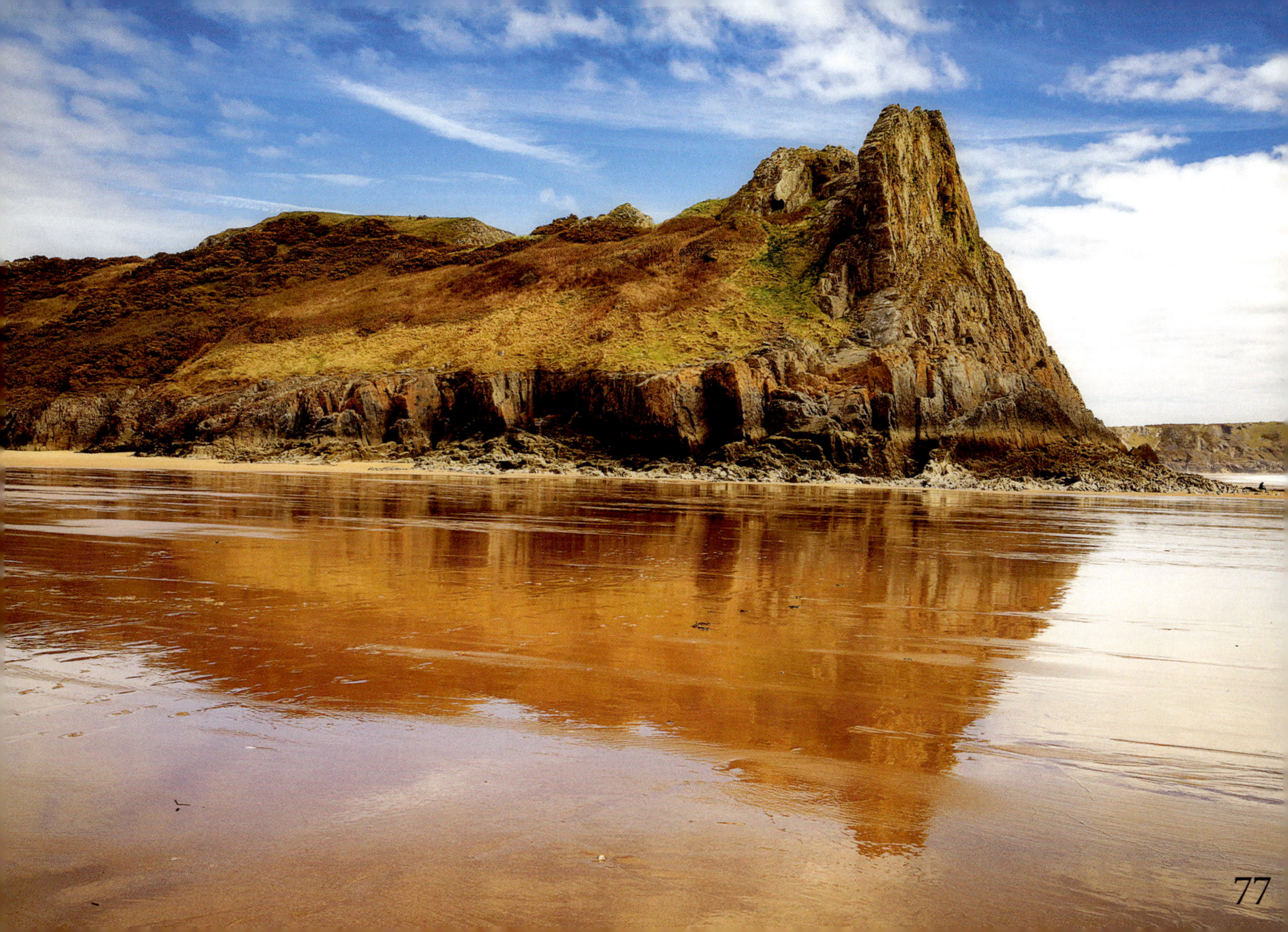

Tor Bay

This is Little Tor which lies on the west side of Tor Bay. Little Tor, made from limestone, is popular with rock climbers with 29 routes described on the South Wales Climbers website. To get to Tor Bay, the most popular path is from Penmaen Burrows. At the top of this path lies a lime kiln. In the 19th century, limestone was taken from the immediate area and converted to quicklime by heating in the lime kiln you see. It was then plunged into water to convert it into lime, a process called 'slaking'. This lime was then mostly transported to the West Country for use in fields and the building industry.

There has been a lot of trade between Gower and the West Country over time. Cornwall and Wales even have the same base language, for example, Good Night is Nos Dha in Cornish and Nos Da in Welsh. The Ancient Britons were Celtic people who lived in Britain from the Iron Age into the Middle Ages. They spoke the Common Brittonic language. Following various events, by the 11th century the Ancient Britons had split into groups with colonies living in Wales, Cornwall, Brittany (now part of France) and southern Scotland/northern England. Over time, the Common Brittonic developed into the distinct languages of Welsh, Cornish, Breton and Cumbric. Separated, their languages developed differently but retained some similarities.

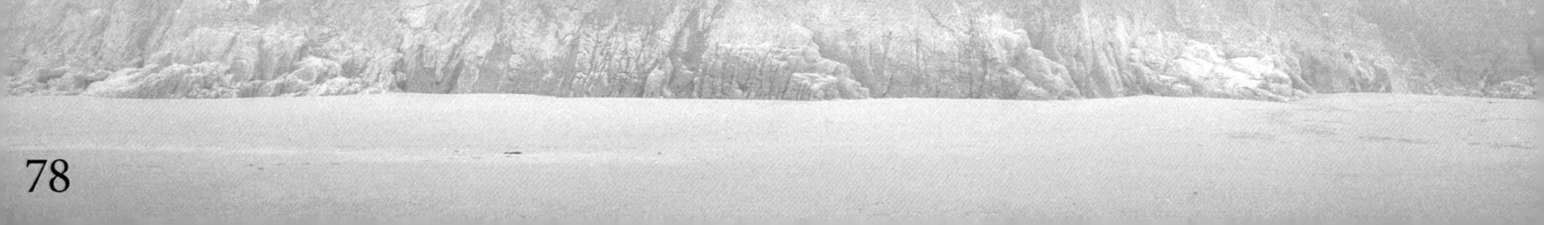

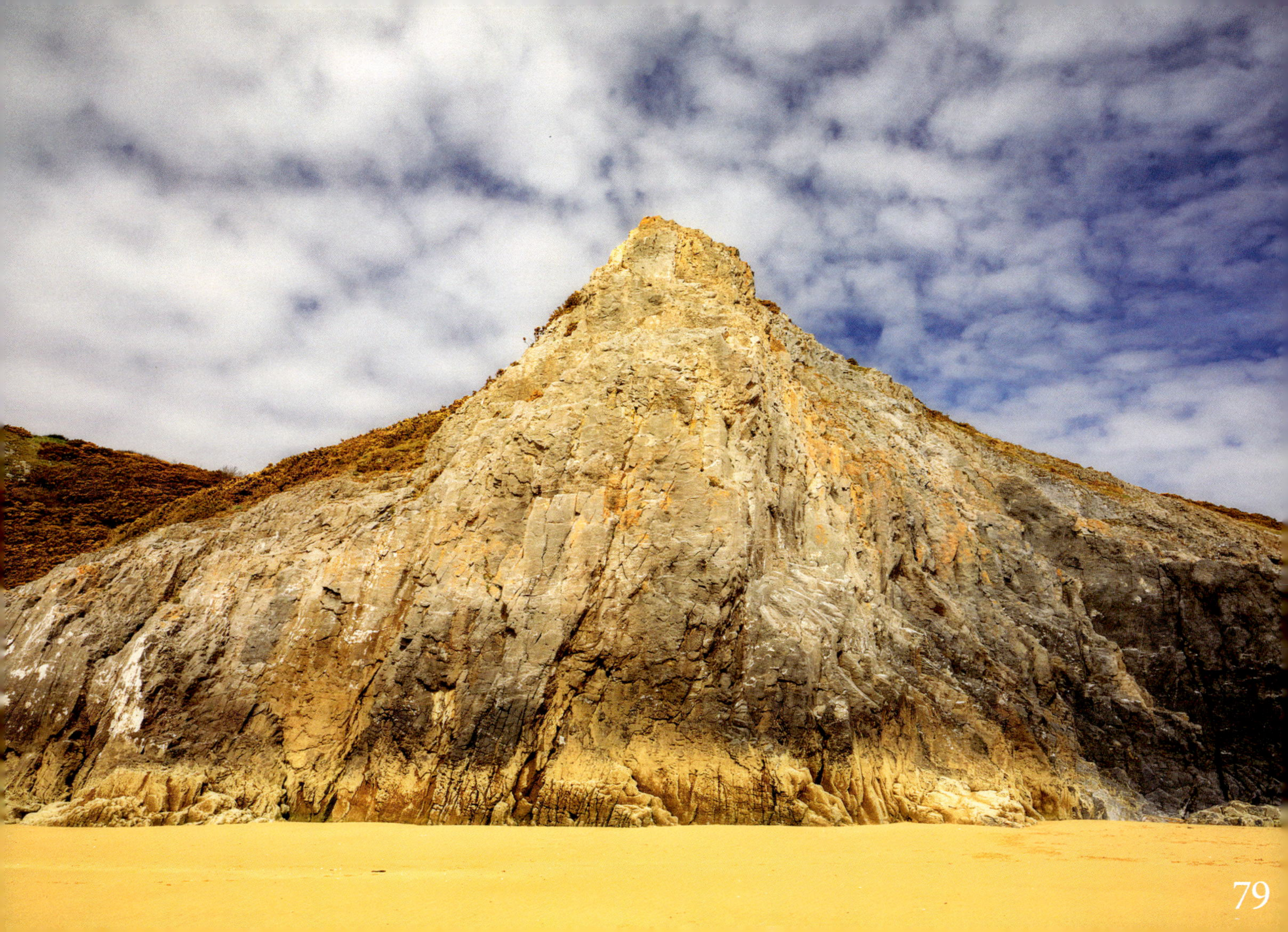

Tor Bay

This photo is taken from Little Tor looking across Tor Bay to Great Tor. The colour of the sea and the landscape makes it look more like New Zealand than Gower! The path to this viewpoint isn't very obvious and the only way I found it was thanks to Google Earth. There is an indistinct path leading off the main coast path. If you follow it, pushing through brambles, you reach an open area where wild flowers grow and you can admire the view with Tor Bay on one side and Oxwich Bay on the other.

The photo was taken around high tide. When the water is in, it can seem somewhat unbelievable that in a few hours you will be able to walk around the base of Great Tor. Swansea actually has one of the highest tidal ranges in the world at 14 metres, with the Bay of Fundy in Canada being the biggest at around 15 metres! Much of the world only has a tidal range of just two or three metres.

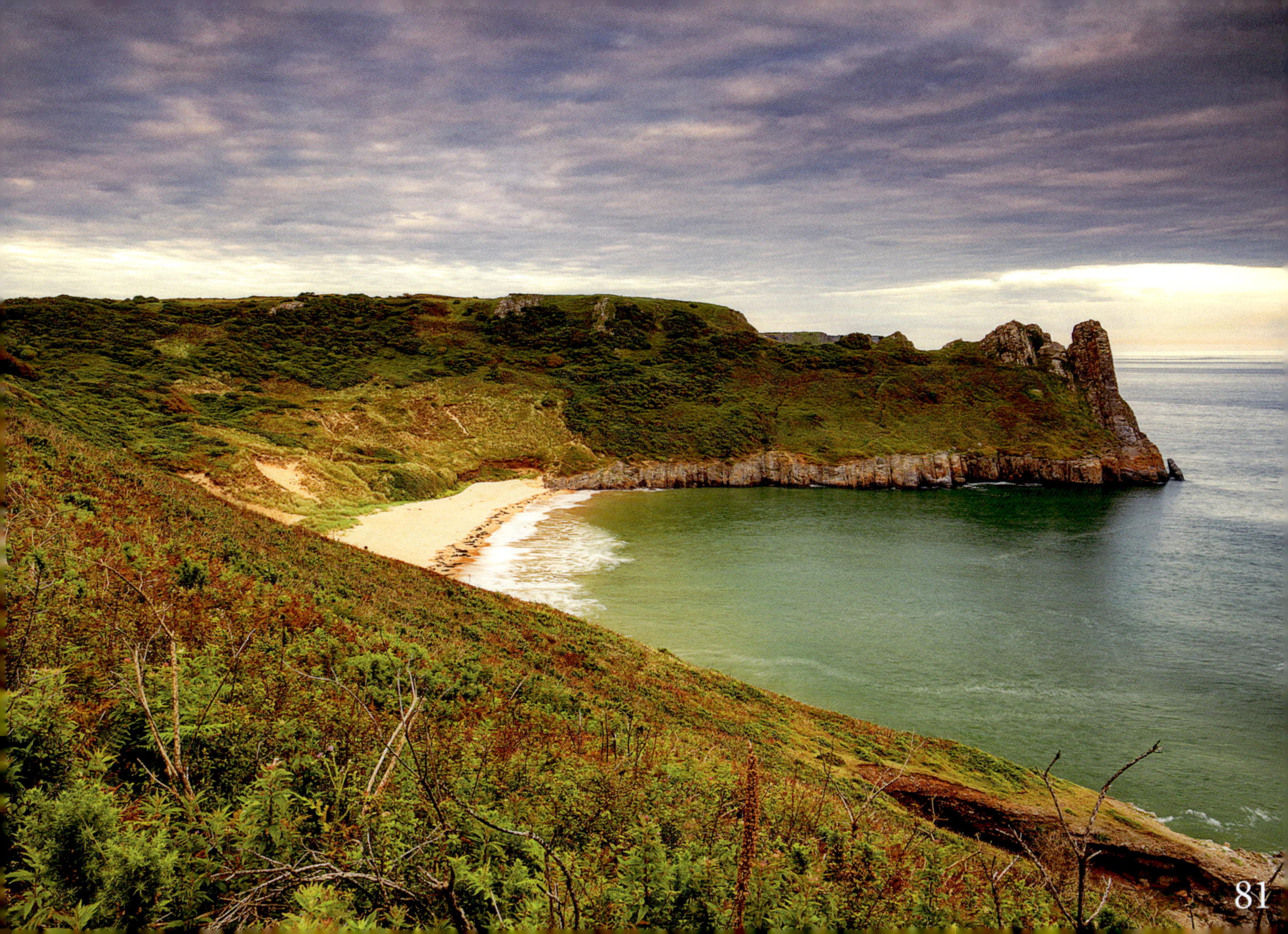

Oxwich Bay

Oxwich Bay is a huge sweeping bay from Great Tor to Oxwich Point. To the east is Crawley Woods, Crawley Beach and Nicholaston Burrows where relative peace can be found thanks to the separation of Nicholaston Pill and the long distance from the main access to Oxwich. At the far west of the bay, partially hidden in the trees, is the tiny, picturesque Church of St Illtyd. Oxwich Bay is popular with sunbathers, wind surfers, divers and for boating sports. With the car park practically on the beach, access is very easy.

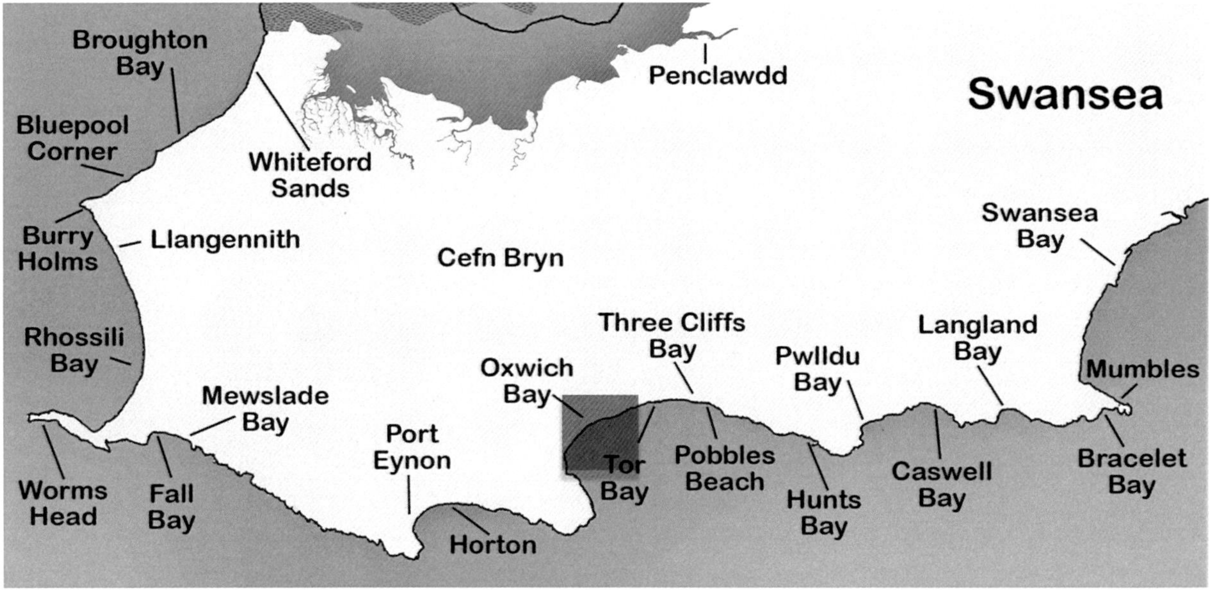

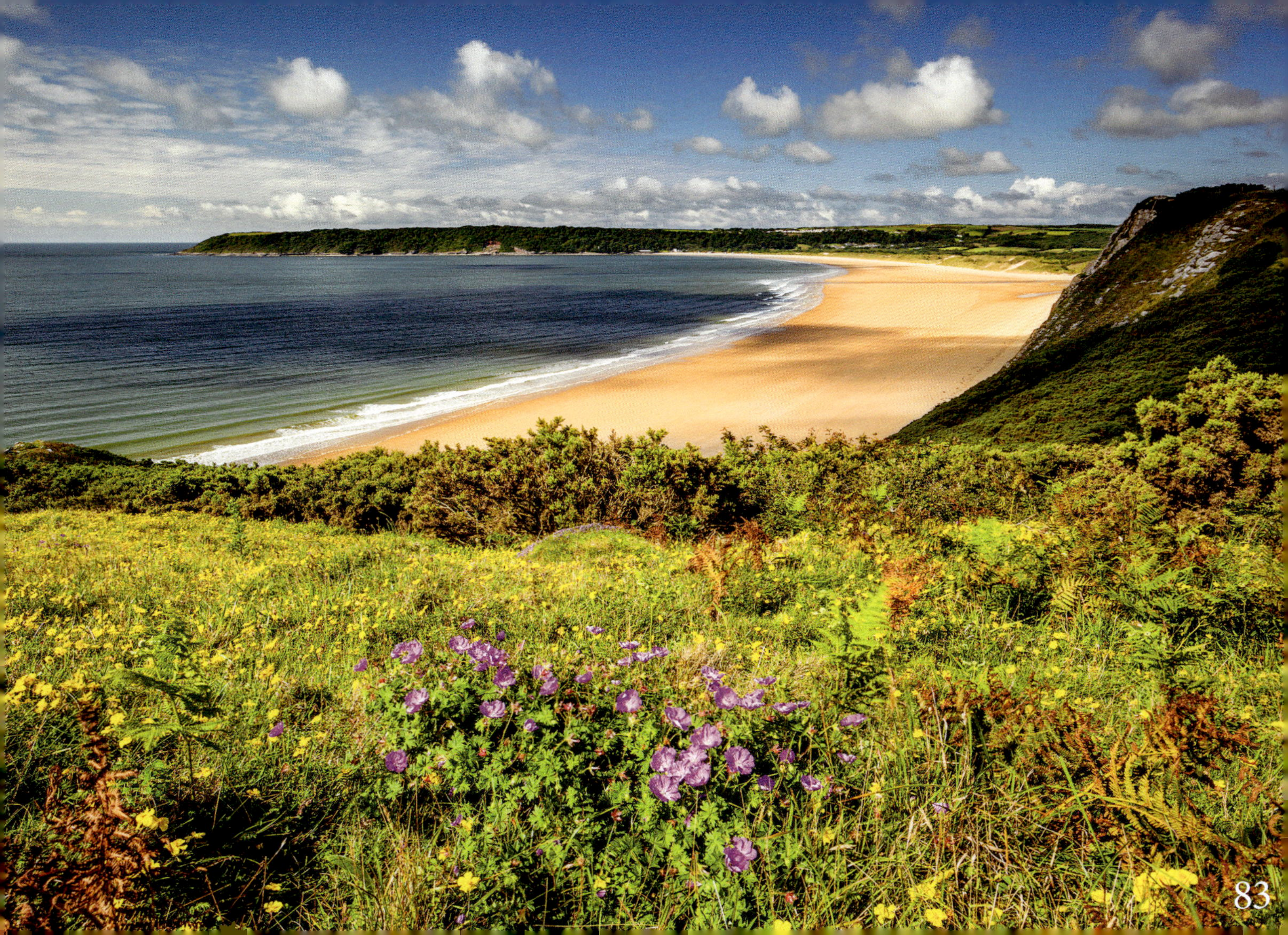

Oxwich Bay

This photo is from the last cliff before the dunes was taken just after the sun had set. Standing here isn't for the faint hearted, though, as directly to the left is a precipitous drop to the sand below!

Oxwich National Nature Reserve, to the rear of Oxwich Bay, is managed by Natural Resources Wales and has one of the richest coastal habitats in Britain, with hundreds of species of flowering plants and many birds rarely found in Britain. It is made up of sand dunes, lakes, woodlands, salt marsh and freshwater marsh. This rare combination supports over 600 varieties of flowering plants! A seawall was built in 1790 to create a serpentine lake to mimic the Serpentine Park in Hyde Park, London. The rest of the land was grazed by cows and sheep. The lake has since silted up and created a marsh.

Nicholaston Woods is an ancient woodland with many different trees, which is great for supporting a wide variety of wildlife. There are plenty of walks around the nature reserve.

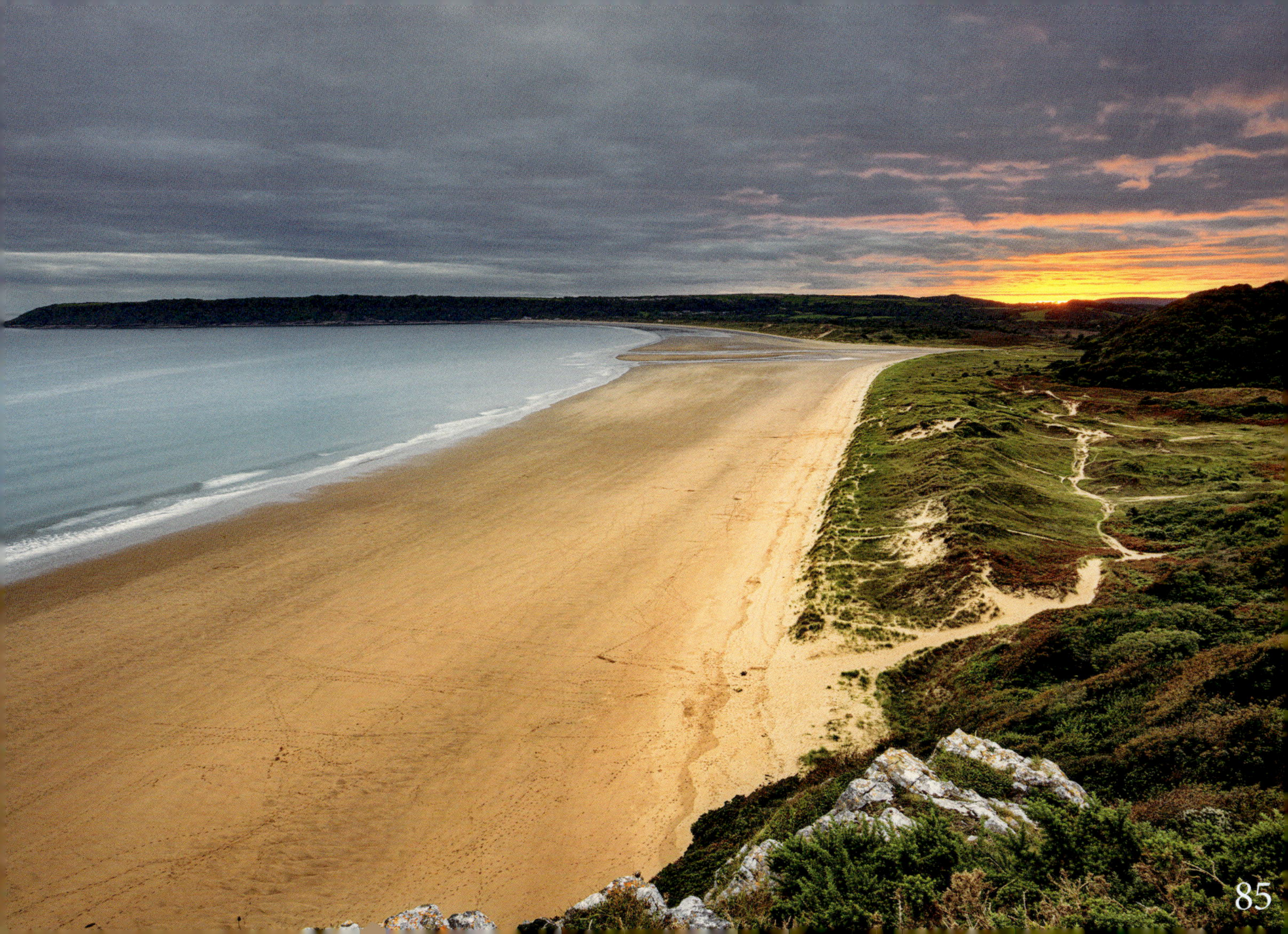

Oxwich Bay

This picturesque scene hides a more important purpose. There are several undersea cables that leave the UK at Oxwich Bay! One is the TAT 11 which runs from New Jersey in America to Oxwich and then onto France. Another is Gemini North which from Oxwich Bay to Rhode Island in America. There is also the SOLAS cable which runs to Ireland. You wouldn't know by looking at it, but Oxwich Bay has an important role in international telecommunications!

Another claim to fame is in 1911 when Oxwich Bay was the site of the first aeroplane flight in Wales! Going further back in time, Oxwich was known for 'wrecking'. You might assume that wrecking means the ship was deliberately run aground by false lights shone from shore, but whilst this exists in many stories, there is no evidence that this ever happened. What wrecking actually refers to is salvaging valuables from shipwrecks.

The Mansel family from Oxwich Castle made use of the fact that they were so close to the coast and often wrecked ships that they didn't have the right to. Perhaps the most well known was on 27th December 1557 when Sir Rhys Mansel wrecked a French ship that Sir George Herbert of Swansea had the rights to. A fight ensued and Sir Rhys Mansel's daughter got struck on the head by a stone and died six days later. It went to court and the Mansel family were compensated by having their wrecking fine waived.

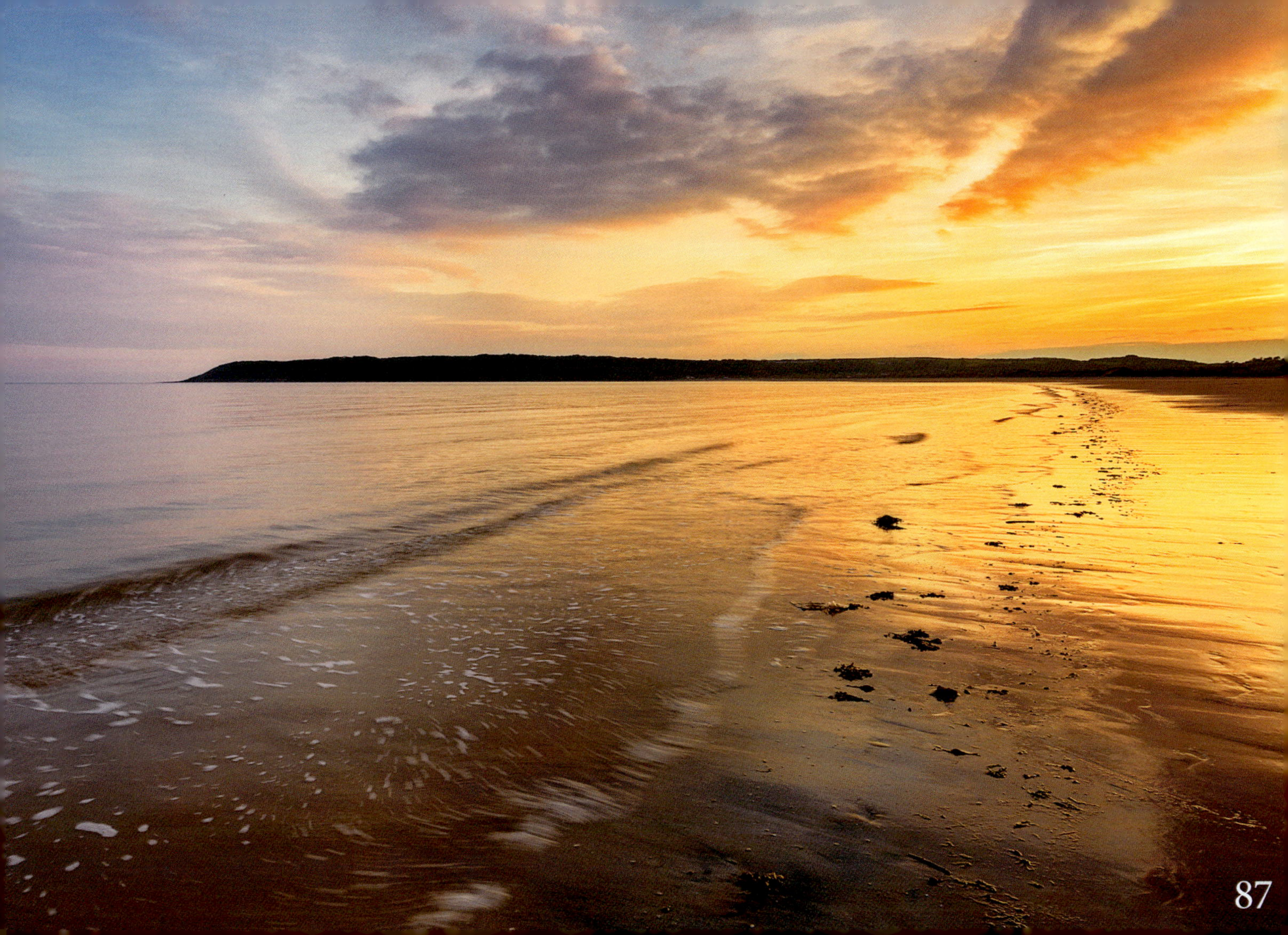

Oxwich Bay

This photo was taken from the beach near to the Church of St Illtwyd. The church, hidden amongst the trees, dates to around the 12th century but the site was used for religious purposes as far back as the 6th century. There is little definitive knowledge of St Illtwyd, but he was known to be very popular during the end of the 5th and start of the 6th century and founded Llantwit Major in the Vale of Glamorgan. There is a long distance footpath called St Illtwyd's Walk, which starts in Pembrey Country Park and finishes in Margam Country Park, 64 miles later.

At the back of the churchyard, there is a grave of an unknown Royal Navy soldier whose body was washed up at Oxwich during the First World War. In the upper churchyard, there is a well that is now dry. It was reportedly haunted many years ago when a water horse was seen before disappearing into the well waters.

Behind where I was standing is the Oxwich Beach Hotel, a popular venue to get married. There is also a campsite, Oxwich Camping Park, with easy access to the beach.

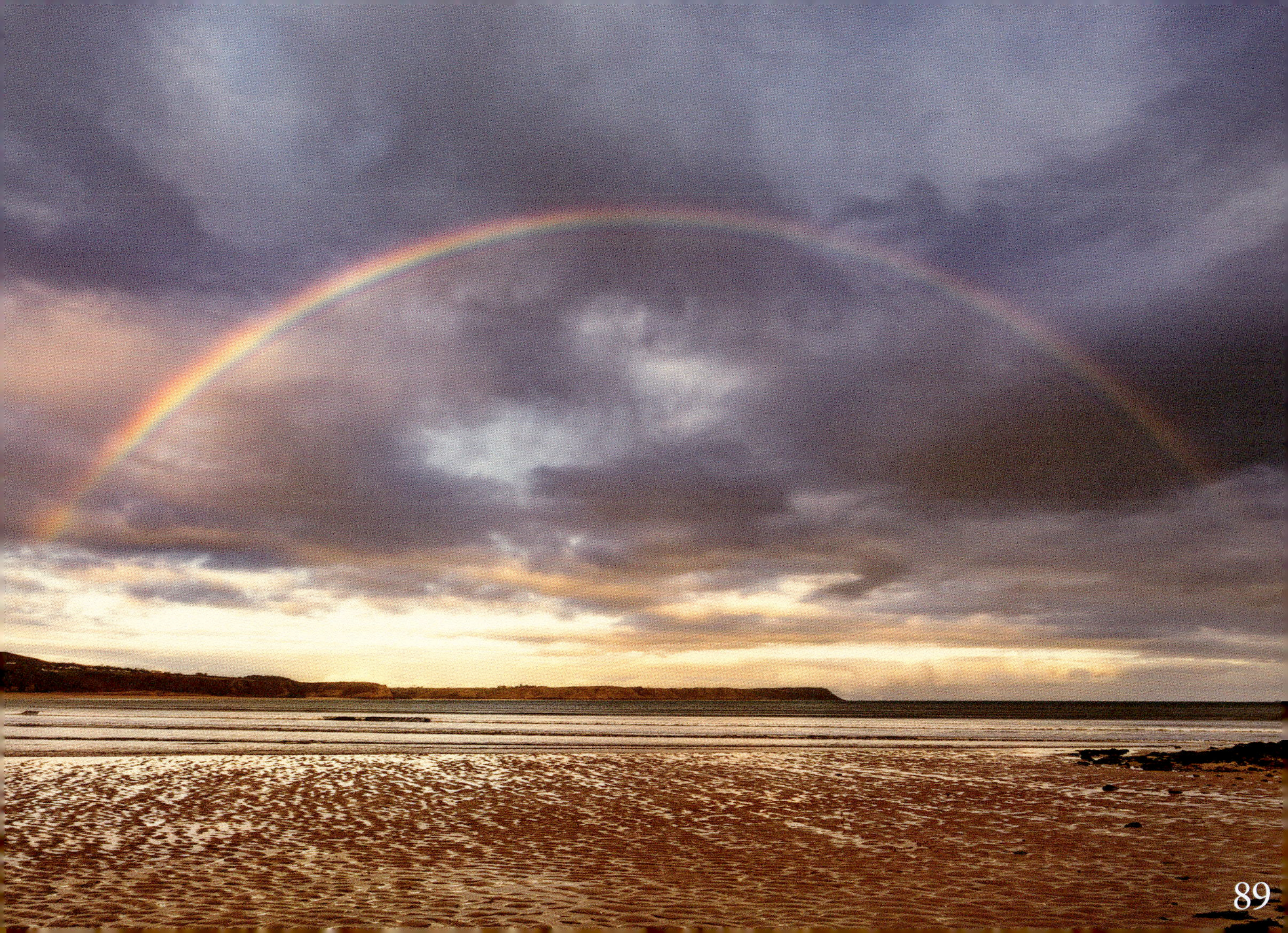

Slade

Slade, also known as Slade Sands or The Sands, is a sandy beach accessible from the coast path from either Oxwich or Horton. There is a path from Slade, but there isn't any parking to speak of. Getting down to the beach is a scramble using a rope that has been placed there and you will almost always have it to yourself. I took this photo after the sun had set but before the colours had disappeared. The headland in the distance is Port Eynon Point and just around the corner is Horton.

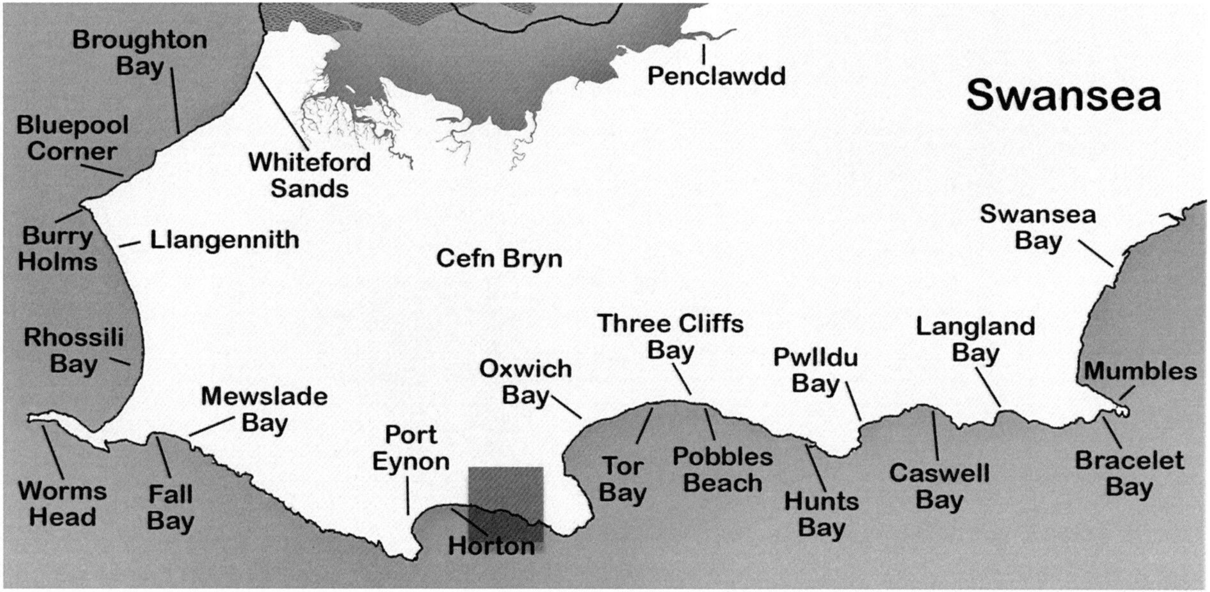

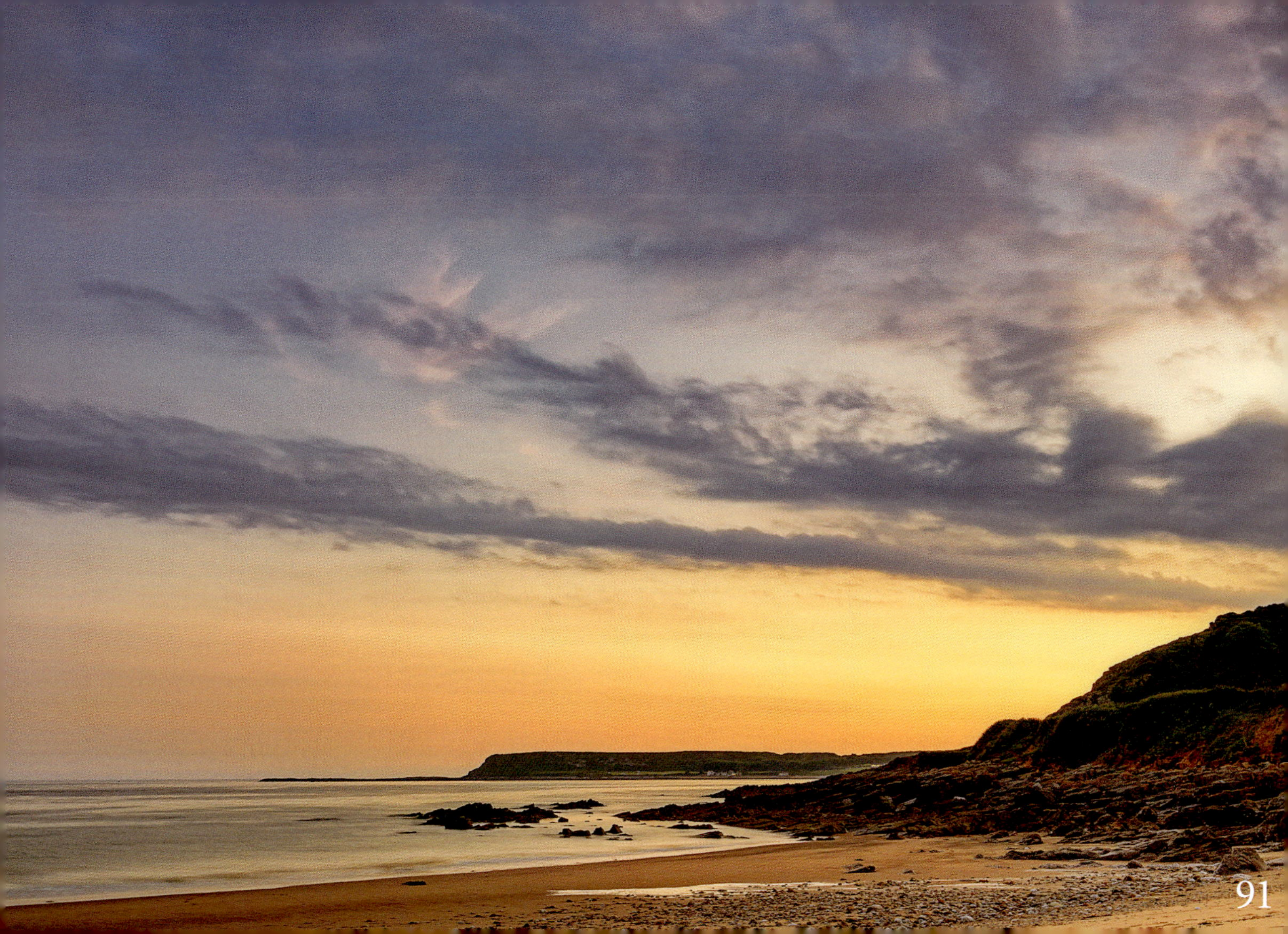

Horton and Port Eynon

As you walk from Slade towards Horton and Port Eynon, you get views like this. Horton is a small village and shares the bay with Port Eynon. There are numerous campsites around and the beach has seasonal lifeguard support. The bay is safe and is great for water sports and sunbathing. Despite the number of campsites and safety of the beach, it is large enough to find your own spot. But be warned, both of the car parks in Horton and Port Eynon are locked in the early evening!

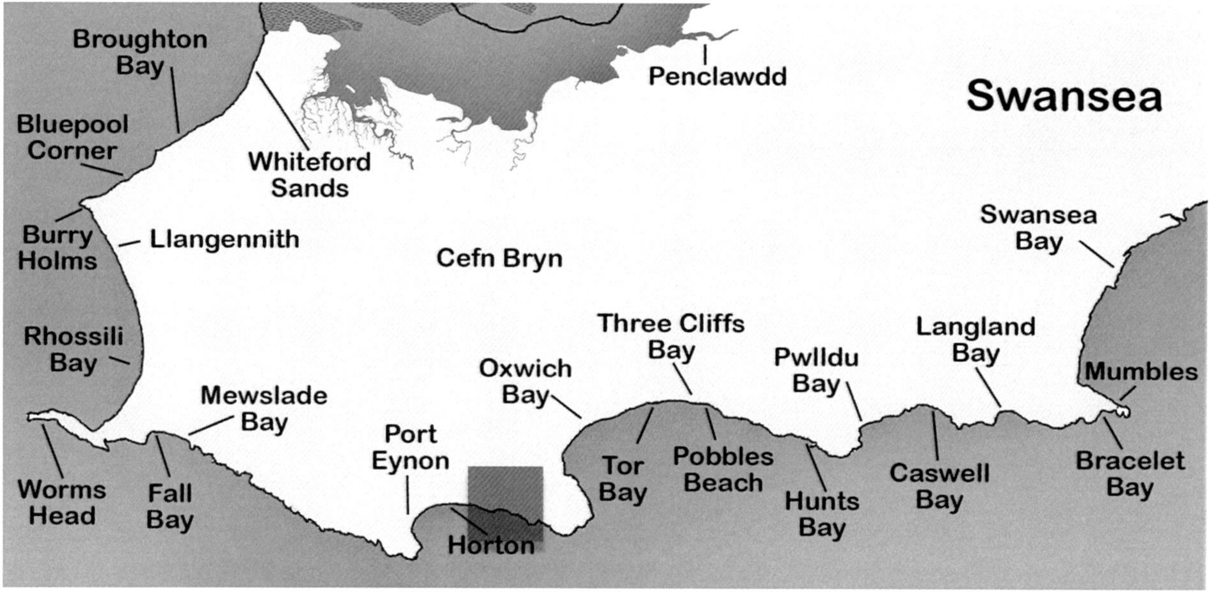

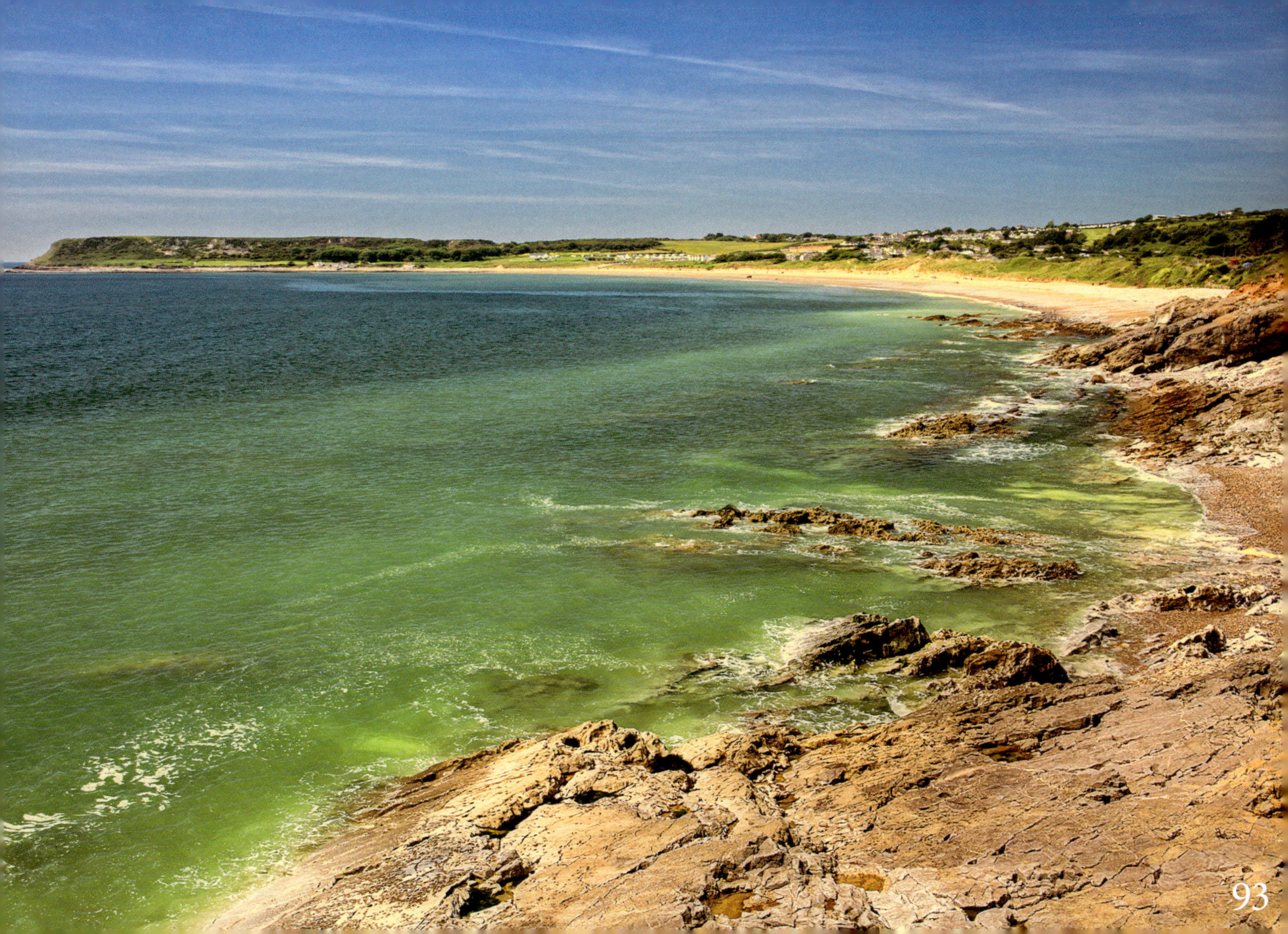

Horton and Port Eynon

This photo was taken near the lifeboat station in Horton. The lifeboat station was originally established in Port Eynon in 1884. Whilst out on a call to the steamship Dunvegan on 1st January 1916, the lifeboat capsized twice and three crew members lost their lives. This caused the station to be temporarily closed. In 1919, the lifeboat station closed for good and in 1920 the lease surrendered.

In 1968, a new lifeboat station was established at Horton and is known as the Horton and Port Eynon lifeboat. During the inauguration ceremony, the crew were called out to a bather who had got into difficulties. Whilst searching for the bather, the lifeboat capsized and three crew ended up in the water. Fortunately, they returned to shore safely. In 1992, a new boathouse was constructed to house both the tractor and lifeboat.

The old lifeboat station in Port Eynon is now a Youth Hostel, possibly the youth hostels with the best view in the country!

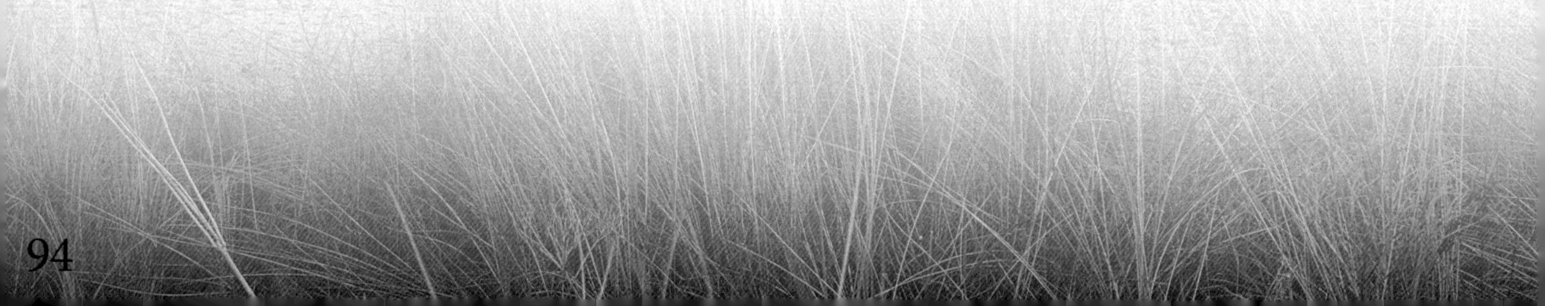

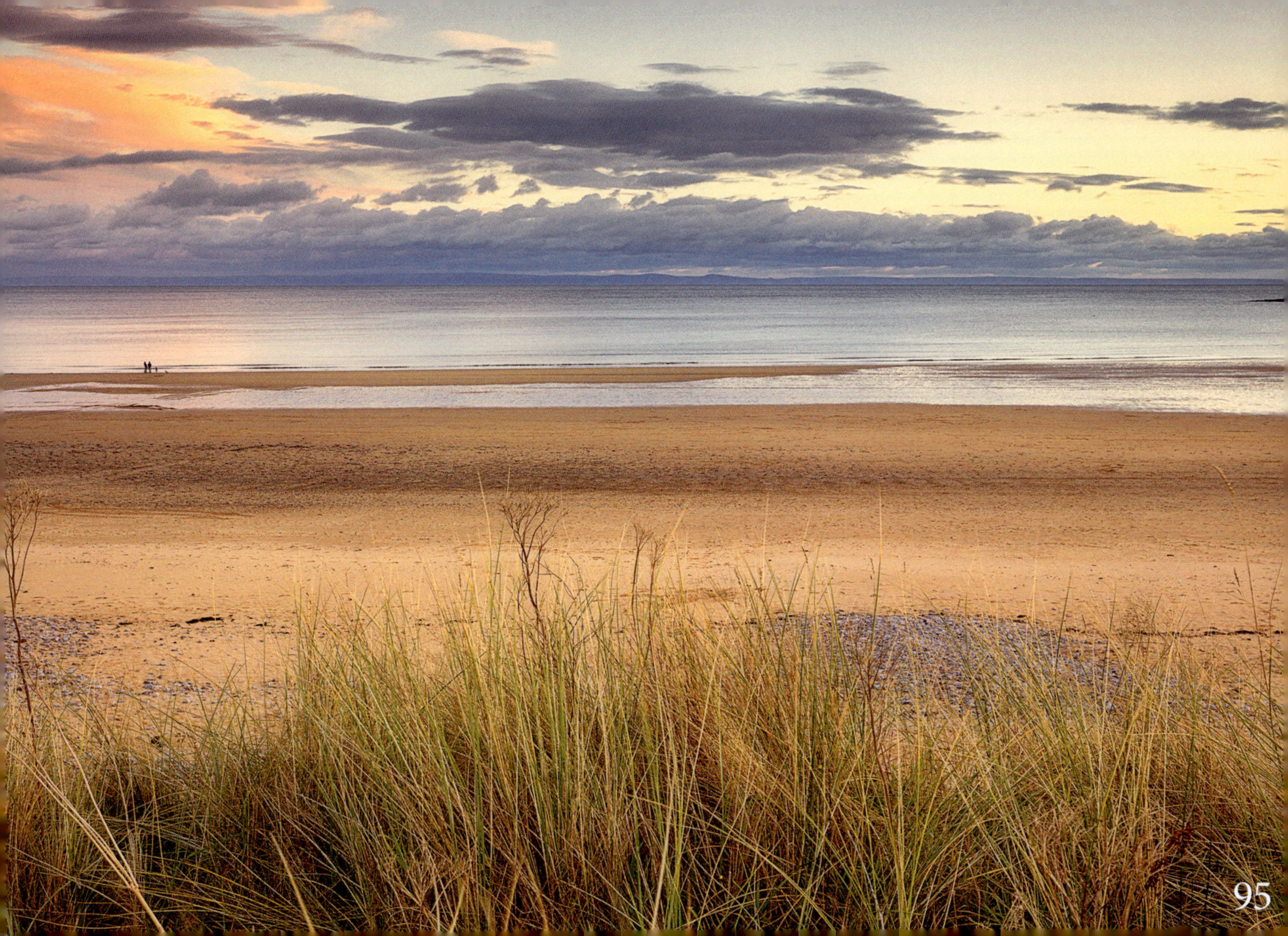

Horton and Port Eynon

The Salthouse is actually the remains of two 18th century cottages. At low tide, other structures can be seen that are remains of the salt pans and a quay. They are possibly part of the former Salthouse mansion, owned by the Lucas family. The family became rich from the salt but also by other not so legal means, which has led to rumours of smuggling and an alleged tunnel to Culver Hole. The Great Storm of 1703 destroyed much of the mansion and two cottages were built in their place, the remains of which are what you see today.

The actual salt house, thought to be the oldest salt works in Wales, was thought to have been lost until the Glamorgan-Gwent Archaeological Trust excavated the site in 1986 and found over 4000 artefacts. A defensive sea wall was constructed in 1992 when a grant was allocated to prevent further erosion.

This photo was taken at 1:51am. I knew that the Galactic Core of the Milky Way would be visible so I headed to this location where I would see the Salthouse along with the Milky Way. The conditions were perfect for astrophotography and I always find being under the starry sky an absolute privilege. Later on, the air temperature dropped to the dew point and my lens condensated constantly so I had to stop. I got home in time to have two hours sleep before getting up for the day!

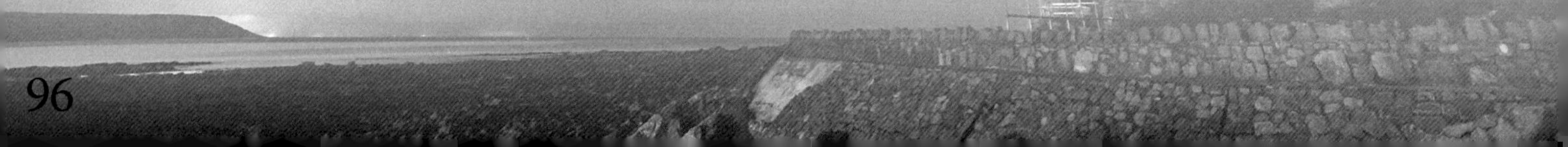

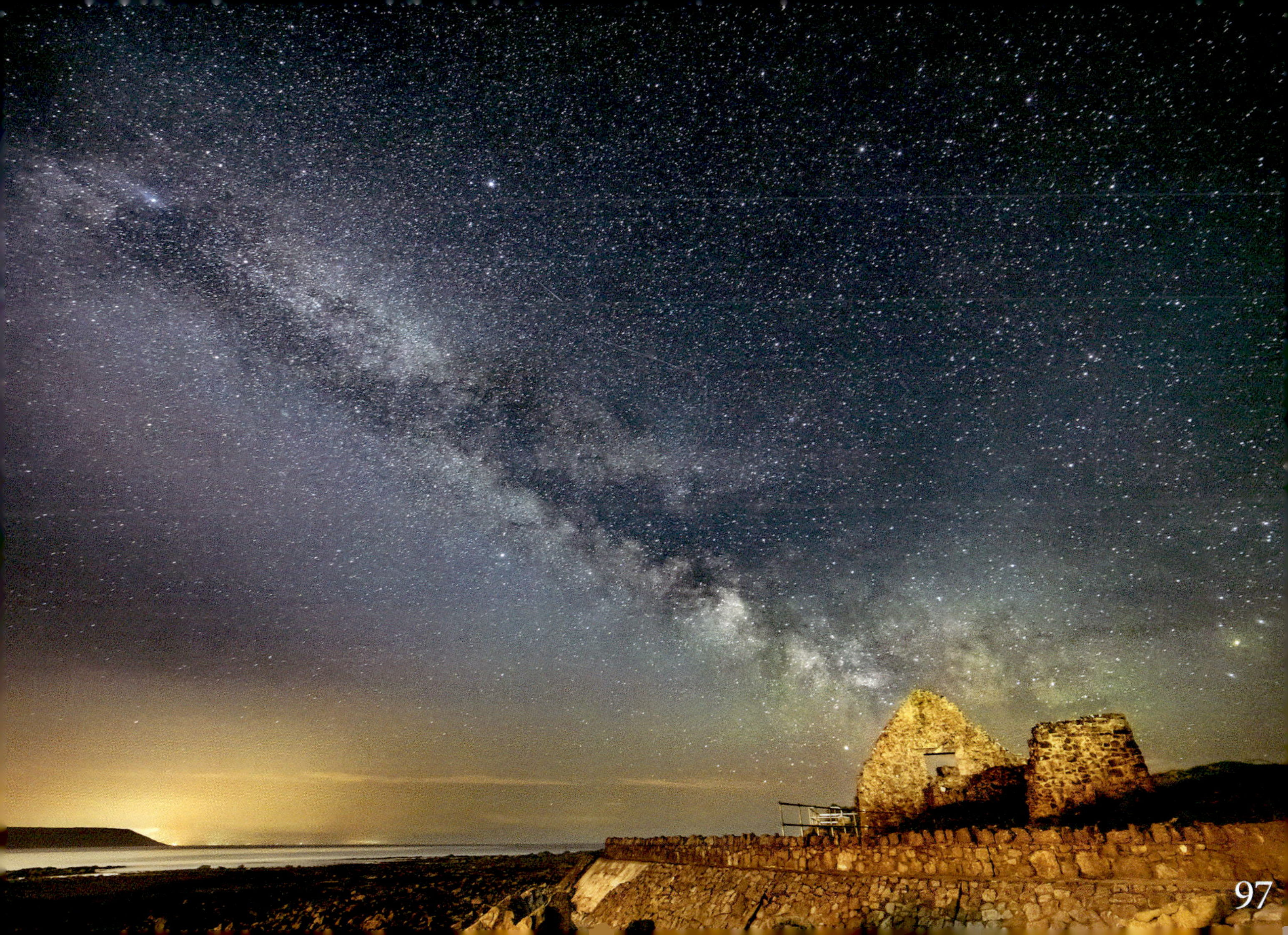

Horton and Port Eynon

On a June Saturday night, I took a test photo from a hill on Horton for some reason and in that photo I spotted something unusual down at Port Eynon. I very quickly realised what it was and was very excited. I've always wanted to see Bioluminescent Plankton so the next evening I headed to where it had been. What I saw took me by surprise - I had no idea how visible to the naked eye it was, I thought only the camera would pick it up. The waves lit up the most intense blue colour. It got so intense at one point, I'm sure another colour was invented!

Bioluminescence is the result of dinoflagellates phytoplankton, also known as fire plants. The light, produced through a process called chemiluminescence, is a defence mechanism. When they are disturbed, they give off a bright blue light for a fraction of a second. The light is intended to attract a predator to whatever is disturbing the plankton and to startle any attacker off.

When waves break, or you throw a stone amongst the plankton, the water lights up. If you kick the wet sand where the sea has recently been, blue sparkles can be seen. On one occasion, I waded into the water to take photos and still had my shoes and trousers on – they were sparkling blue as the water ran off my clothes! It is a phenomenon that everyone should see at least once and if 2018 is anything to go by, Gower and the Welsh coast further to the east is the place to see it!

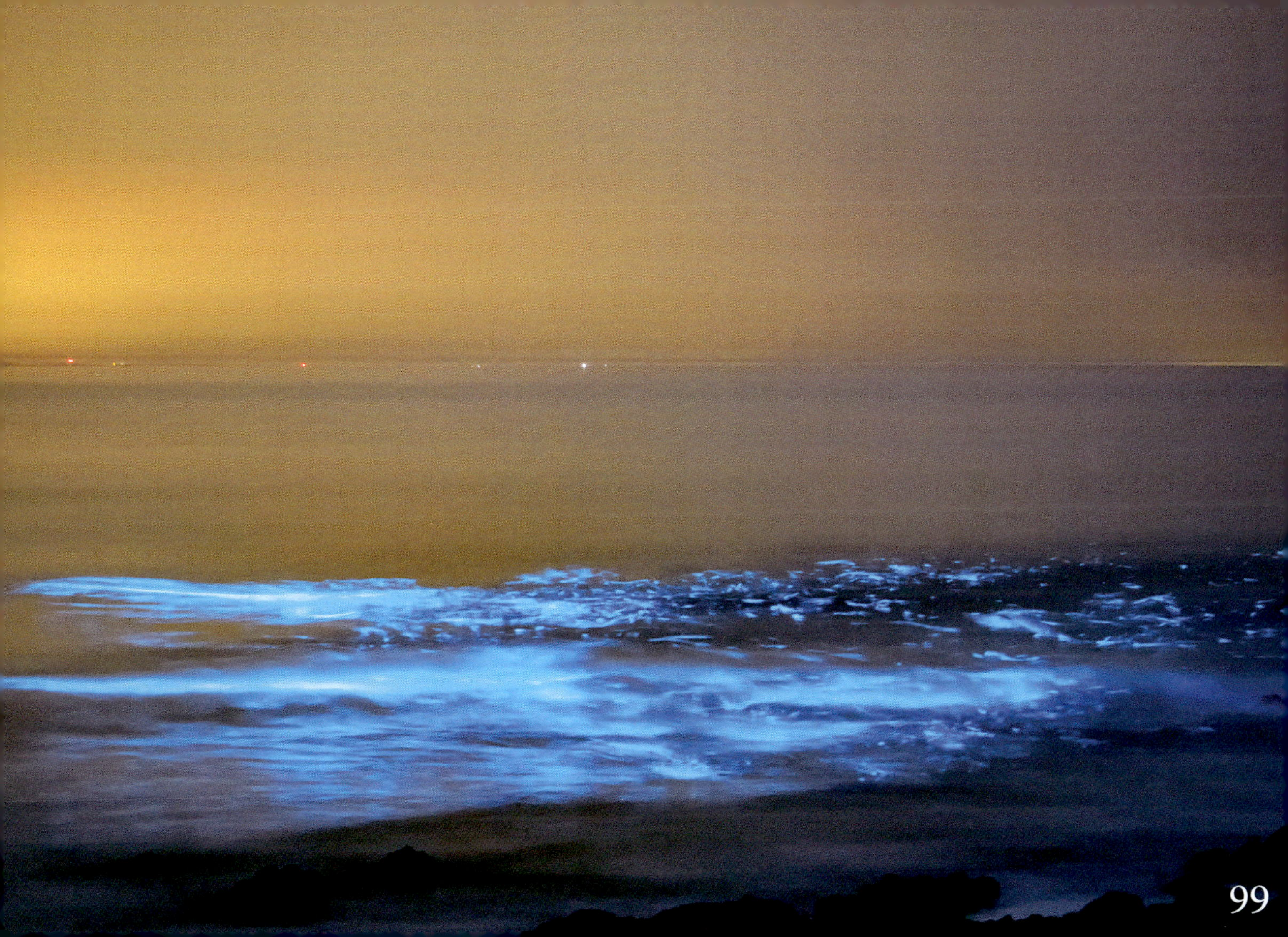

Horton and Port Eynon

This photo was taken as the sun set behind Port Eynon Point. This part of Port Eynon is known as Sedger's Bank and is a nature reserve managed by The Wildlife Trust of South and West Wales. Only a small part of the reserve is above high tide and that is a small storm beach. The rest is covered by sea water at various times depending on the tide. The limestone rocks provide shelter for the typical beach life such as mussels, whelks, barnacles, etc. At the lowest point, a forest of kelp borders the whole site. You might be lucky enough to see seals here too! The reserve is part of the South Gower Coast Site of Special Scientific Interest.

According to the Woodland Trust, "A Site of Special Scientific Interest (SSSI) is a formal conservation designation. Usually, it describes an area that's of particular interest to science due to the rare species of fauna or flora it contains - or even important geological or physiological features that may lie in its boundaries. SSSIs often contain important habitats such as grasslands, parkland and woodland. Some even contain ancient woodland and ancient trees. In other words, these areas have high conservation value, and need to be protected." Wales has around 1000 SSSIs covering approximately 12% of the land! Natural Resources Wales is the authority that looks after the SSSIs in Wales.

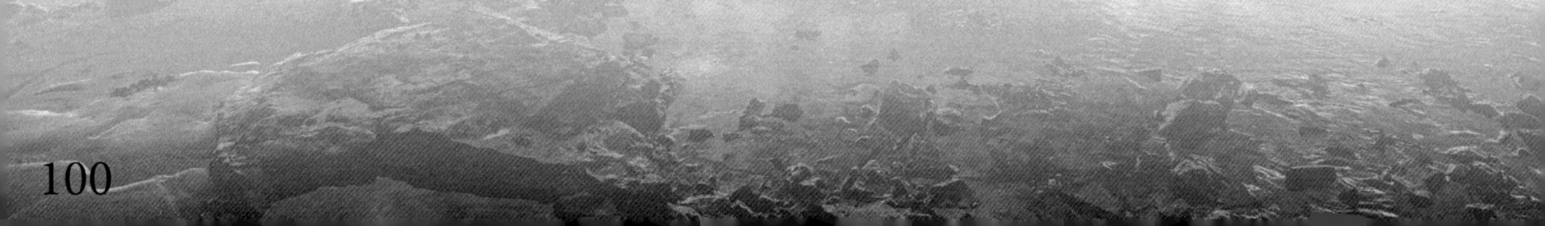

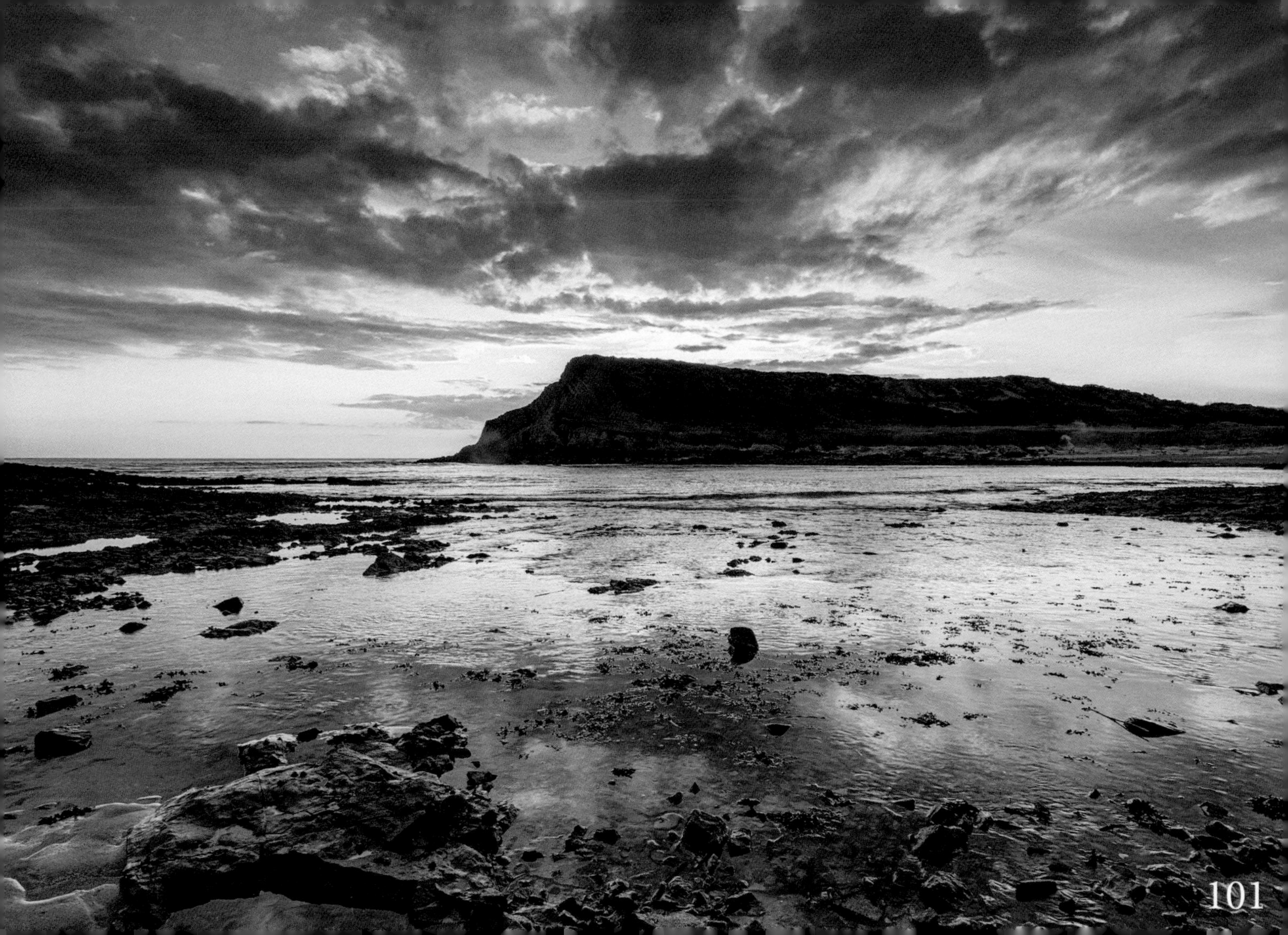

Horton and Port Eynon

The coast path leaves the Salt House and starts the short climb to the top of Port Eynon Point. Whilst the rocks around the Salt House are Oxwich Head Limestone, Port Eynon Point is mostly made from Hunts Bay Oolite Group which stretches all the way to Mewslade Bay. The rocks the sea washes over and some of the lower cliffs are made from High Tor Limestone. They are all different types of Carboniferous Limestone, of which much of Gower is made from.

A part of Port Eynon Point has been used for quarrying this limestone, which you will see as you make your way to the top. Managed by The Wildlife Trust of South and West Wales, Port Eynon Point is another nature reserve. The quarry provides habitats for rabbit and fox as well as birds such as the Stonechat and Rock Pipit. Interesting birds are usually present all year round.

Point Eynon Point Cave, below the headland, was once inhabited by animals when sea levels were lower. Bones from lion, bear, rhinocerous, mammoth and deer have been found. The cave can be accessed depending on the tide.

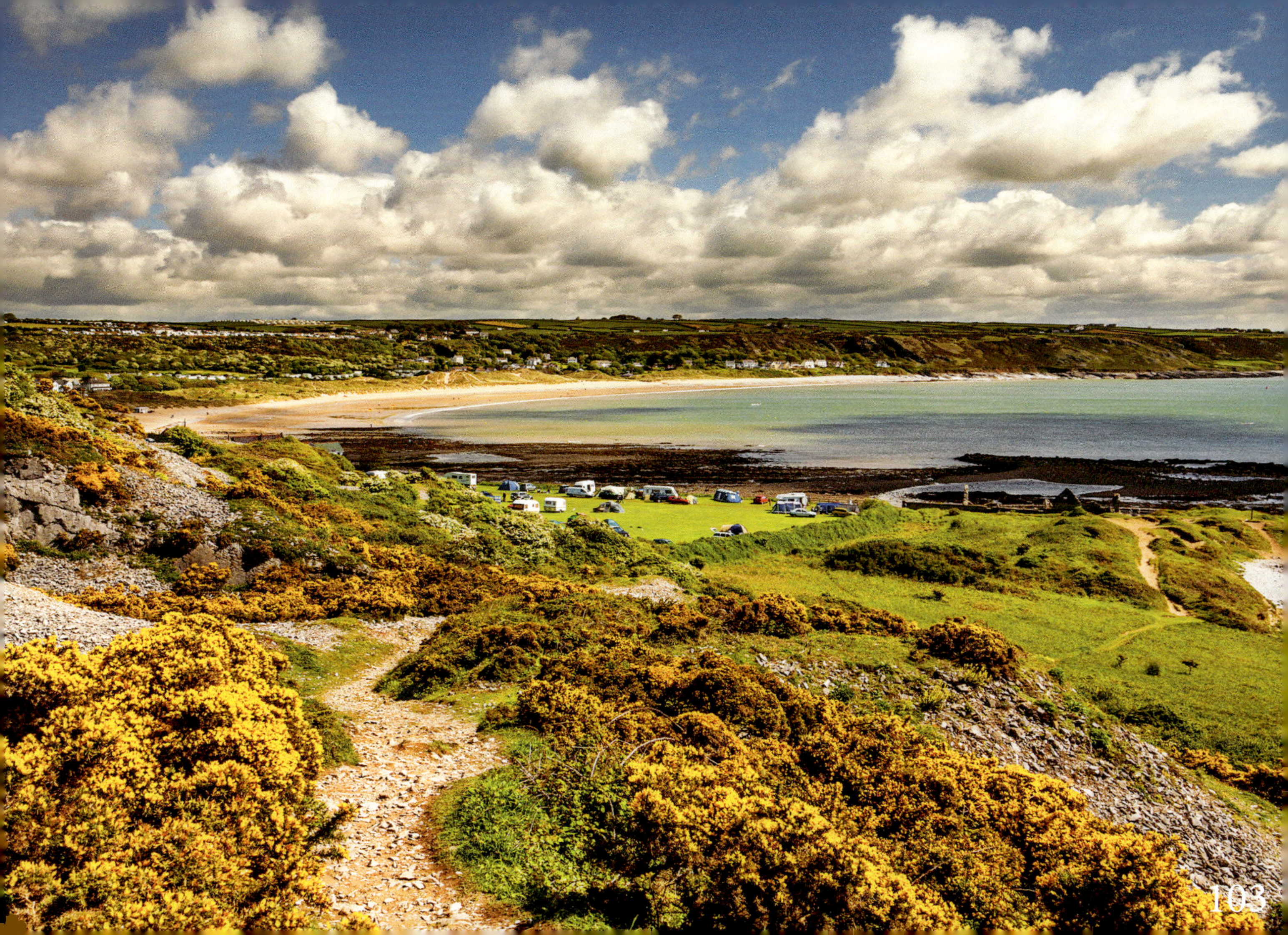

Horton and Port Eynon

This photo of the moon was taken from the top of Port Eynon Point. I run Astrophotography Workshops where I teach people how to take wide-field photos of the sky using their normal DSLR and lenses. Wide-field means it also includes part of the landscape and many stars; Deep-field means focusing on one star or a cluster of stars.

On this particular workshop, it was a day time workshop combined with night time. We started off during daylight at Penmaen Burrows where we spent a few hours on the cliffs teaching my client how to use his camera for daylight photos and then moved to Rhossili for a while. We then drove to Port Eynon and walked the coast path to Overton Mere for sunset. After sunset, it takes roughly an hour for stars to start appearing and two hours for it to be completely dark. We waited around as it got cloudier and cloudier. In fact we saw no stars at all!

The moon made an appearance for around five minutes, which is when I took this photo. We waited around a bit longer but decided to go home. The weather forecast is wrong more times than it is right, I have found. I've met up with people for an astrophotography workshop when the forecast says it will be 100% clear and it's been pouring down with rain. When we can't see the stars, we postpone as it seems a little pointless running a workshop about photographing stars when you can't see any stars!

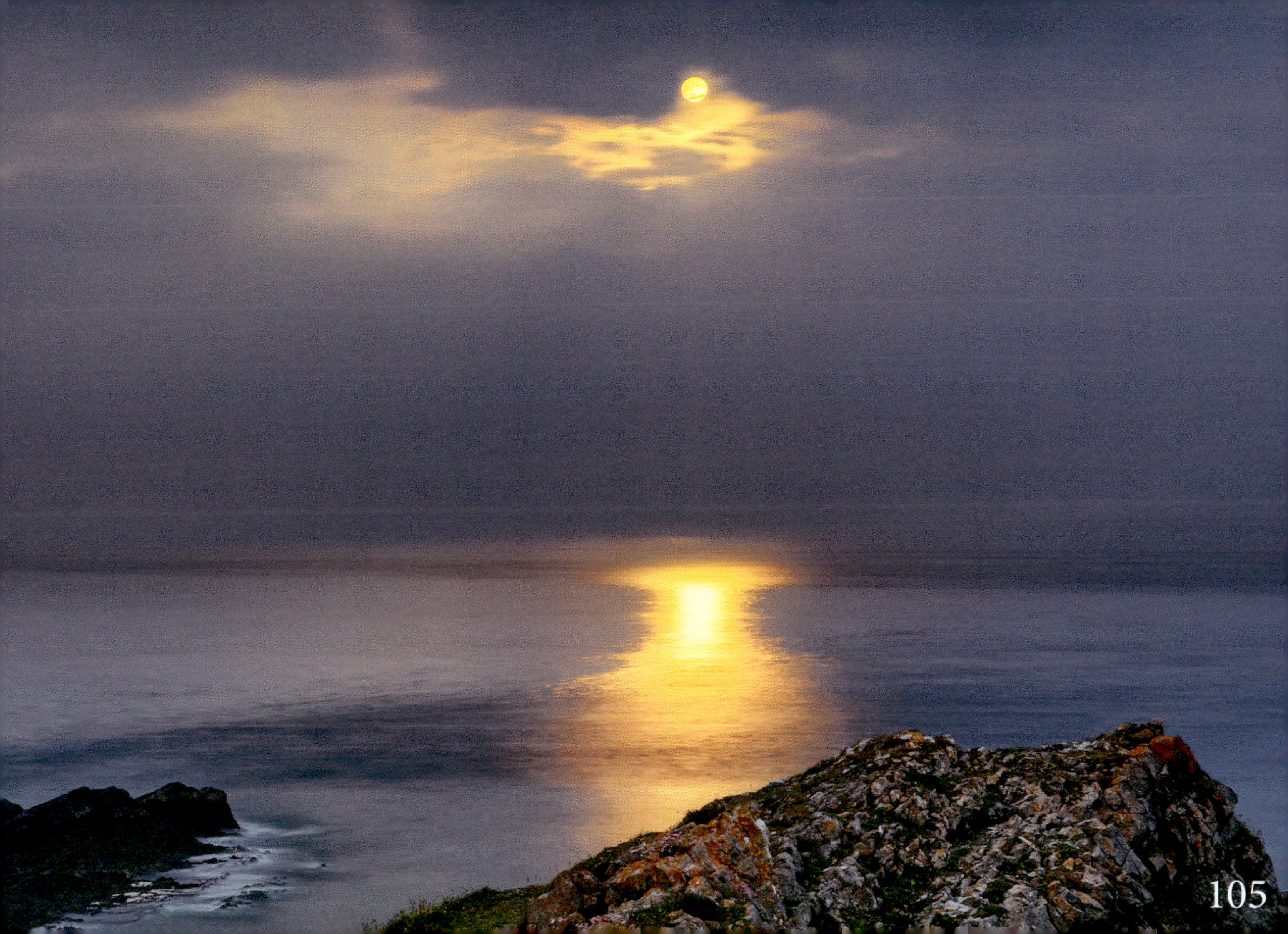

Horton and Port Eynon

A short distance along the coast path on the other side of the headland is the somewhat mysterious Culver Hole. There is some evidence in its construction and in the written records that it may have begun its life as a stronghold for the long since vanished Port Eynon Castle.

In the 16th century, it is thought that the owner of the Salt House repaired the Culver Hole for his own use, and given the rumours of his involvement in smuggling, it is easy to see where the suggestion of a smugglers' haunt came from. There is even a rumour of a tunnel leading from the Salt House to the Culver Hole, but no trace of a tunnel has ever been found.

When the tide has pulled rocks away from underneath it is possible to climb inside the structure. The inner construction makes it look like a dovecot and culver is an English word derived from the Old English of culfre, which means dove or pigeon so this was almost certainly its use at some point. However, the romance of smuggling will always be the favourite suggestion.

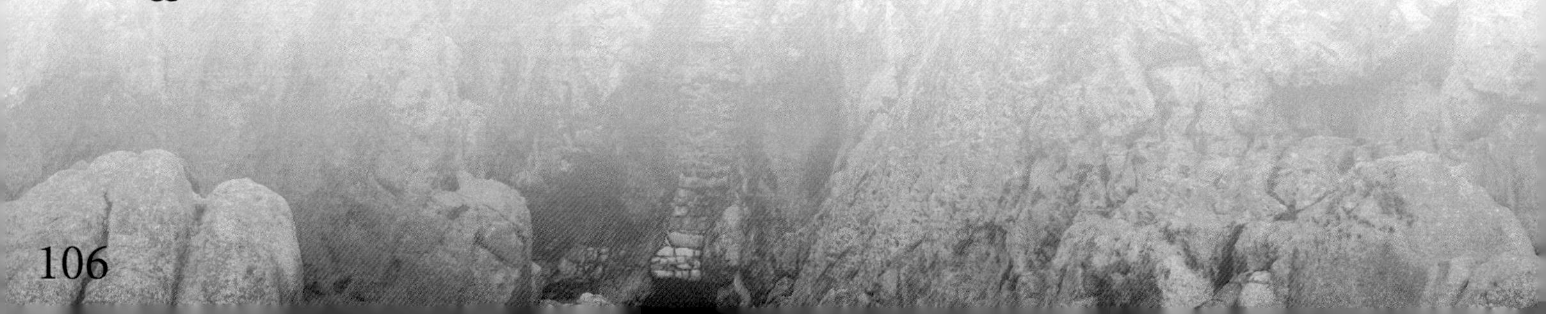

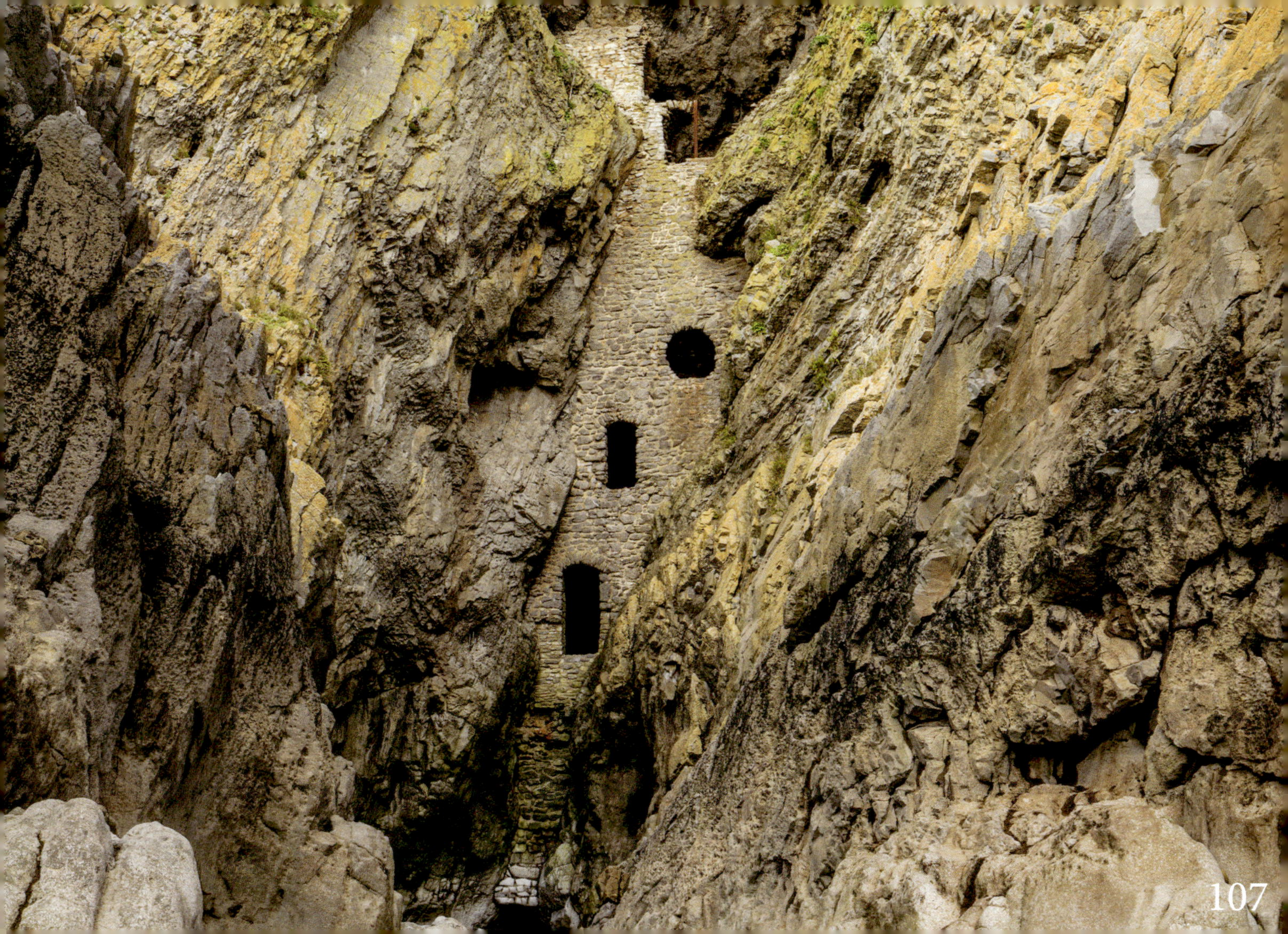

Overton Mere

Just on from Culver Hole is Overton Mere. It is a very rocky bay and largely unvisited as it isn't really suitable for swimming. There are a few shipwrecks around that emphasise how dangerous this bay can be, the most well known being the Wittezee from Holland which was shipwrecked on 12th November 1940. Before 2009, much more of the wreck used to exist but it was sadly removed during the construction of an outflow pipe. The limestone rocks have created some great rock pools, which is ideal for kids (and adults!) not wanting a sandy beach.

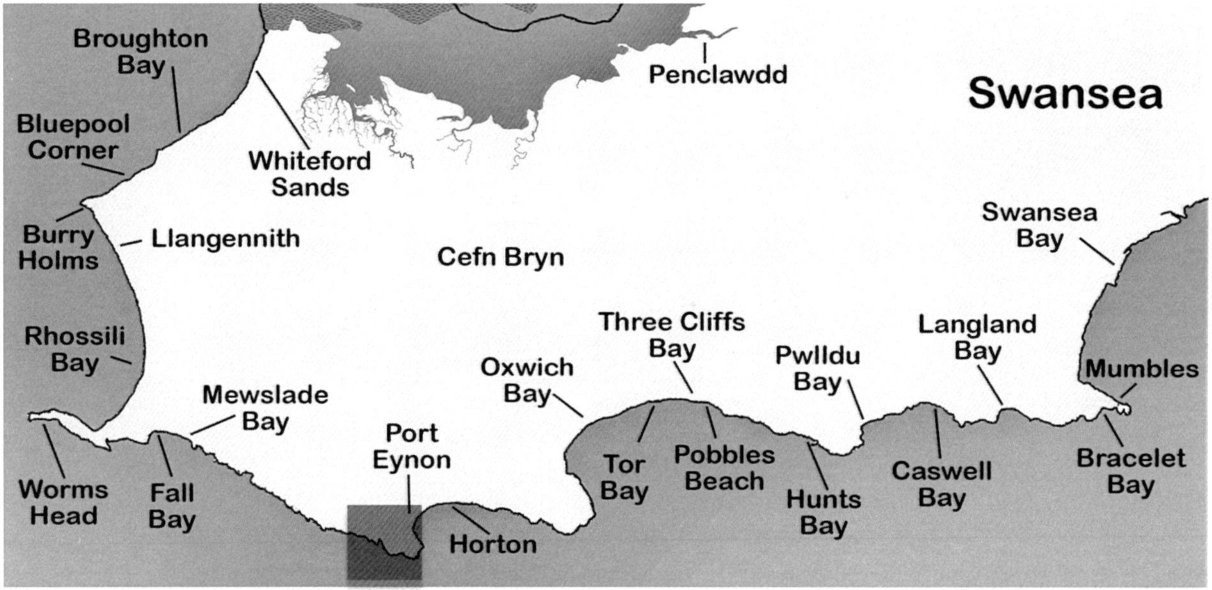

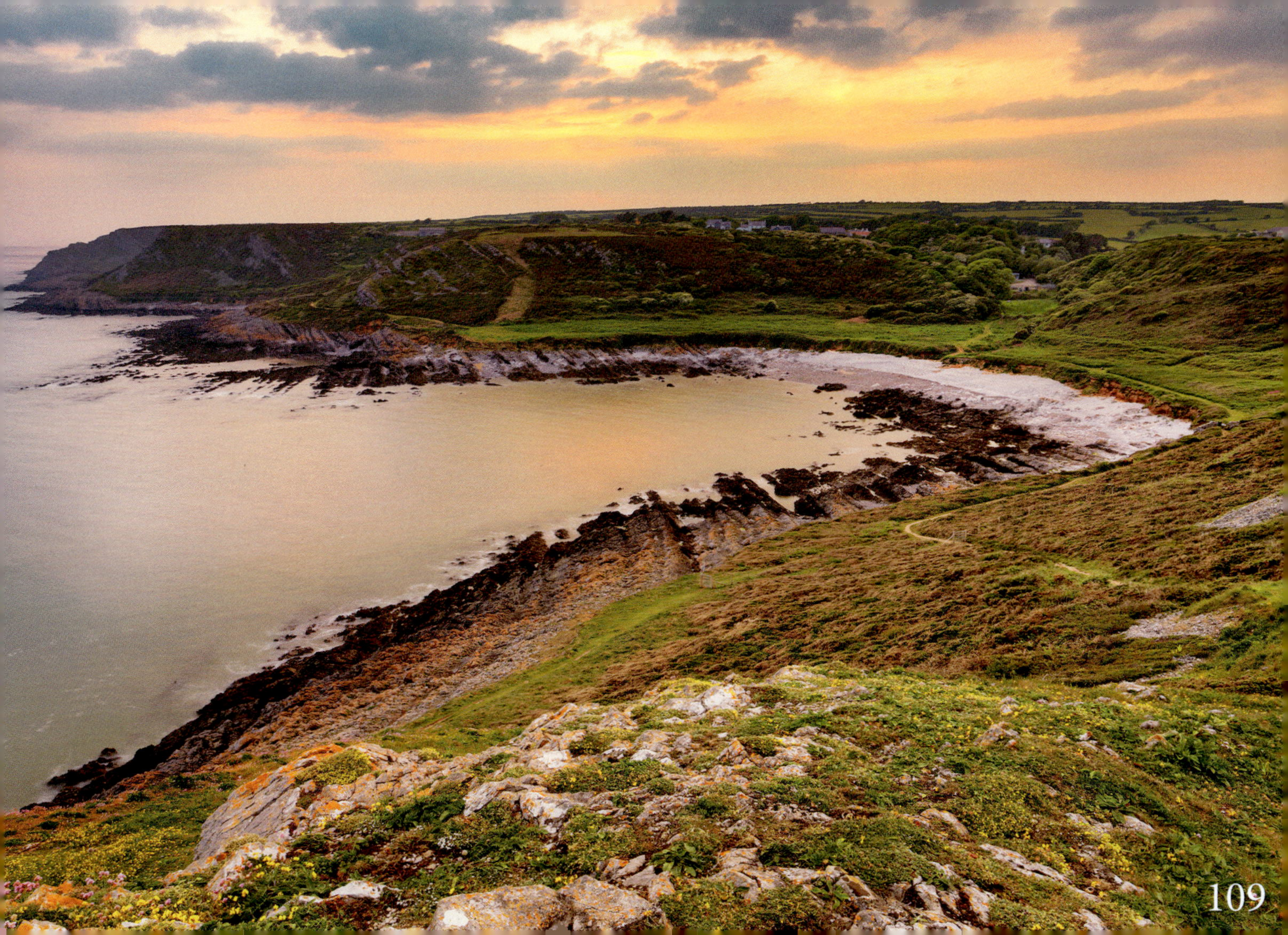

Goat's Hole Cave / Paviland Cave

This unassuming, picturesque gully called Foxhole Slade looks innocent enough, but it is actually the way to access the most important cave on Gower – Goat's Hole Cave, which is more commonly as Paviland Cave or Red Lady Cave. To get to it, you have to wait until low tide – not just any low tide, it has to be a low tide on a high tide swing day. Low tides are different heights each day and some low tides aren't low enough to be able to cross the small beach to get to the cave. I didn't realise this myself until I'd spent two hours on the cliff waiting for the tide to get lower, but it never did.

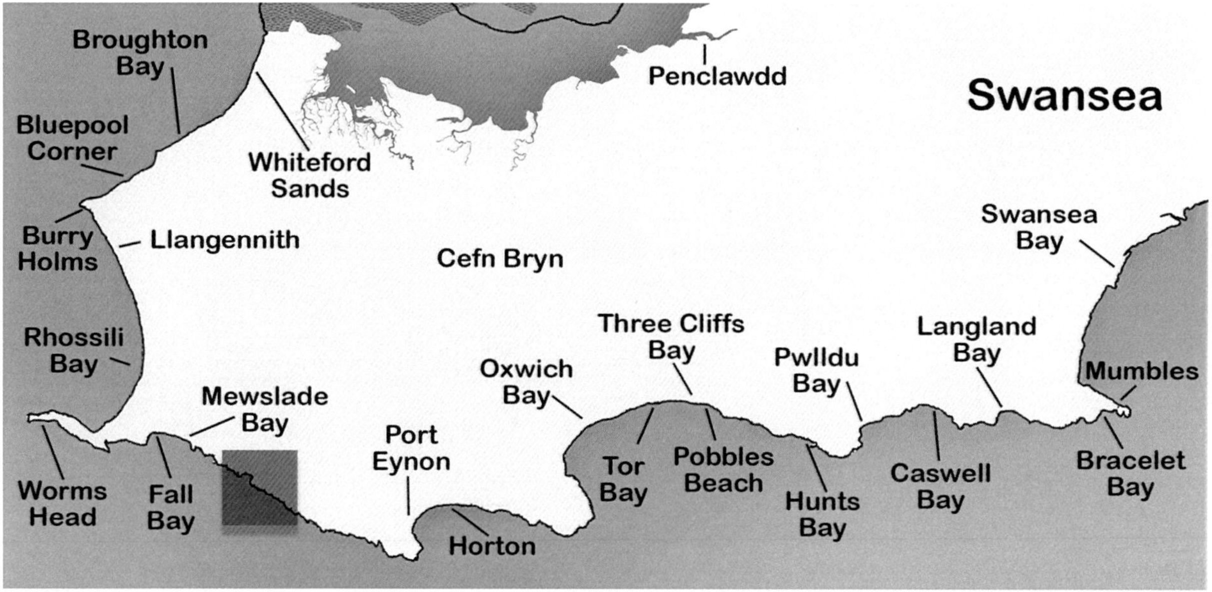

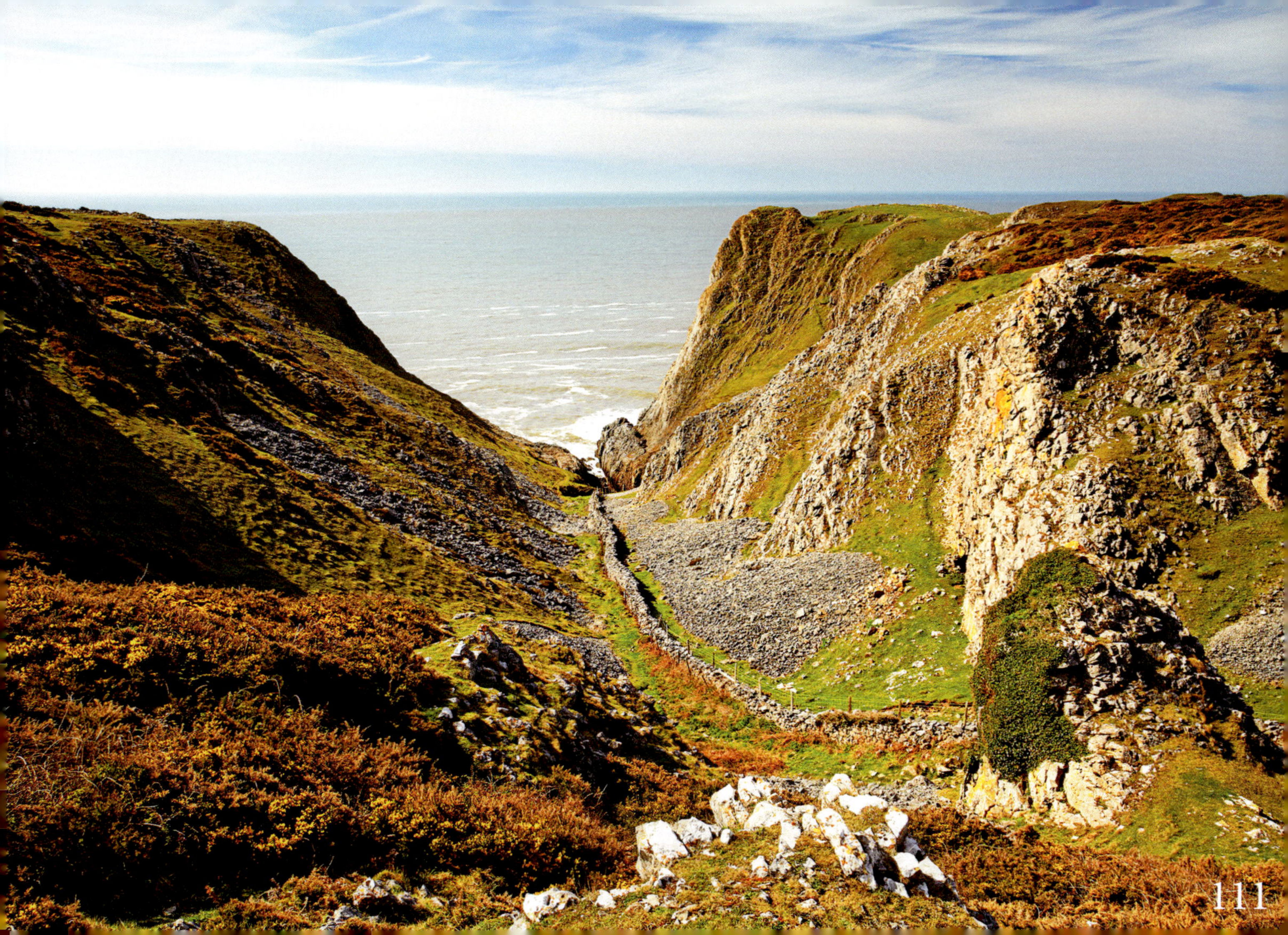

Goat's Hole Cave / Paviland Cave

Goat's Hole Cave / Paviland Cave on the south coast of Gower is where the remains of the 'Red Lady of Paviland' were discovered. 'She' was originally thought to be a Roman female, as the bones were dyed with red ochre and accompanied with grave goods. However, it was later discovered that 'she' was a Stone Age male, but the name of Red Lady has stuck. It was thought for many years that the Red Lady was from around 24,000BC, but the bones were recently re-examined and discovered to be older. At the time of the ritual burial, about 34-34,000 years ago, the landscape was very different. Sea levels were much lower, possibly 70 miles away, so the cave would have provided views over grassland rich in game with the Bristol Channel a mere river.

The bones were found by during a geological dig by Rev William Buckland in 1823. The 'Red Lady' was laid to rest with carved ivory and shell beads. It is one of the oldest examples of a ceremonial burial in Western Europe! The bones have been in Oxford University, where William Buckland was a Professor of Geology, since they were discovered. There have been repeated calls for them to be returned to Swansea where they can be put on display in the museum.

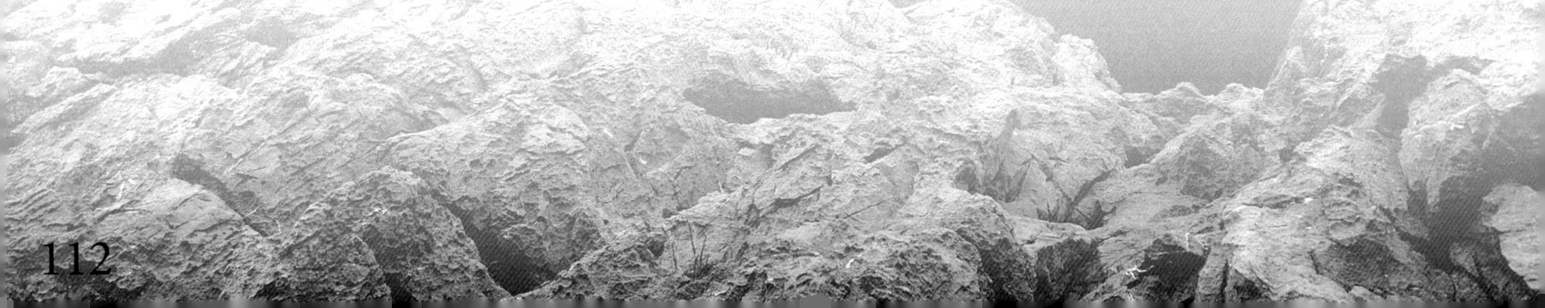

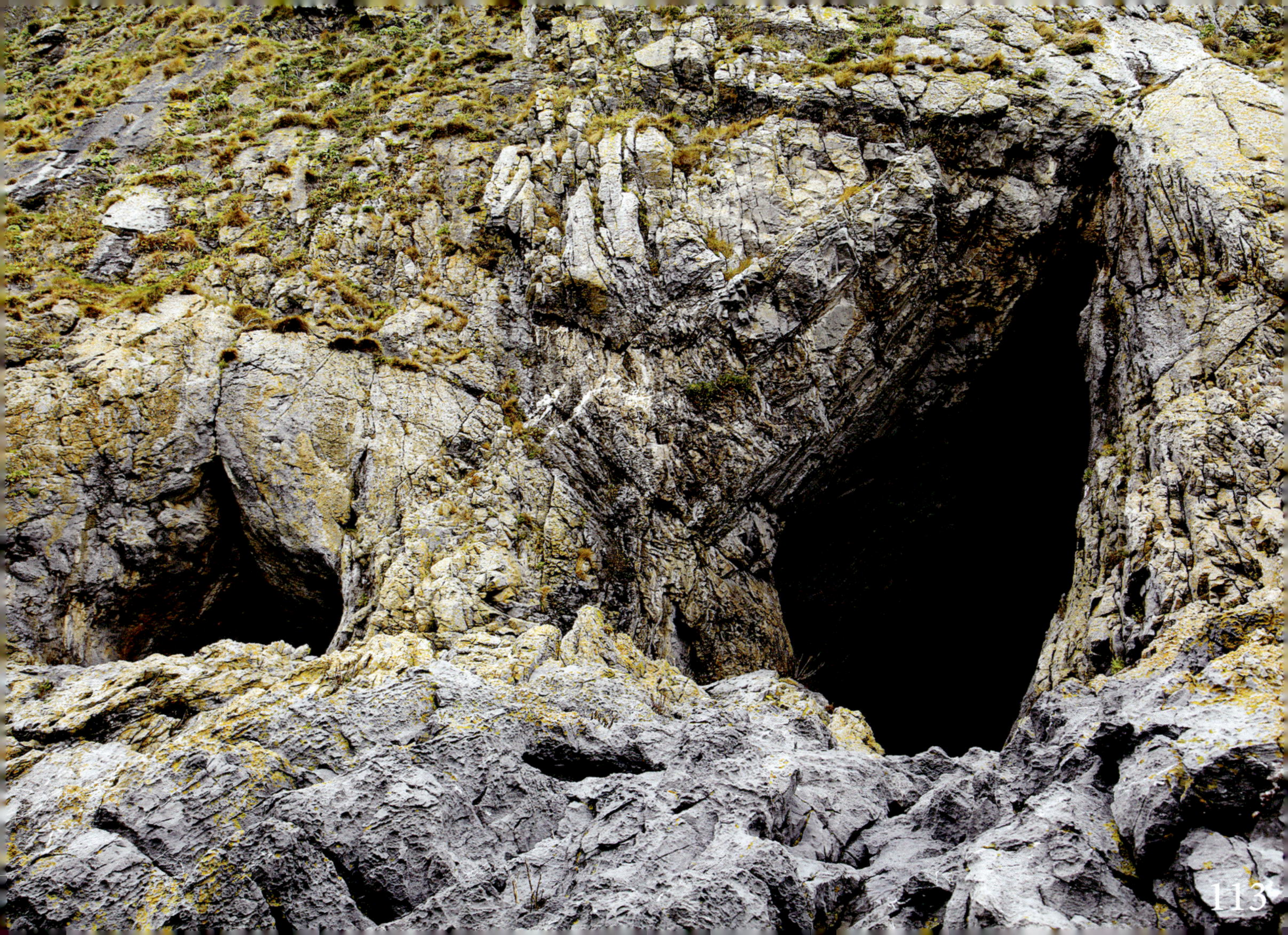

The Knave

You could be forgiven for thinking that this isn't Gower with the rock formations here. The tilted High Tor Limestone has made this into a spectacular bit of landscape. This stretch of coastline between Port Eynon and Rhossili is my favourite and it isn't unusual not to see anyone else for a good while when walking. You can park at Pilton Green Common and walk across the fields to the coast path and turn right or, if you fancy a walk, start in Rhossili or Port Eynon. Worms Head is in the distance.

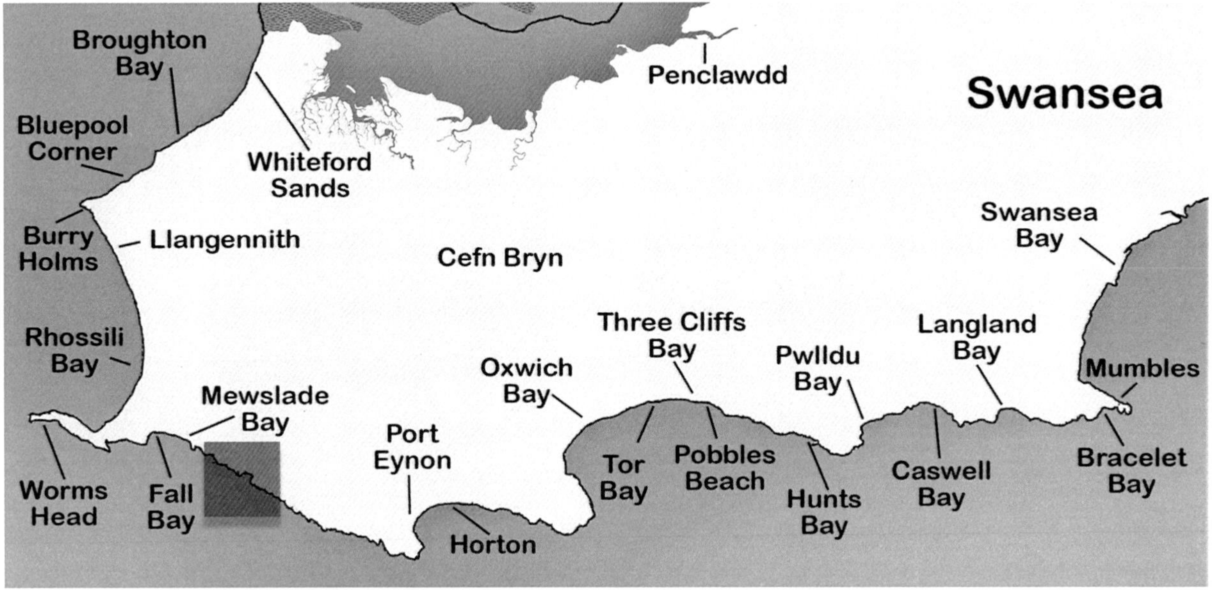

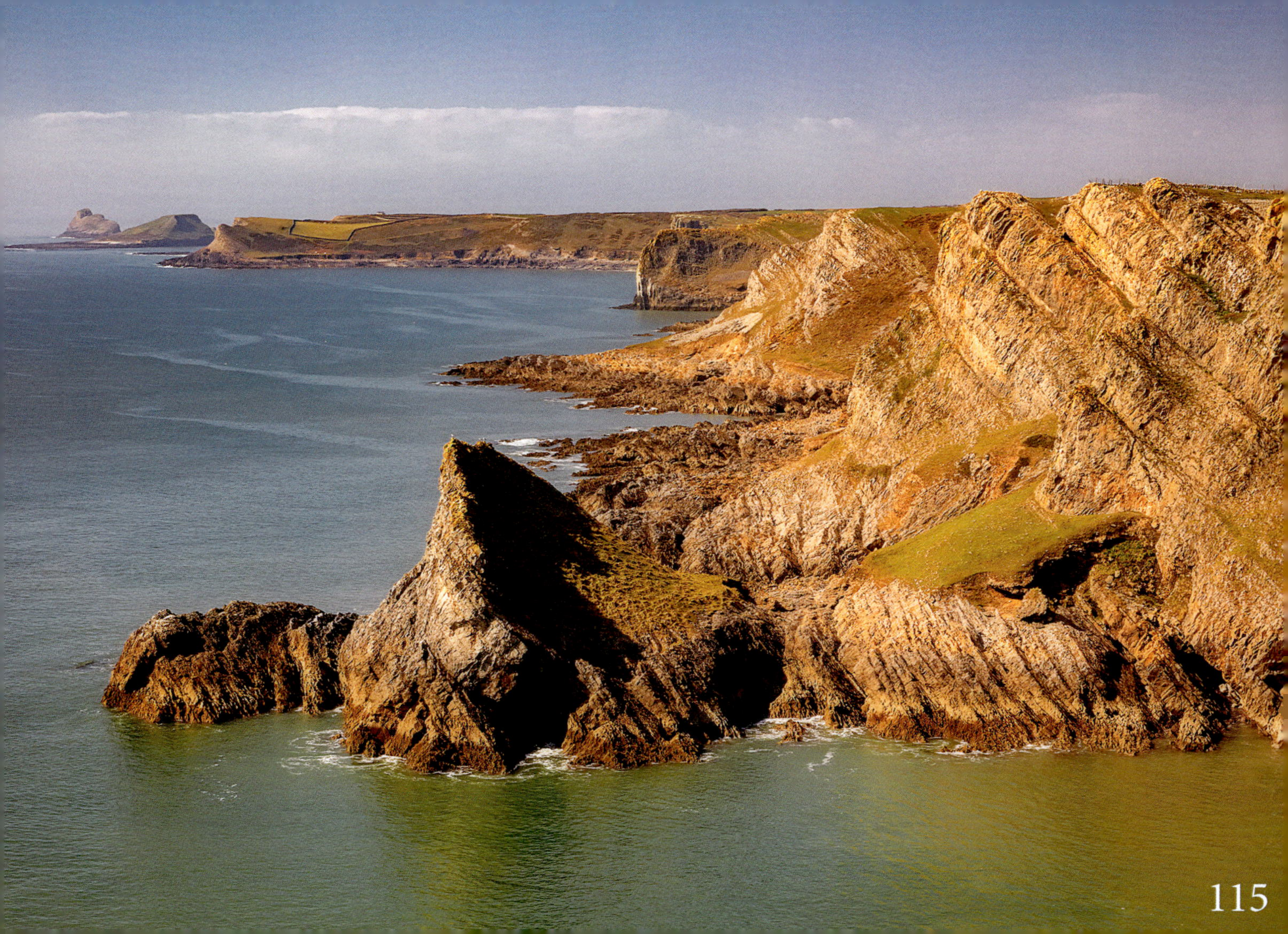

The Knave

It is possible to get down to The Knave by scrambling down a gully, but there isn't really any beach. Water erodes limestone, which in turn creates caves over many thousands of years. Much of Gower is made up of limestone and is notable for the vast amount of caves, especially what are called 'bone caves'. Bone caves are caves which have been excavated and have been found to contain bones of animals or maybe even humans.

The area around The Knave has more than its fair share of caves: Highcliff Shelter, Short Cave, Ogof Arllechwedd, Ogof Ffynnon Wyntog or Deborah's Spring, Samphire Hole, Ogof Wyntog, Knave Sea Cave, Ogof Asgwrn Mochyn or Deborah's Cliff Shelter and, perhaps the most well known due to it being on the OS map, Deborah's Hole. There is even a metre high rock arch on the headland near the Knave.

Sat on the cliff above The Knave is an Iron Age promontory fort. Much of it has fallen into the sea thanks to erosion, but around one third of the fort circle is still there. Being a promontory hill fort, however, it might not have been the complete circle to start with as the cliff would have served as a defence on one side. The site was excavated in 1939 by Audrey Williams, a well known archaeologist.

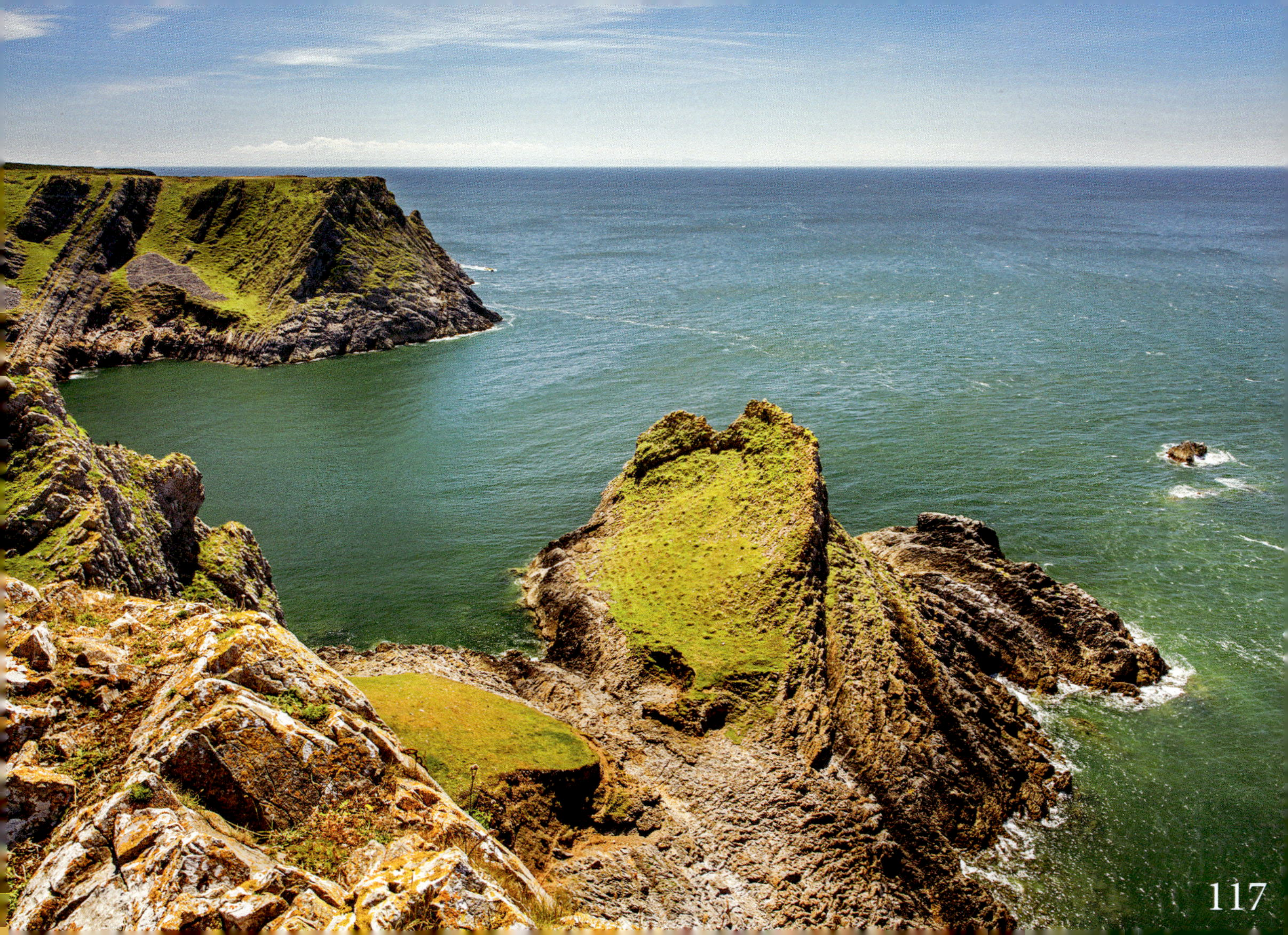

Ramsgrove

Ramsgrove is a pebble beach that is almost always deserted. It can be reached from the coast path after parking at Pilton Green Common or, if you stay at Pitton Cross Caravan and Camping Park, you can walk through fields directly to it. Walking down through the valley between the limestone cliffs is like no other place on Gower. I always view it with a sense of awe. Looking at the cliffs in the photo with the rocks dipping either side, it seems obvious there is a minor fault that the water made use of to carve the valley.

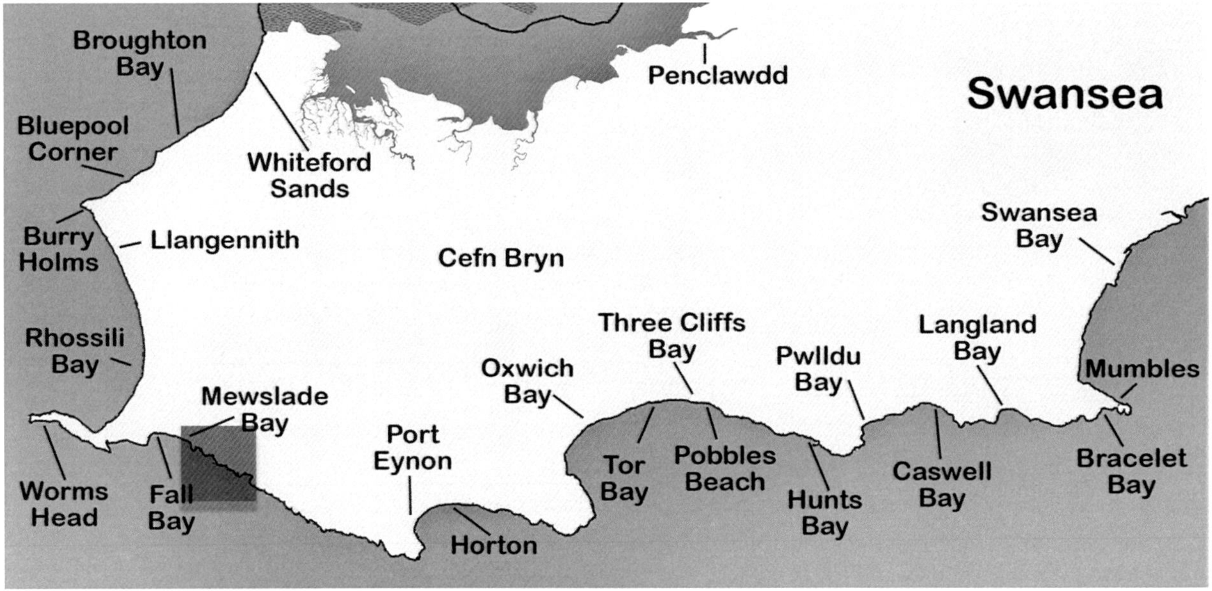

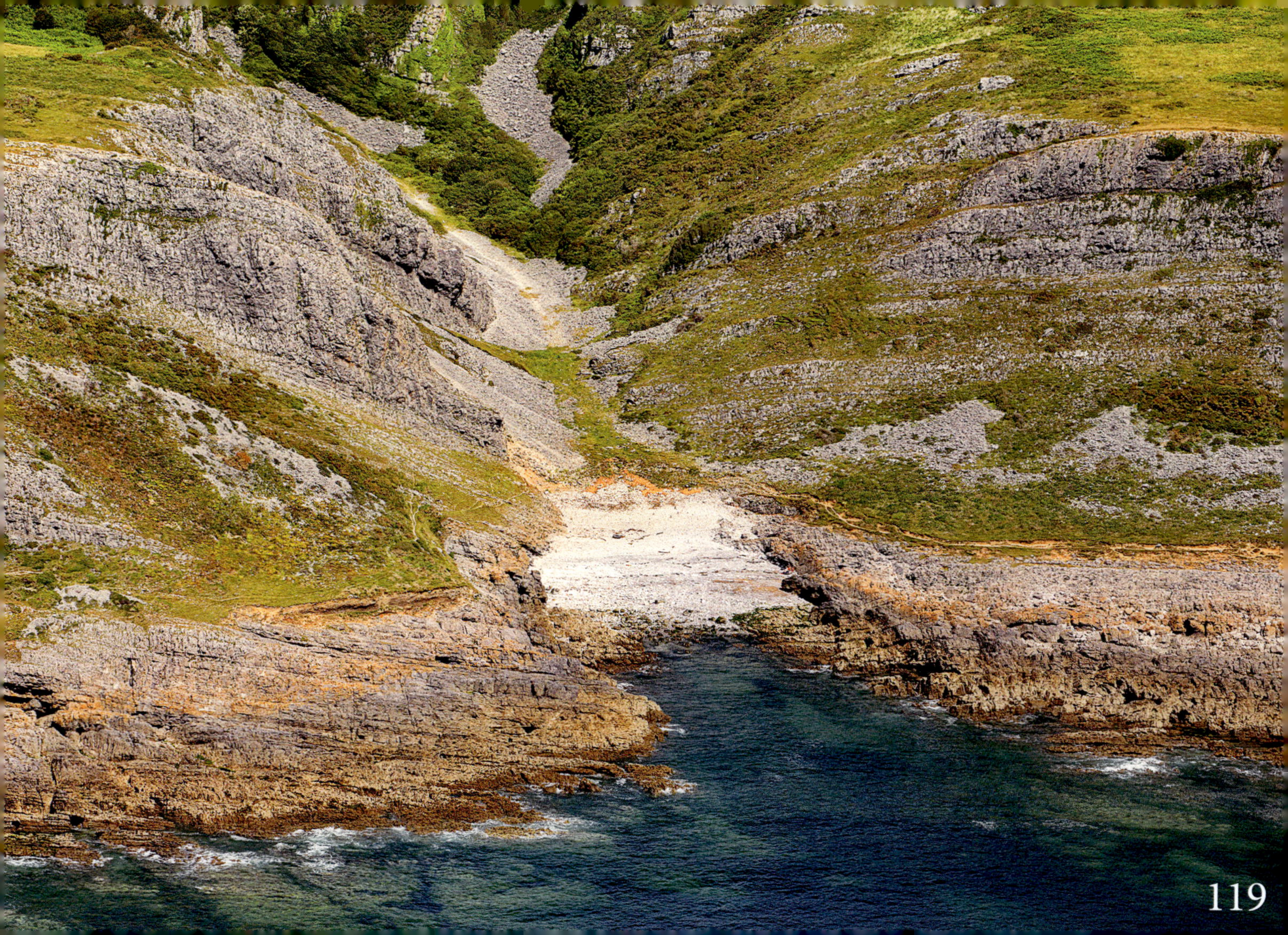

Ramsgrove

Ramsgrove is sometimes called Ramgrove or Rams Grove. At the top of the beach, just below the high tide, is Ramsgrove Resurgence. A resurgence is where an underground river reappears on the surface. The limestone cliffs of the valley on the walk to Ramsgrove are good for rock climbing as is the rocky crag just by the beach. The climbs always have interesting sounding names, such as Insatiable Appetite, Don't Tell Ann, Malaysian Lust, Ram Bam Thank Ewe Lamb, and so on.

Ramsgrove is a lovely place to sit in the warm sun, watch the waves and tune out from the hecticness of modern life. Thirty minutes spent here with no phone, no interruptions and just the sounds of nature can make you feel so much better. Thirty minutes can often turn into sixty…

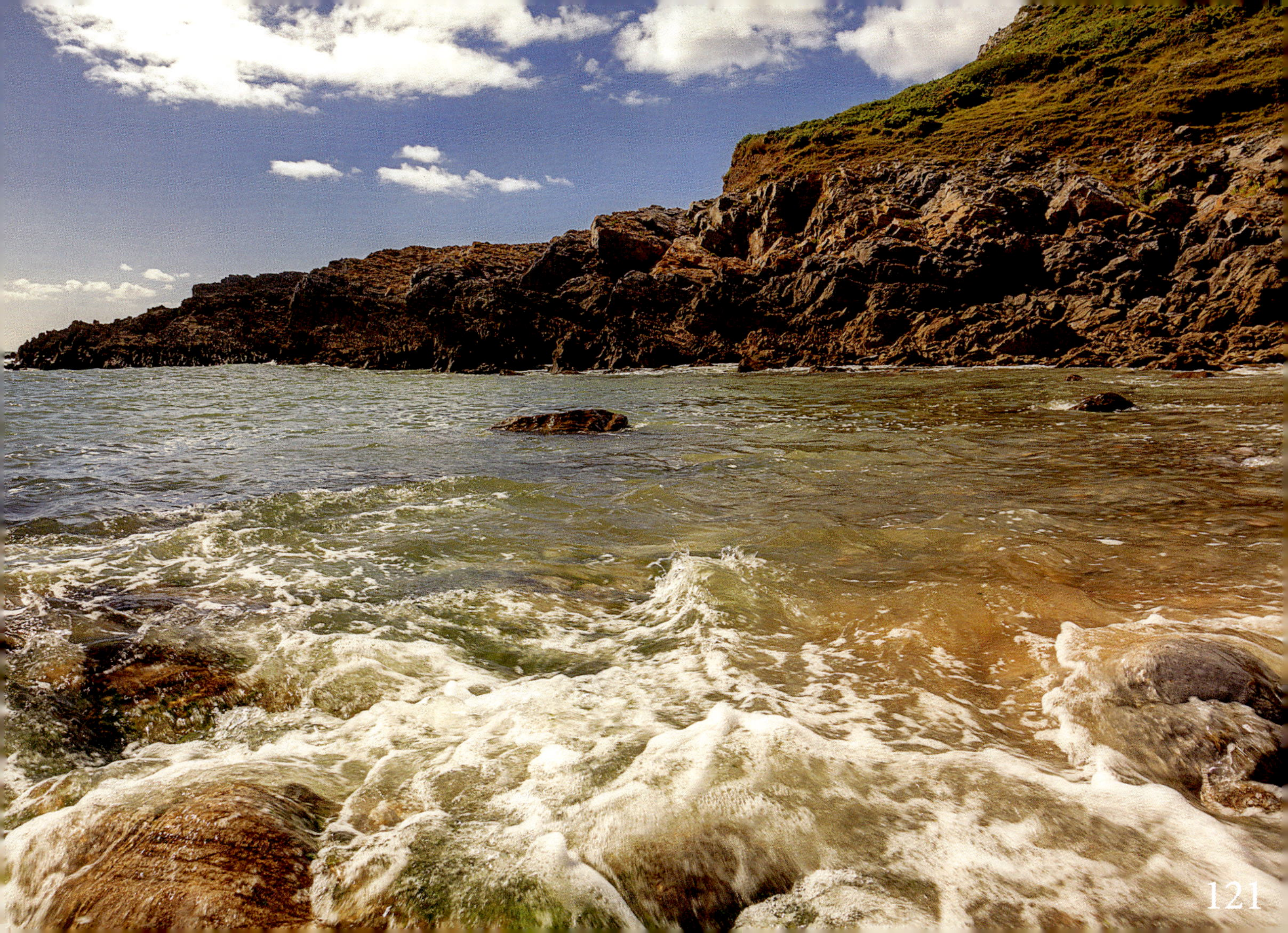

Mewslade Bay

Mewslade, owned and managed by the National Trust, is a pretty, sandy beach that is very popular with surfers and sunbathers alike. There is a nice walk through woodland and then through Mewslade Quarry which has some interesting looking caves. Although they look tempting, only the properly equipped and experienced should attempt entry as much of the passage is a crawl. The sandy bay is completely submerged when the tide is in, but turning right along the path just above the beach gives some lovely places to sit and watch the waves.

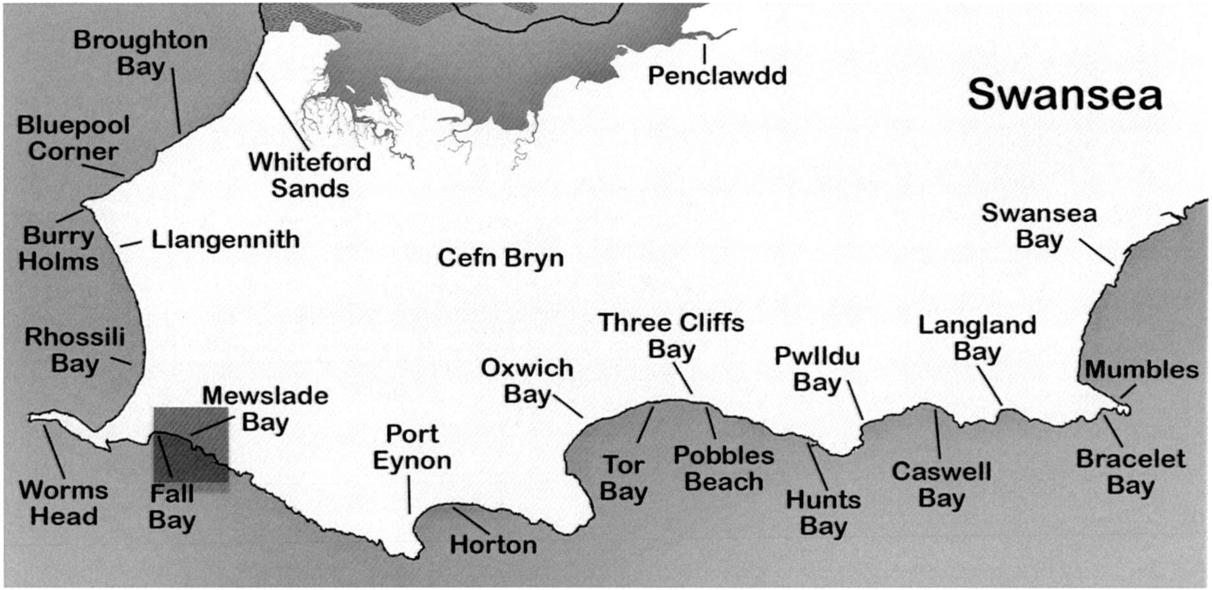

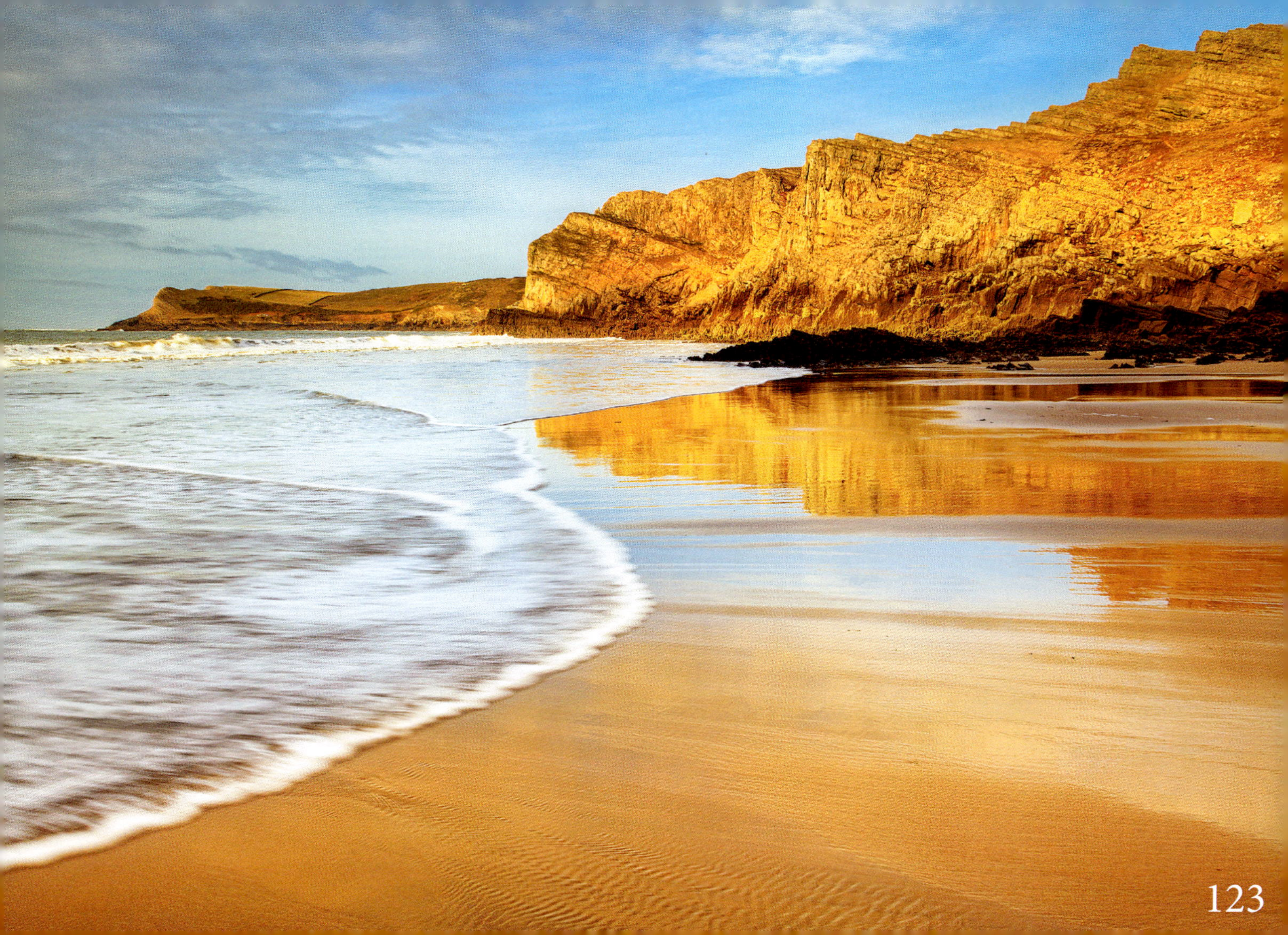

Mewslade Bay

Standing guard over Mewslade is Thurba Head and, being limestone, is great for rock climbing. Down on the beach, the limestone sticking out from the sand looks more like a moonscape in places. Whilst the beach is well known, it doesn't get too crowded like, say, Caswell Bay and Langland Bay. It is a beach well worth visiting whether you want to sunbathe, paddle, surf or walk.

I took this photo in early November. The sun was out, the weather was warm and the sea looked very inviting so I took my shoes off so I could take a photo looking back to the beach with the waves breaking in the foreground. The pain of the cold water on my feet was excruciating! It took several goes going in and back out again, but I got used to it and took this photo. I used my night time wide angle lens to capture as much of the waves as possible and to include that lovely blue sky with fluffy white clouds.

If you follow the path around the coast from just above the beach towards Rhossili, the views are spectacular, but the path isn't for the faint hearted as there are drops to the beach below close to the path.

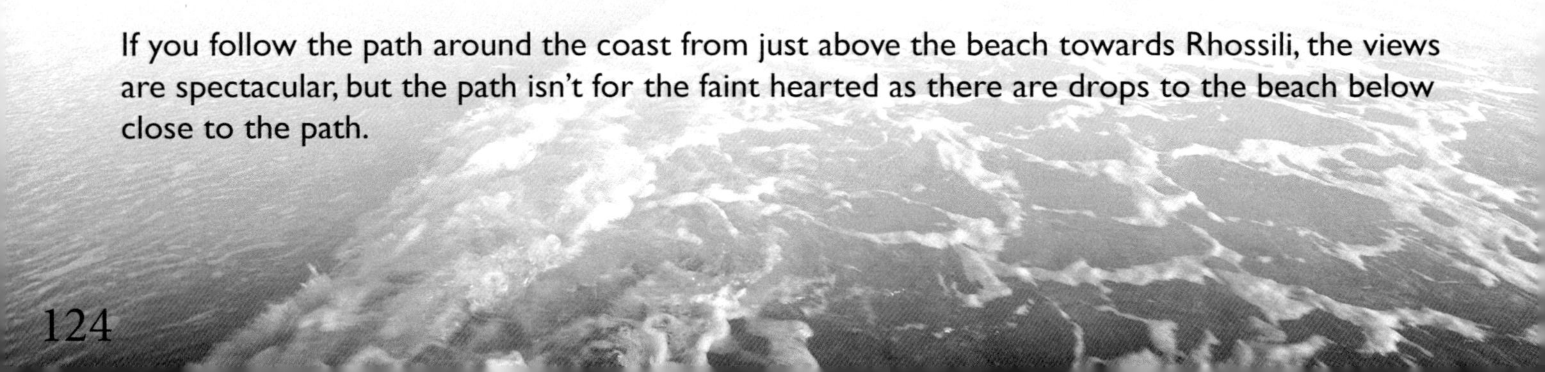

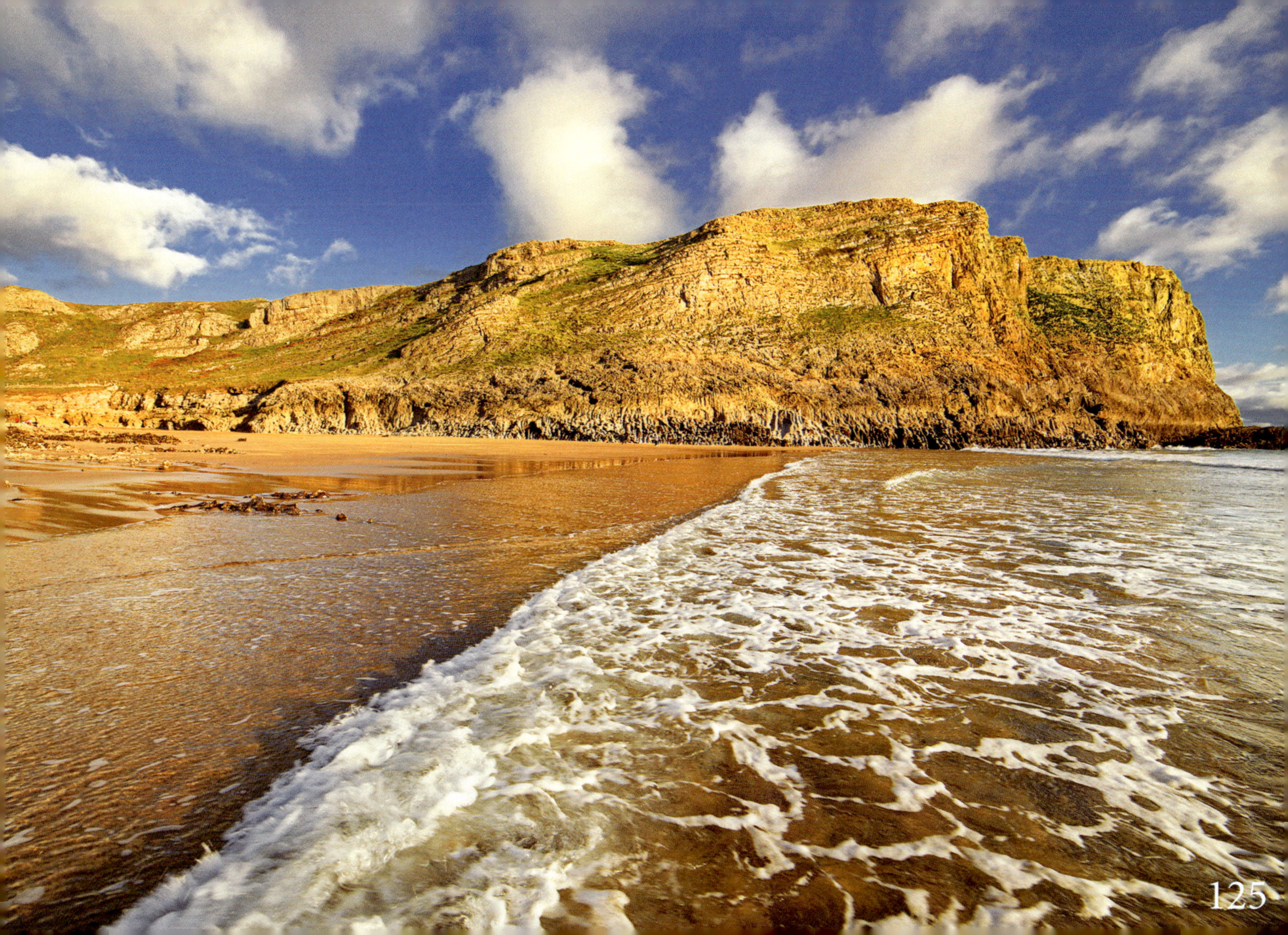

Fall Bay

Fall Bay is just along the coast from Mewslade Bay and during very low tides it is possible to walk along the beach between the two. Fall Bay is one of the quieter beaches on Gower, often overlooked in favour of Mewslade and Rhossili, and is well worth a visit. You can walk from Mewslade or Rhossili along the coast path or on public footpaths through fields from Rhossili. The headland in the distance is called Tears Point and is good for fishing.

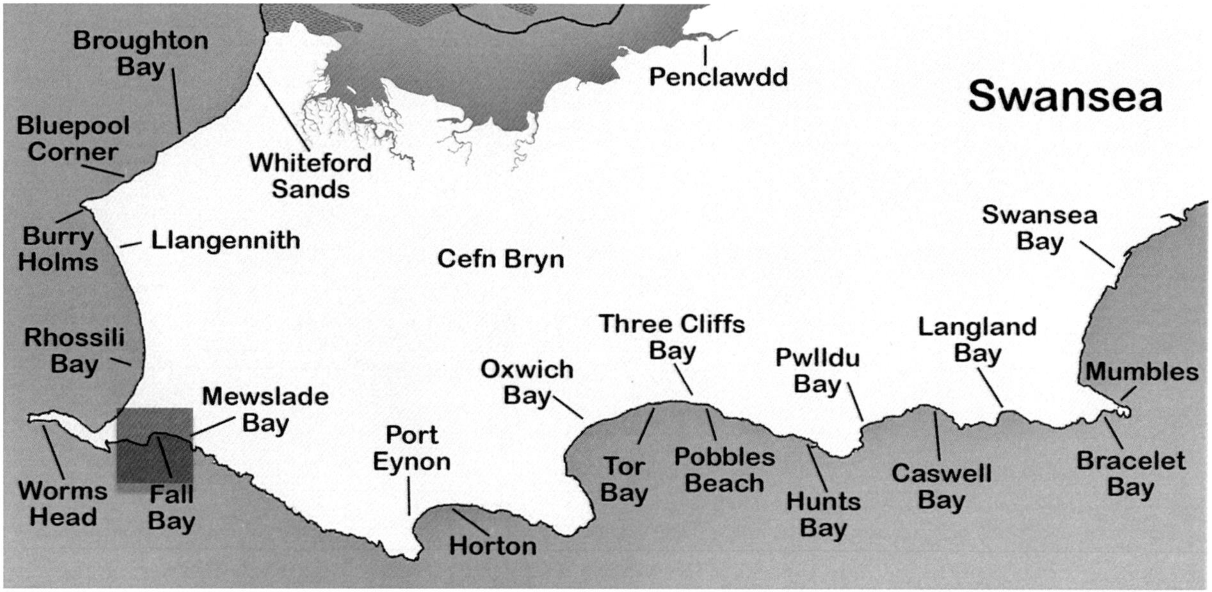

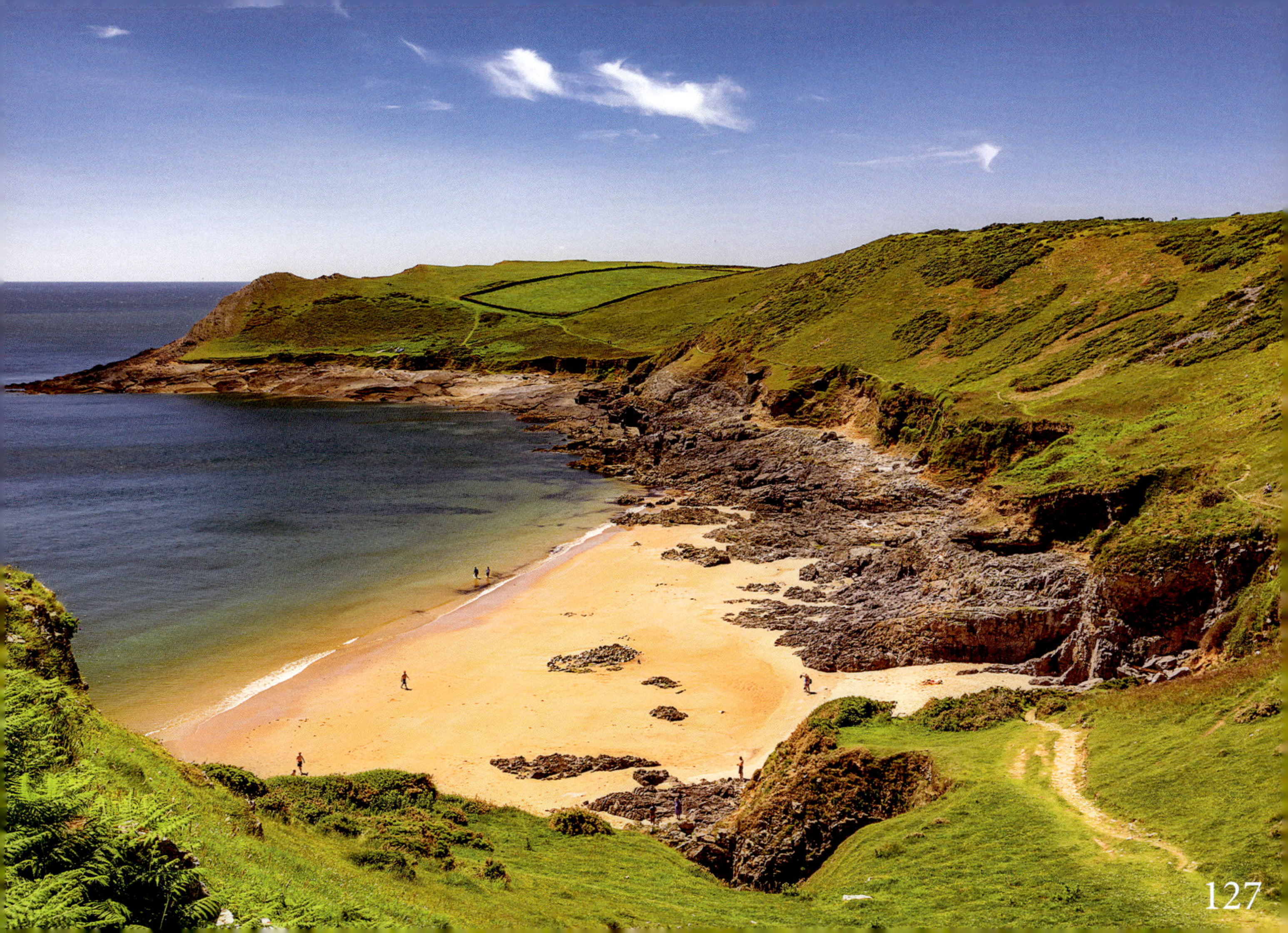

Fall Bay

Fall Bay has a great example of a 'Pleistoscene' raised beach. At the back of the beach is a raised wave cut platform, which provides evidence that sea levels were once around 10 metres higher than they are today. Pleistoscene is often referred to as the 'Ice Age' which was the most recent period of glaciation on Earth, from around 2.5 million years to 12,000 years ago when there were repeated freeze-thaw cycles. During the freeze cycles, water was locked up in massive ice sheets – some of the UK was a mile beneath the ice! The last massive ice sheet ended roughly along the M4, leaving Gower just outside of it. There is evidence on Gower that the glaciers did dip further south, for example, Arthur's Stone on Cefn Bryn.

When glaciers covered much Britain, the water was locked up in glaciers which meant the sea levels were much lower than they are today. This has been seen through the occupation of the sea caves along the Gower coast when the Bristol Channel was more like a Scandinavian tundra and the sea 50 to 70 miles away. When the glaciers melted around 20,000 years ago, the sea levels rose rapidly and flooded the low lying land. There is evidence there was once a land bridge between Britain and France where people lived that rapidly flooded when the glaciers melted. The Bristol Channel also flooded. The sea level was so high that it cut wave platforms above where the beaches are today.

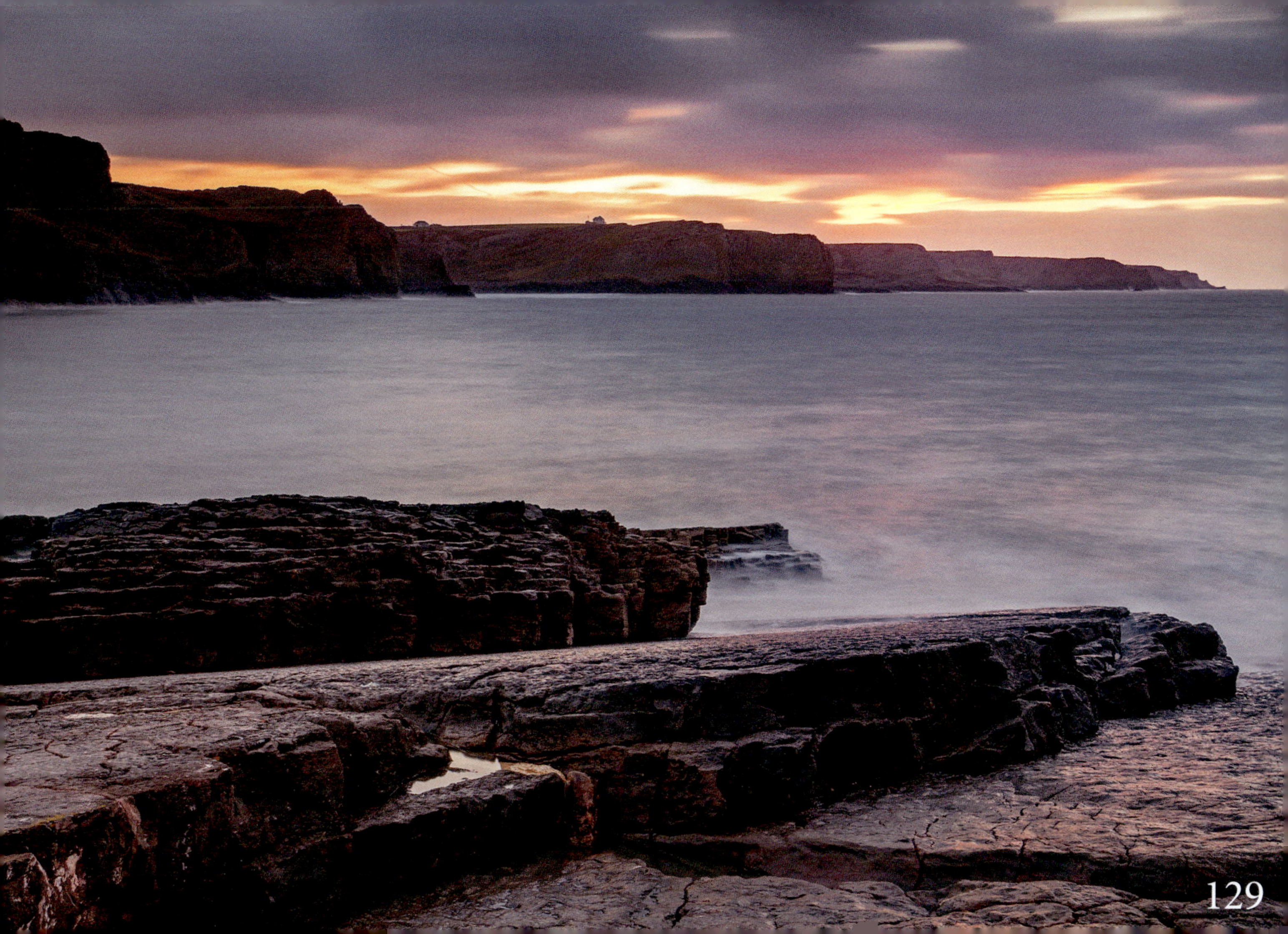

Fall Bay

When the ice melted, the massive weight of the ice was removed and the north of Britain slowly lifted whilst the south of Britain slowly sank. In 2009, the University of Durham studied this and found that today, 20,000 years after the ice melted, Britain is still feeling the effects and even now the south of Britain, including Gower, is still slowly sinking- possibly up to 5cm over the next 100 years!

I particularly like this viewpoint of Fall Bay because you are seeing so much history in one spot! From the tropical Rheic Ocean bed forming the rocks we see 300 to 400 million years ago when Britain was closer to the equator; to tectonic plate movement moving us to where we are now; to glaciers changing the climate and seas eroding the rocks to form what we see today. Looking at the landscape, it seems very permanent and set in stone, but it is actually very fluid and changing, just over a long period of time.

In this photo, the slabs dipping into the sea are Black Rock Limestone. Looking across the bay, the rocks above Fall Bay are mostly Gully Oolite before changing to High Tor Limestone at Mewslade Bay. These 3 types of rock are all part of the Pembrokeshire Limestone Group which is Carboniferous Limestone.

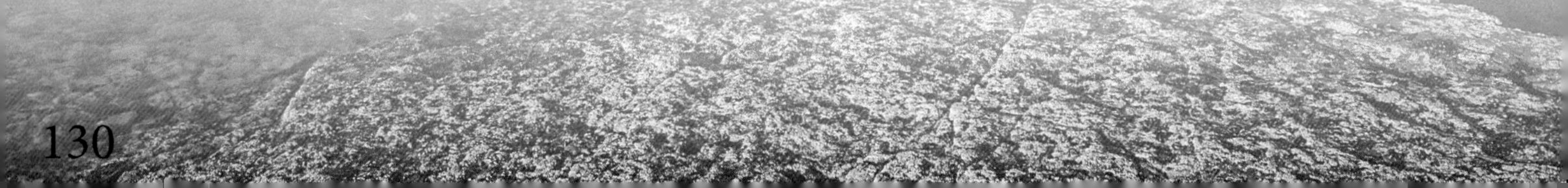

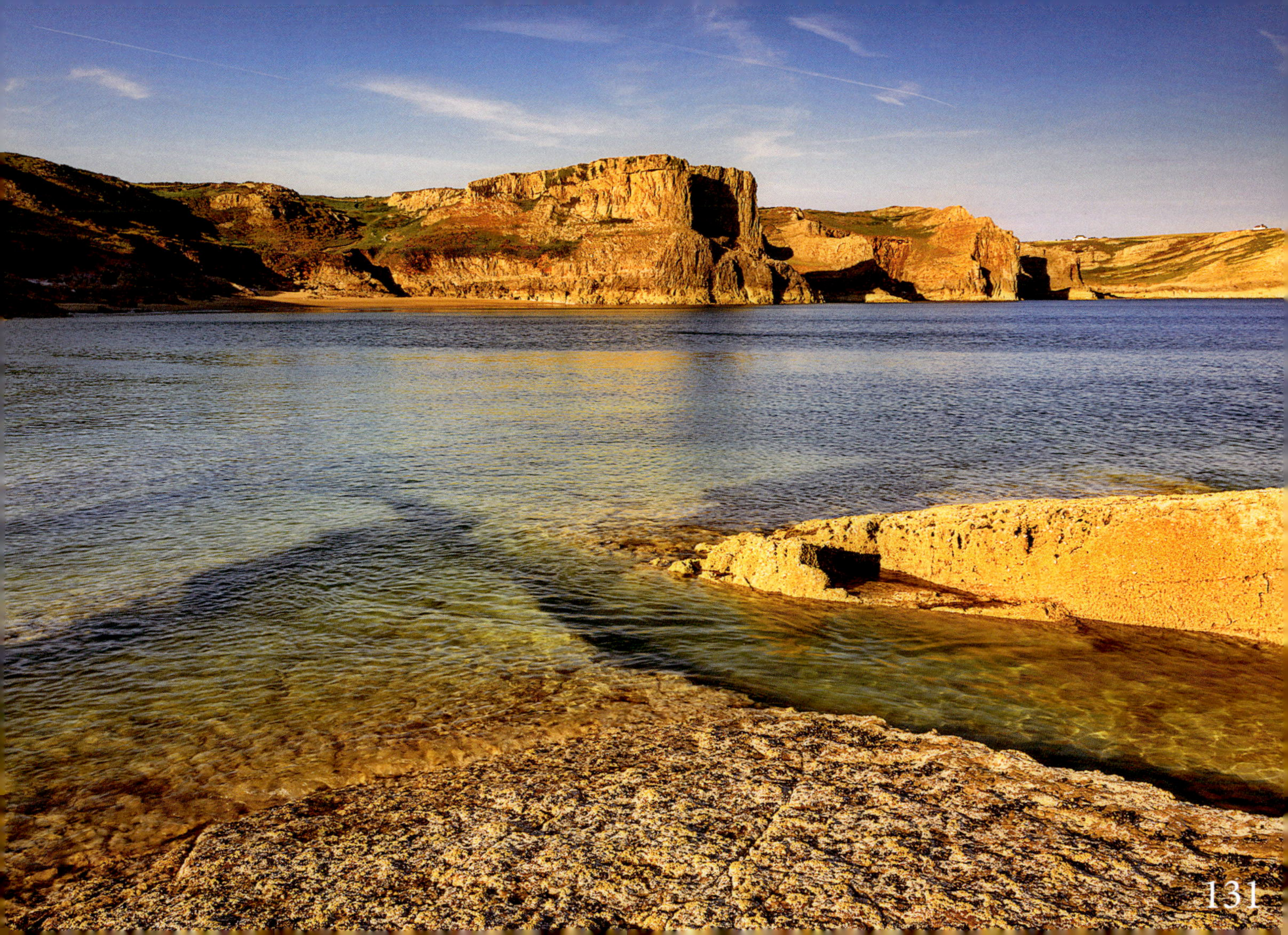

Worms Head and Rhossili Bay

Above Worms Head is the moon setting and the line in the top left is called an "Iridium Flare". Iridium is a communications network for satellite phones and their satellites are very highly polished. When they go overhead and reflect the sun, they get brighter and brighter and then dimmer and dimmer causing this effect. They are in a Low Earth Orbit and circle the earth at 1200 miles above our heads. I studied Iridium at University when I did my degree in Satellite Communications. They have now been deorbited as they have been replaced.

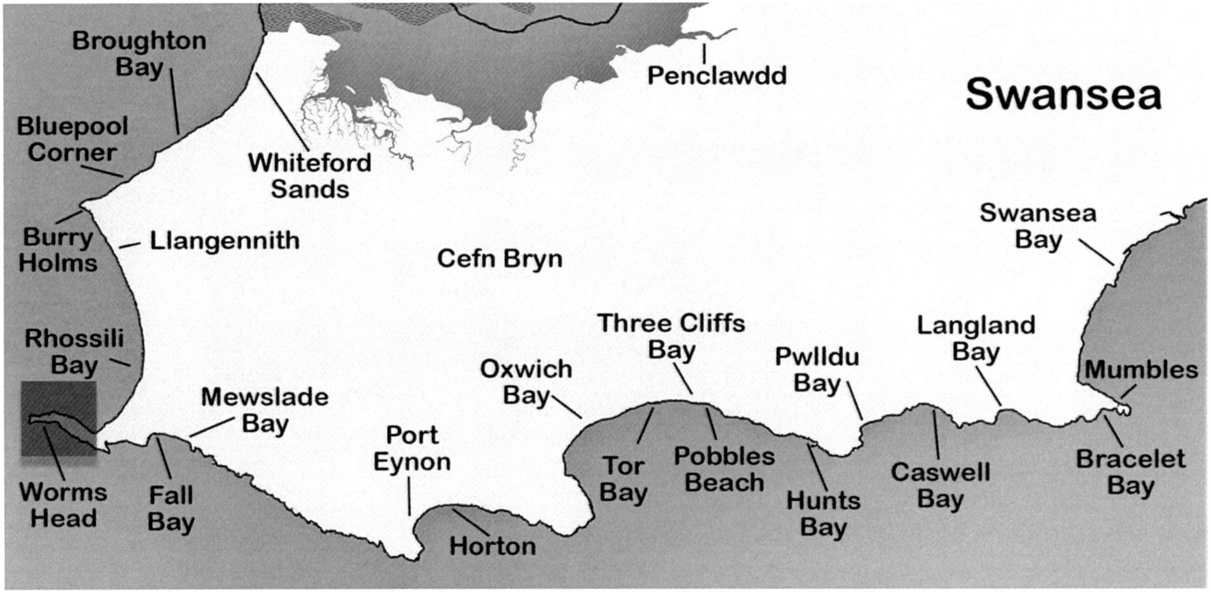

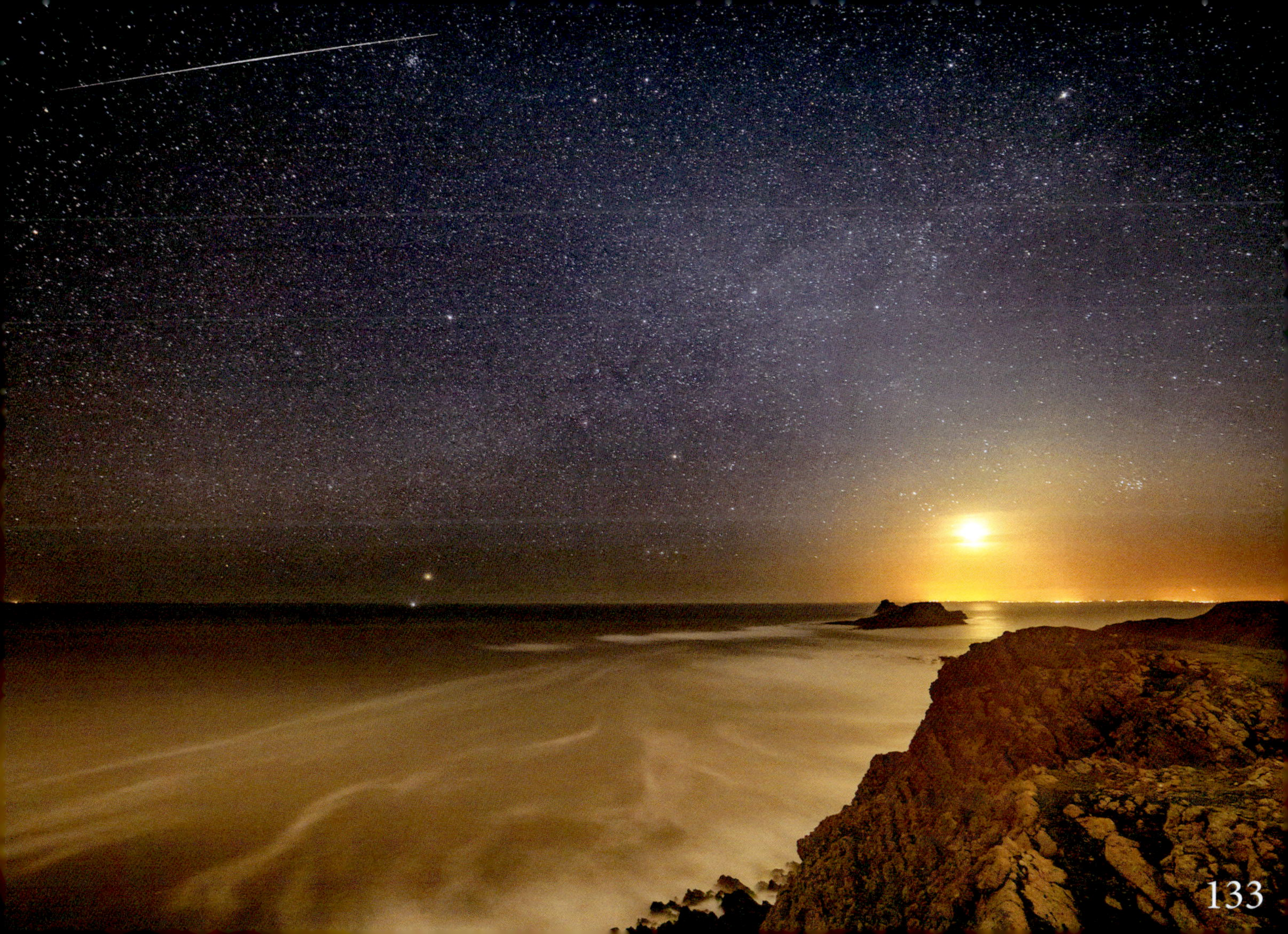

Worms Head and Rhossili Bay

For around two hours either side of low tide, it is possible to scramble across the uneven and sometimes slippery rocks out to the end of Worms Head, although access is restricted from 1st March to 31st August to protect nesting birds. A natural rock bridge called Devil's Bridge links Middle Head to Outer Head. Dylan Thomas himself got caught out once when he famously missed the tide and had to stay on Worms Head until the waters receded again. He wrote about this in his story Who Do You Wish Was With Us?

Tide times are displayed in the window of the old coastguard's lookout hut thanks to NCI Worms Head. The National Coastwatch Institution is a volunteer staffed organisation that was founded in 1994 after two fishermen in Cornwall lost their lives by a recently closed Coastguard Lookout. Local people decided to restore the watch and so the NCI was started. Today there are around 50 NCI stations around the England and Wales. The volunteers are friendly and always happy to talk about that they do. At every NCI station I've visited, they've always invited us in and we're been able to look through their telescopes and chat about what they do.

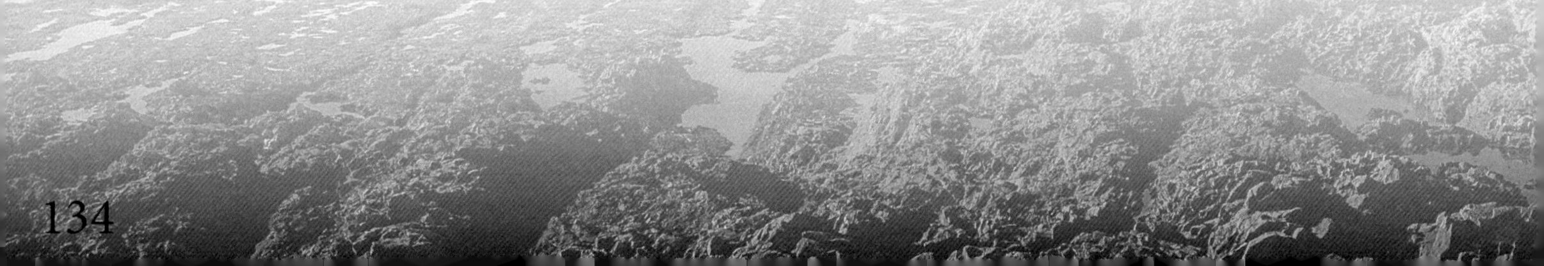

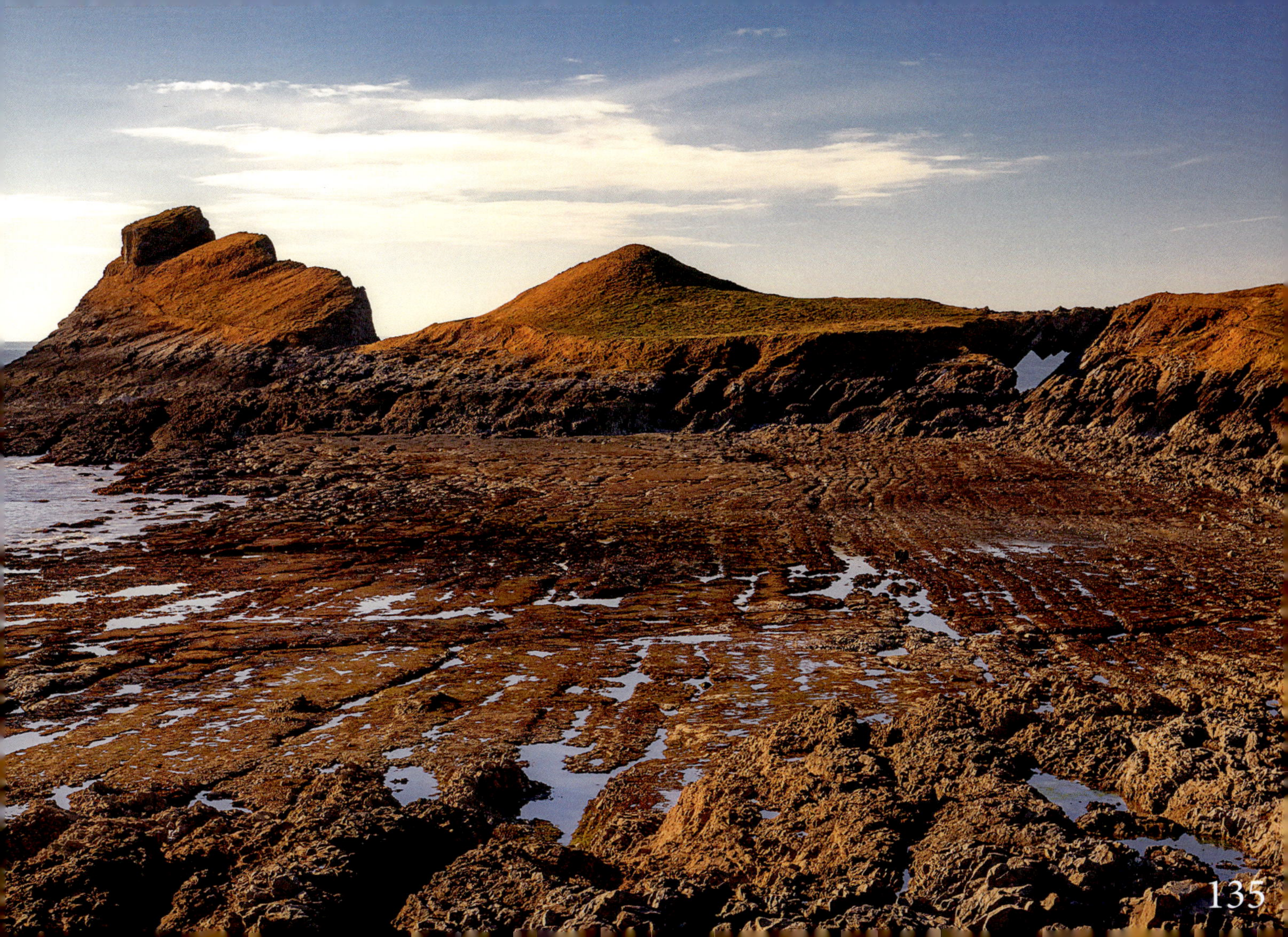

Worms Head and Rhossili Bay

I took this photo of Worms Head whilst running an Astrophotography Workshop where I teach people how to photograph the stars using their DSLR and normal lenses. The moon was a partial crescent with Venus looking nice and bright to the bottom right of it. The star above and to the left is Aldebaran, a red giant. The waves were smashing against Worms Head and, as the day slowly turned into night, the stars started to appear. It always surprises me how much residual light there is even when it appears dark to our eyes. The red in the sky was from sunset which had been an hour before this photo was taken!

Worms Head comes from the Viking/Old English of 'Wurm', which means serpent or dragon. This is perhaps the best angle to see how the Vikings thought this looked like a serpent. For years, I couldn't see it but when I stood on this spot a few years before taking this photo, the head and body finally became obvious to me. The underlying geology has caused this shape to be made by the sea and is part of why Gower is such an amazing place. Where else in the world do you get so many unique beaches and bays in such a small area?

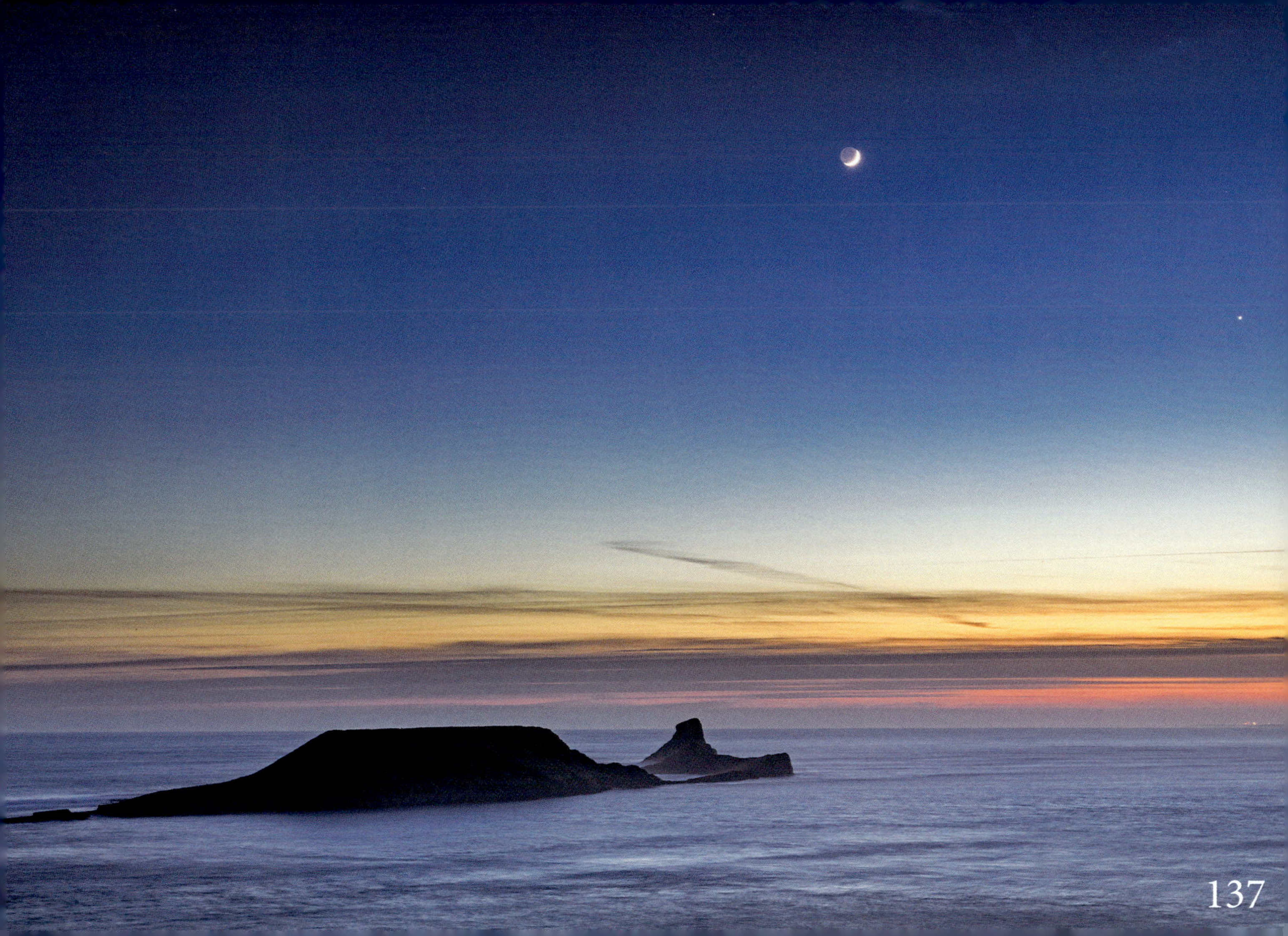

Worms Head and Rhossili Bay

Walking from Worms Head towards Rhossili, there are several iconic views of the vast, sweeping Rhossili Bay where various dips in the cliffs frame the beach in different ways. This photo was taken after snow in March 2018 when the 'Beast from the East' covered all of the UK in snow. Except for a small semicircle around Swansea that is. Where I live in Neath, it was snow free but, just a few miles up the road, the snow was thick. Swansea was also snow free – I went out for sunrise after the definite snow we were promised to find just wet roads.

However, Rhossili seems to have its own microclimate. Driving there, there wasn't any snow until we turned right at Scurlage and suddenly the road was down to one lane with massive snow drifts falling out of the field, it was an incredible sight. Due to the wind, the cliffs at Rhossili had a relatively thin layer of snow, but it was far more than I'd had at home! This isn't the first time I've been at Rhossili when it has had snow whilst the rest of Gower hasn't. A few years before, I was there with it snowing heavily, waiting for it to stop so I could take photos. After a couple of hours I gave up and left. Just outside Rhossili, there was little sign of any snow at all!

The raised plateau below Rhossili Down is a solifluction terrace. During warm periods through the ice age, frozen soil would melt and slip down the hill to create what we see today.

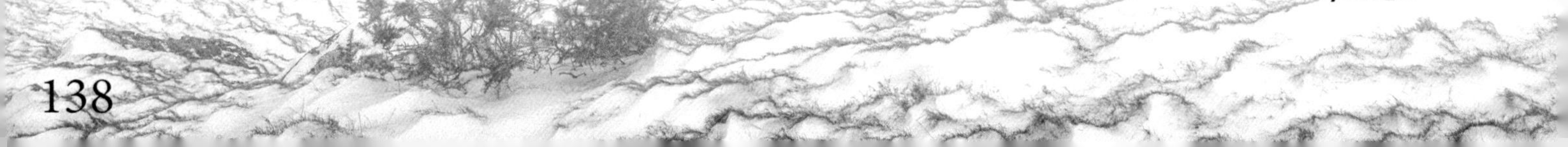

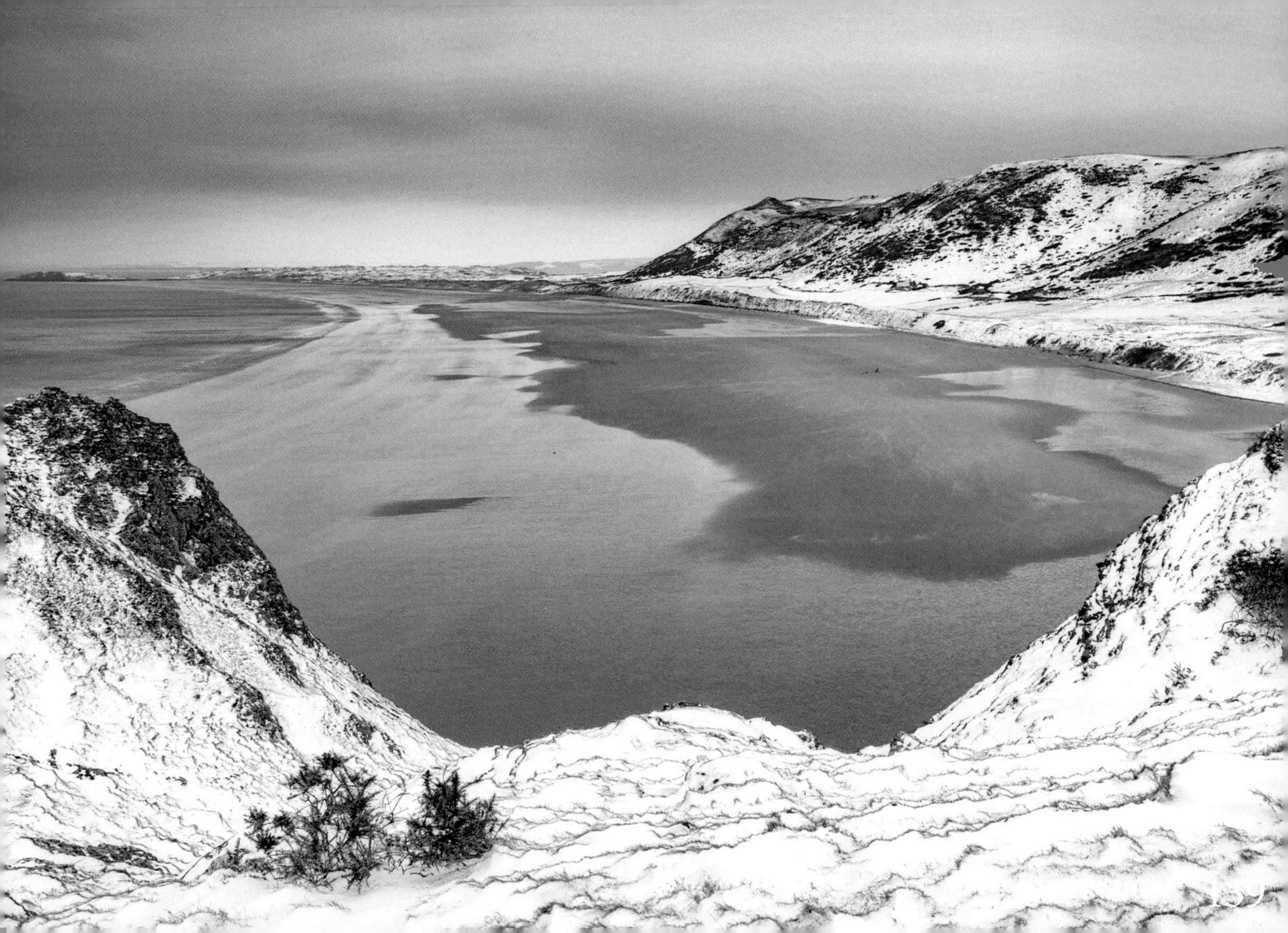

Worms Head and Rhossili Bay

I went to Rhossili for sunset, which turned out to be fairly poor in terms of sunsets I've seen there. As we were walking back to the car, the whole sky turned this incredible pink. We were in a state of disbelief that the sky could do this after such a disappointing sunset. Having left the better viewpoint, I grabbed my camera and ran to different parts of the cliff to try and capture it. I needn't have rushed because the sky stayed this colour for ages. I was in the wrong place with the wrong lens on my camera, but I'm very happy with the photo I have taken it. It really was this colour!

In the 1890s, there were plans to build two railway lines across Gower! One line would run along the centre of Gower from Swansea, terminating at Port Eynon, and the other would run along the south coast from Mumbles, terminating at Worms Head. Rhossili would be turned into a health resort, much like Brighton. One line was to give easier access for people living on Gower and the other was to promote tourism. After meetings, the go ahead was given, surveys were carried out and compulsory land purchase notices were issued. The planning went all the way from the 1890s until 1914, but not a single bit of the railway was ever built. When the First World War broke out, the plans were put on hold and never picked up again. Gower would be a very different place today if it had gone ahead!

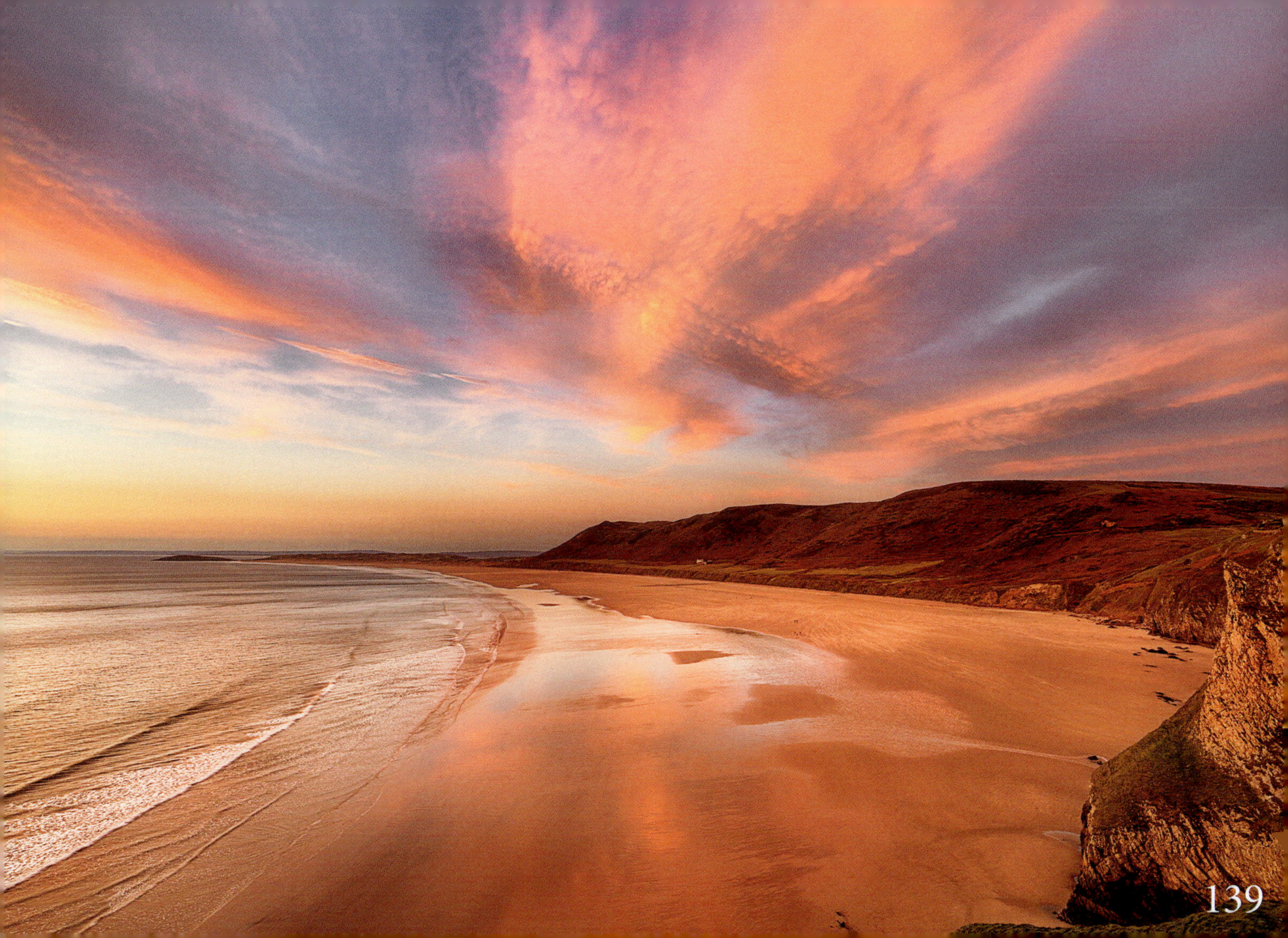

Worms Head and Rhossili Bay

Rhossili is well known for the Helvetia Wreck, but below Old Castle Corner is another wreck. The Vennerne, a 375 ton barque from Denmark, was sailing from Aberdovey to Swansea. On 24th October 1894, she sheltered inside Worms Head during rough seas. However, she spent several hours straining at her cables for several hours before they broke and she was driven onto the beach. The captain, his wife, child and crew of seven all abandoned ship and rowed to the beach where they were helped ashore by members of the Rhossili Rocket Company. Attempts were made to refloat her the next day by a tug called Privateer but they failed and the Vennerne became a wreck. The remains were auctioned with the iron hull selling for £54 and what was left can still be seen today.

At low tide, if you follow the cliffs below Rhossili, you will find the wreck. It is very different to the Helvetia and well worth taking the time to have a look.

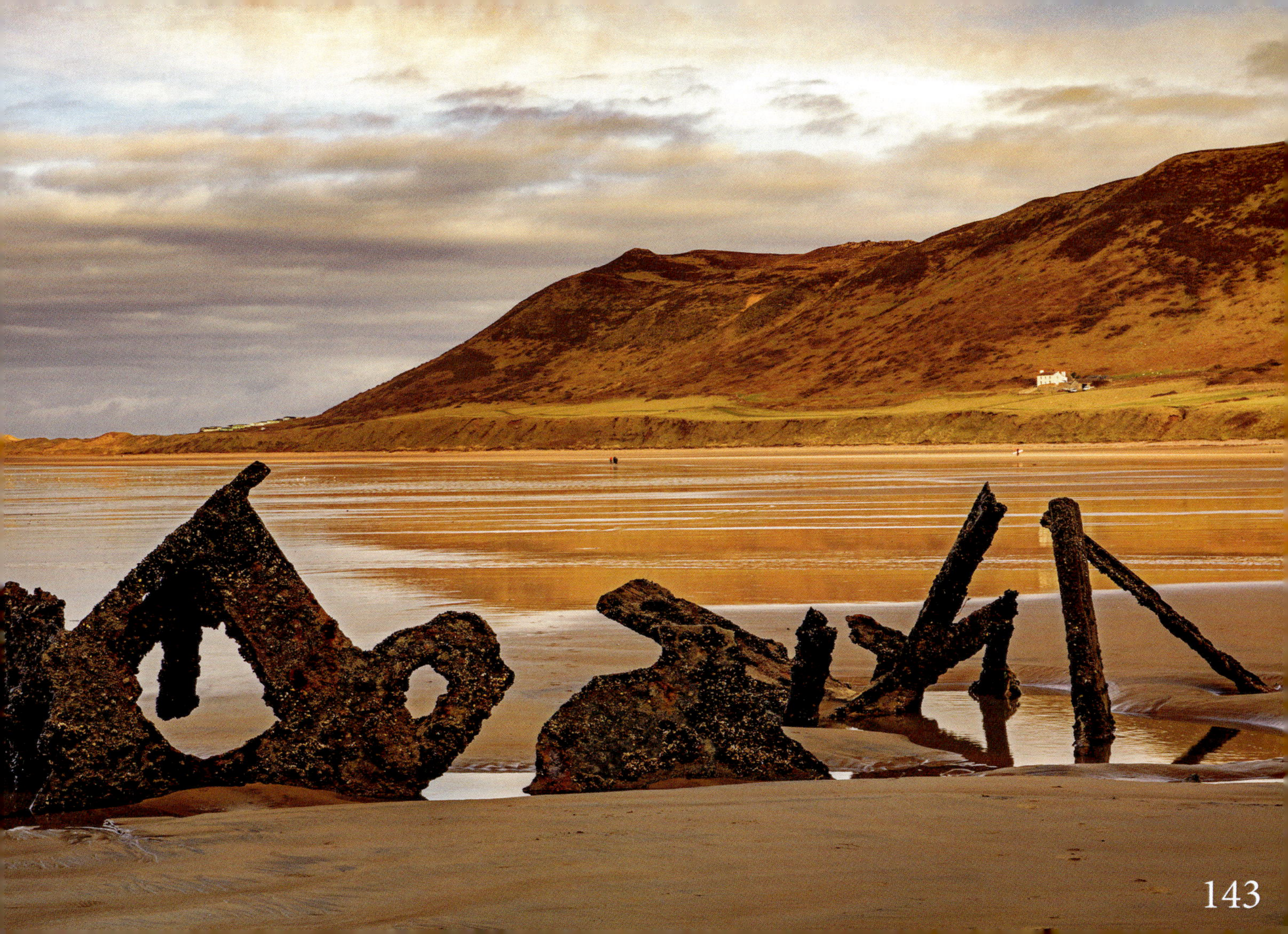

Worms Head and Rhossili Bay

The Helvetia wreck is an iconic landmark on Rhossili Bay, people photograph it, children play around it, surfers try not to hit it and many wonder how it ended up there. The Norwegian barque was sailing from New Brunswick to Swansea. On arrival on 31st October 1887, a request was made for a pilot to take it into the docks but a fresh breeze meant they had to wait. On the morning of 1st November 1887, the wind strengthened and she hit the Helwick sand bank losing part of her load from the deck. She sailed around Worms Head to shelter in Rhossili Bay, but when low tide came she beached. When she refloated at high tide, the crew were able to get off and the Helvetia seemed to have survived, but the wind changed direction. She broke her cables and was driven onto the sand where she lies today. Around 500 tons of cargo were saved and the wreck stripped of everything that could be sold.

The photo I took here is the most exposed I have ever seen the wreck. The constant shifting of sands means that sometimes the wreck seems to be almost gone and other times many of the ribs are poking out of the sand. Rhossili Bay is a great place to see the sunset and the wreck, along with Worms Head, gives a unique photograph. The trek down to the beach might seem arduous, but with these two wrecks to see, it is well worth the effort.

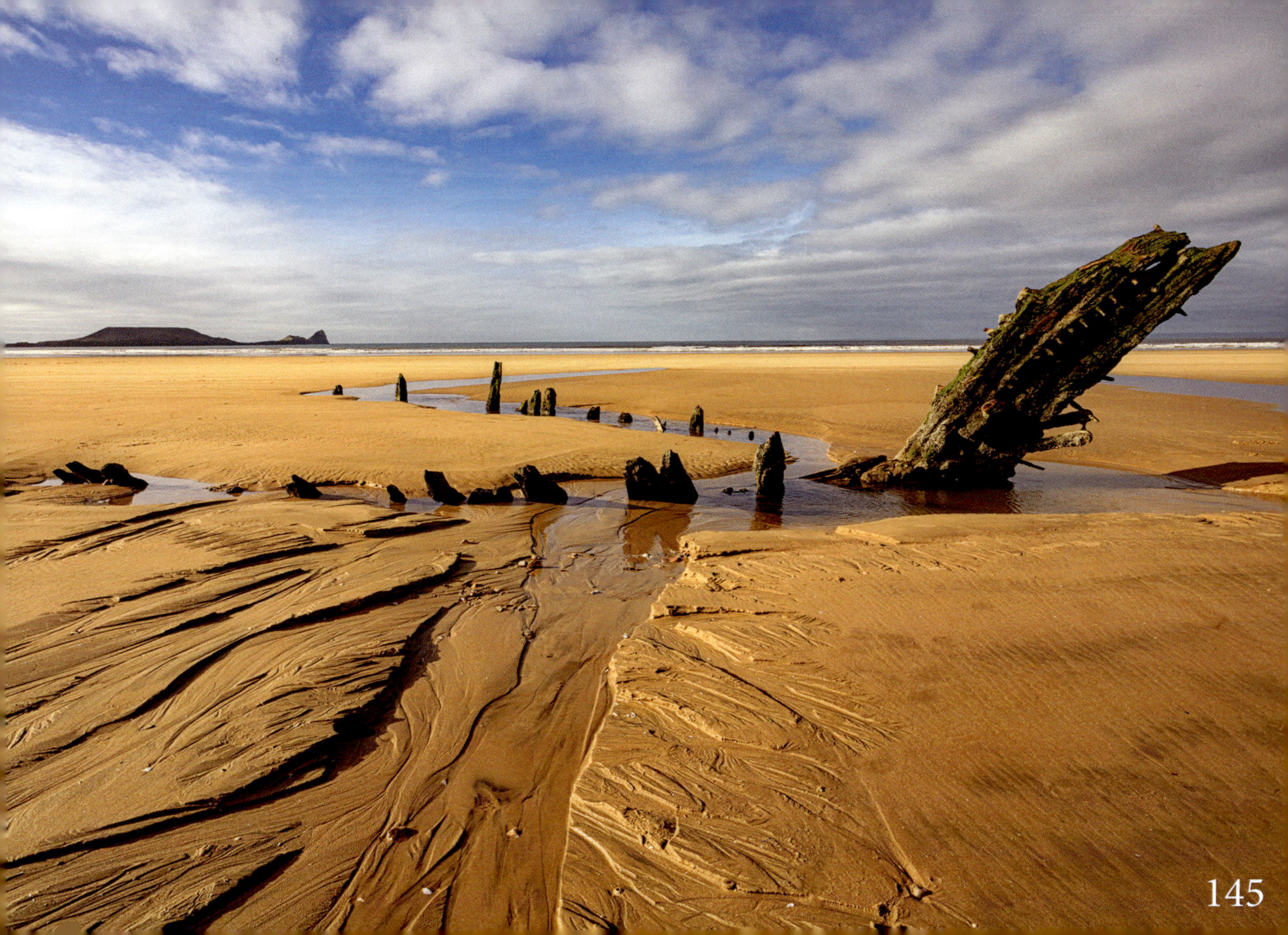

Worms Head and Rhossili Bay

I run Astrophotography Workshops where I teach people to use their ordinary cameras to take photos of the stars. The photos include a landscape element which gives the photo a location and makes it more interesting. I met my client at Three Cliffs Bay at midnight but it was cloudy, so we headed to Rhossili in the hope that the skies would be clear. When we arrived, we were delighted to see the stars so we walked down to the wreck of the Helvetia.

We took our time trying out different compositions and learning the settings to use along with various techniques. Exposure times can be anything from 15 seconds to a few minutes so there is plenty of time for me to take my own photos too. I took this photo just after 2am. At 3am, we headed up onto Rhossili Down to take more photos. When I'm working at night, my tiredness disappears and even though I'm usually out of bed at 5:30am, I can quite happily stay awake all night. Provided I get a couple of hours sleep when I get home, I'm okay for the following day. It was at 4am that we decided to stop. Walking off the hill and an hour's drive home meant I got to bed around 5:30am!

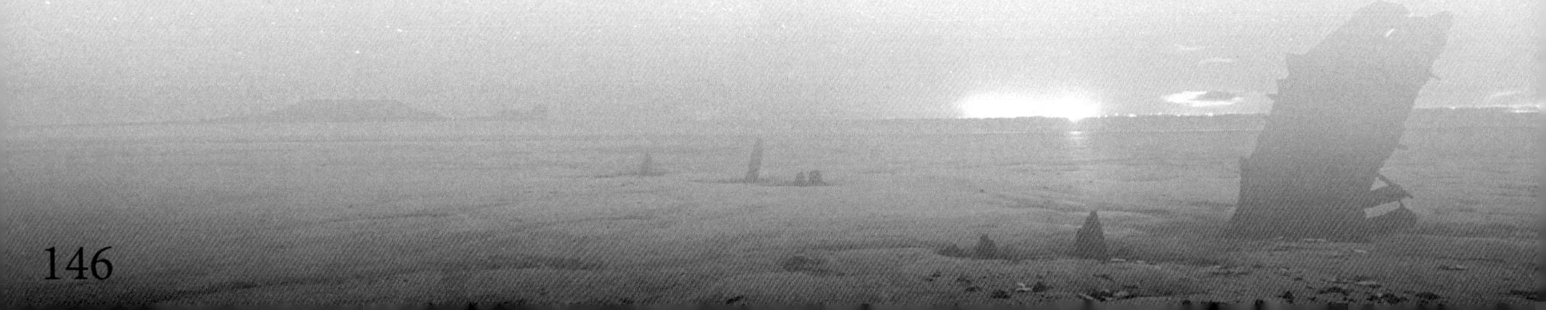

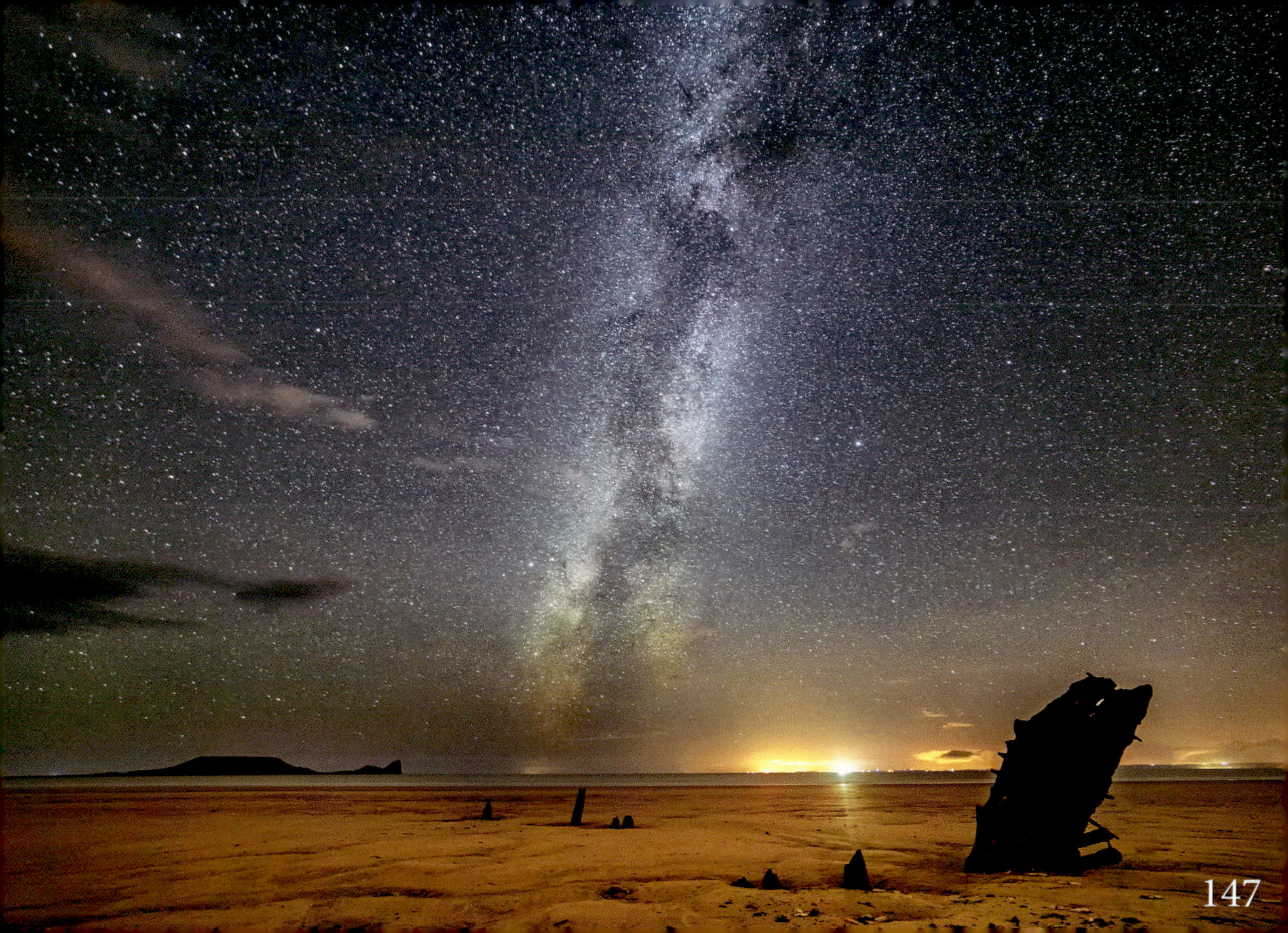

Worms Head and Rhossili Bay

This photo was one that I took on the first ever Landscape Photography Workshop that I ran. When I decided to run workshops, I advertised it on my Facebook page and ran the workshop for free to see how I felt about it and to find out what my customers thought. It went so well that I have been running workshops ever since! We started the day at Penmaen Burrows before heading here for sunset, and what a beautiful sunset it was! I waited until the sun was just about to dip behind The Worm and got into the right position for the sun to reflect in the patch of water.

On Outer Head, the end part of Worms Head, there is a cave and a blow hole. There are narrow fissures from the cave below to the surface above and when the swell comes into the cave, you can feel the rushing air pushed through the rocks. From the cliffs, during the right tide and weather, you can see a massive burst of water rushing up into the sky as high as the Worm itself or even above! With the wind in the right direction, you can hear the boom it causes.

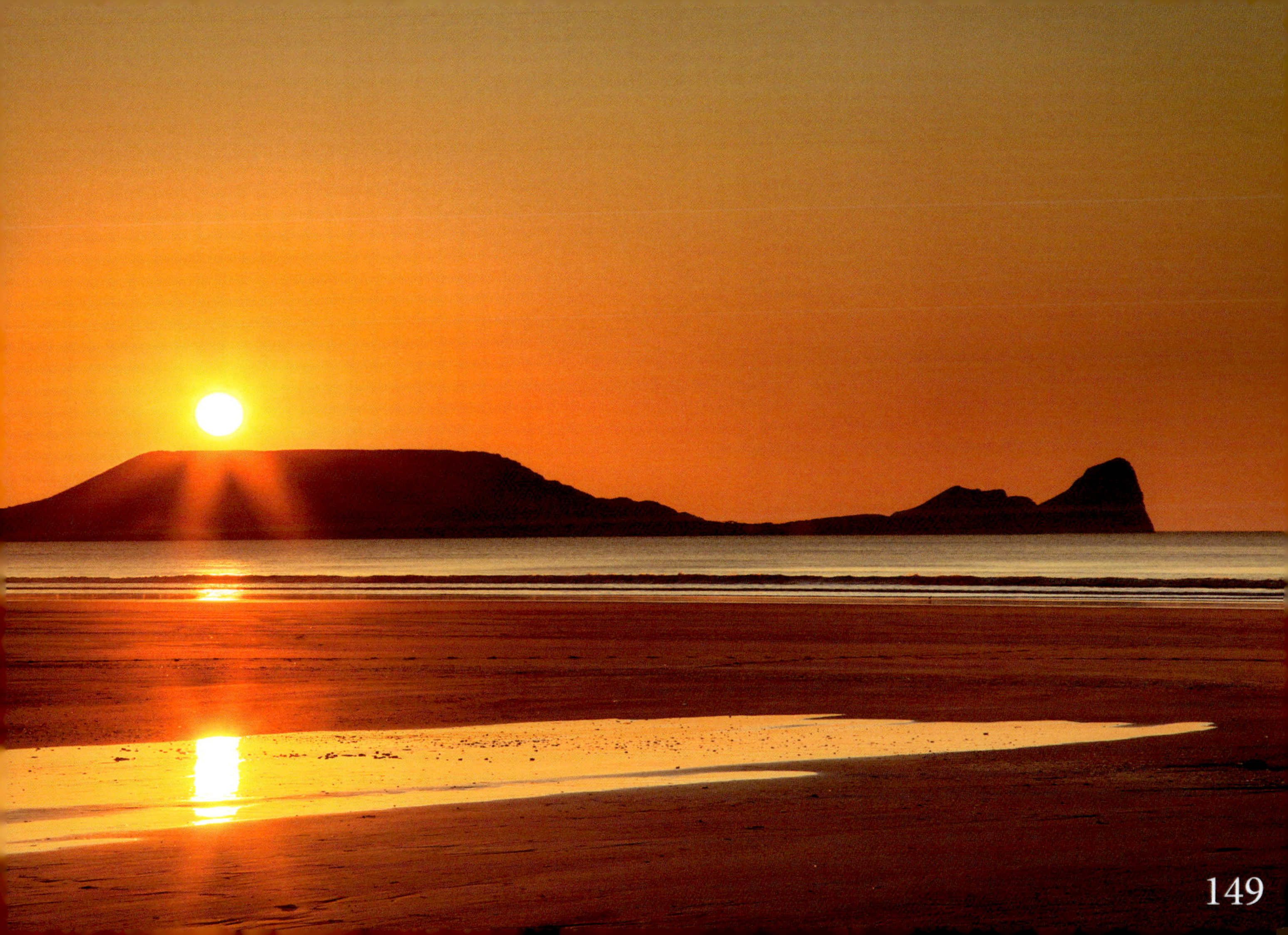

Worms Head and Rhossili Bay

This was taken on yet another of my workshops. We were on the beach for sunset and one and a half hours later, the moon set in roughly the same place. It takes roughly two hours after sunset for the sky to become completely dark and before then, even though it appears dark to our eyes, the camera is incredibly good at picking up the residual light from sunset, which is why there is colour in the sky by the moon. The Milky Way made an appearance over the cliffs too. This combined with the rather high tide made this photo, which I am very happy with.

In 2017, Rhossili Bay was voted to be one of the top ten beaches in the world! It was the only European beach to make the list. Due to its spectacular beauty and ease of access, it has been used multiple times for film and TV. Perhaps the most well known was for Doctor Who and then again for Torchwood, the Doctor Who spin off.

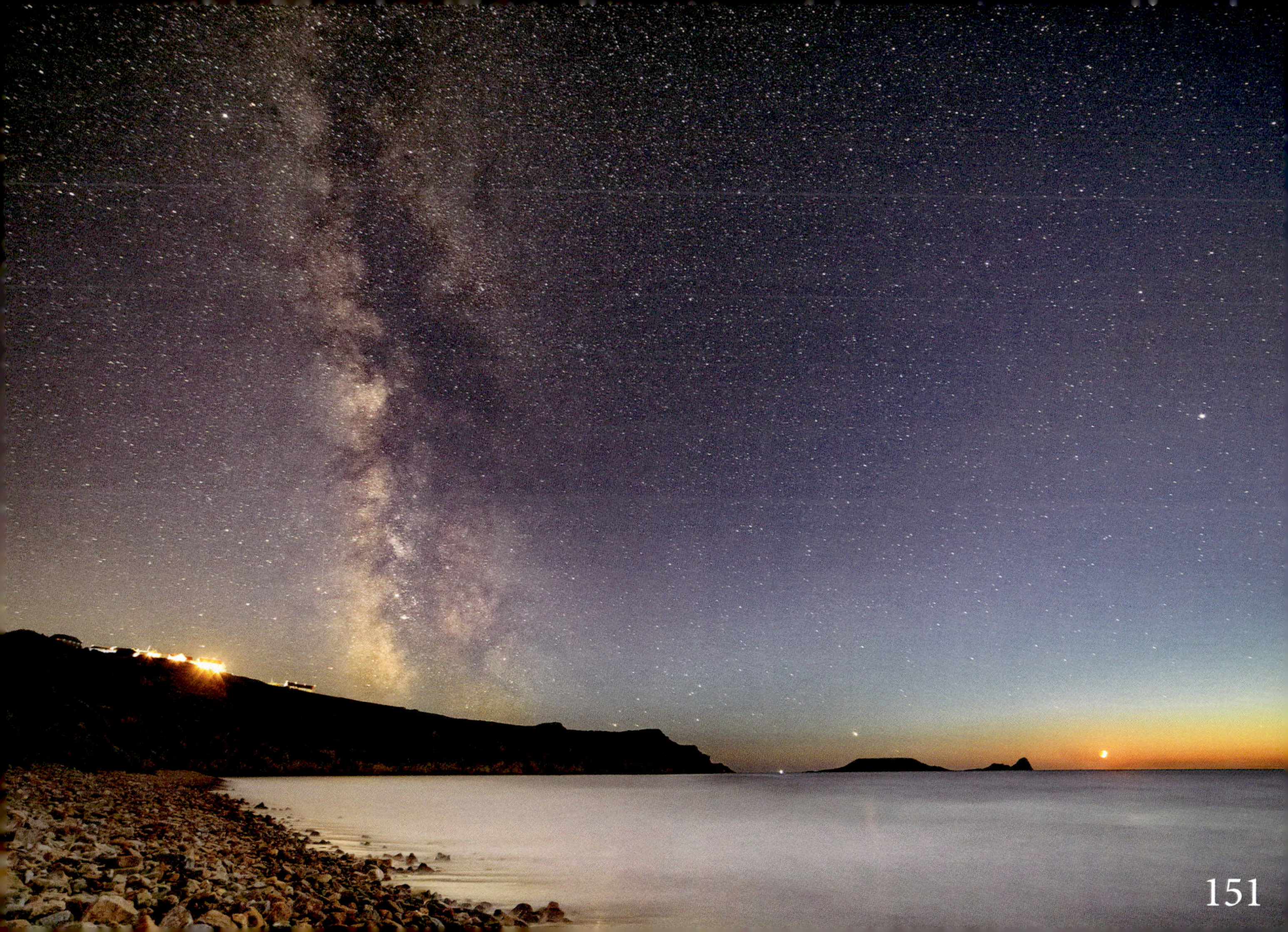

Worms Head and Rhossili Bay

This is the fourth photo in a row to be taken on a workshop I was running! In February 2019, once again the UK had snow across much of the country and, once again, Swansea had none. With its own microclimate, I knew I could rely on Rhossili to have some, so we headed there for sunset and it didn't disappoint. You can't tell, but we fought a bitterly cold wind whilst photographing the sunset.

This is a great viewpoint to look down on what is called The Vile, a medieval strip field farming system. The National Trust has been working hard to restore this field system and in 2018 planted several fields with sunflowers. There were so successful that in 2019 they planted 400,000 sunflowers, poppies, lavender and lupins alongside crops of millet, wheat, oats, buckwheat, spelt, linseed and barley. The wildlife has benefitted hugely from the Trust's work and it is well worth a visit when the crops are growing.

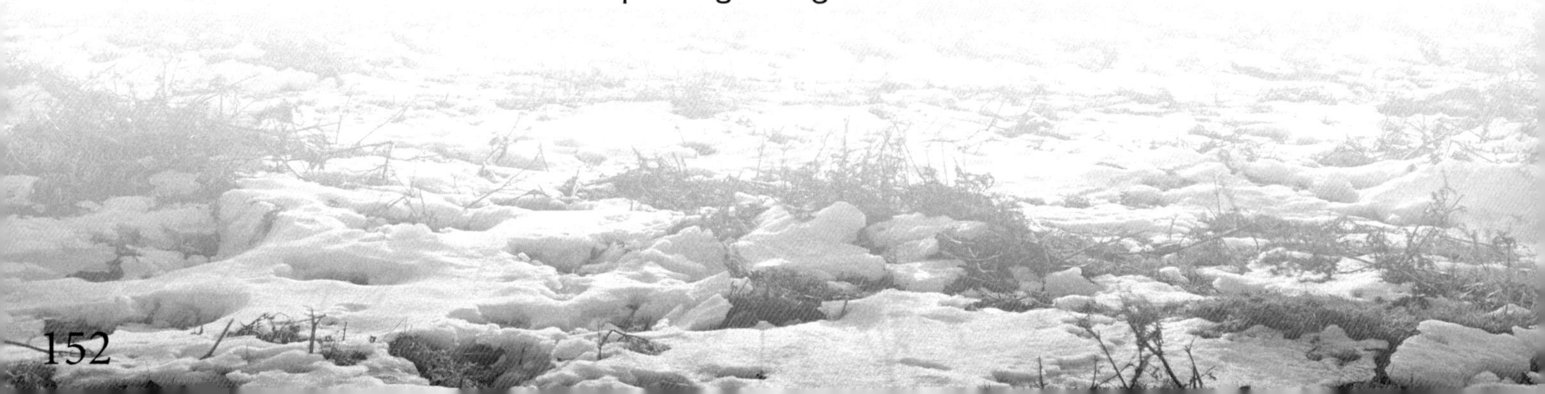

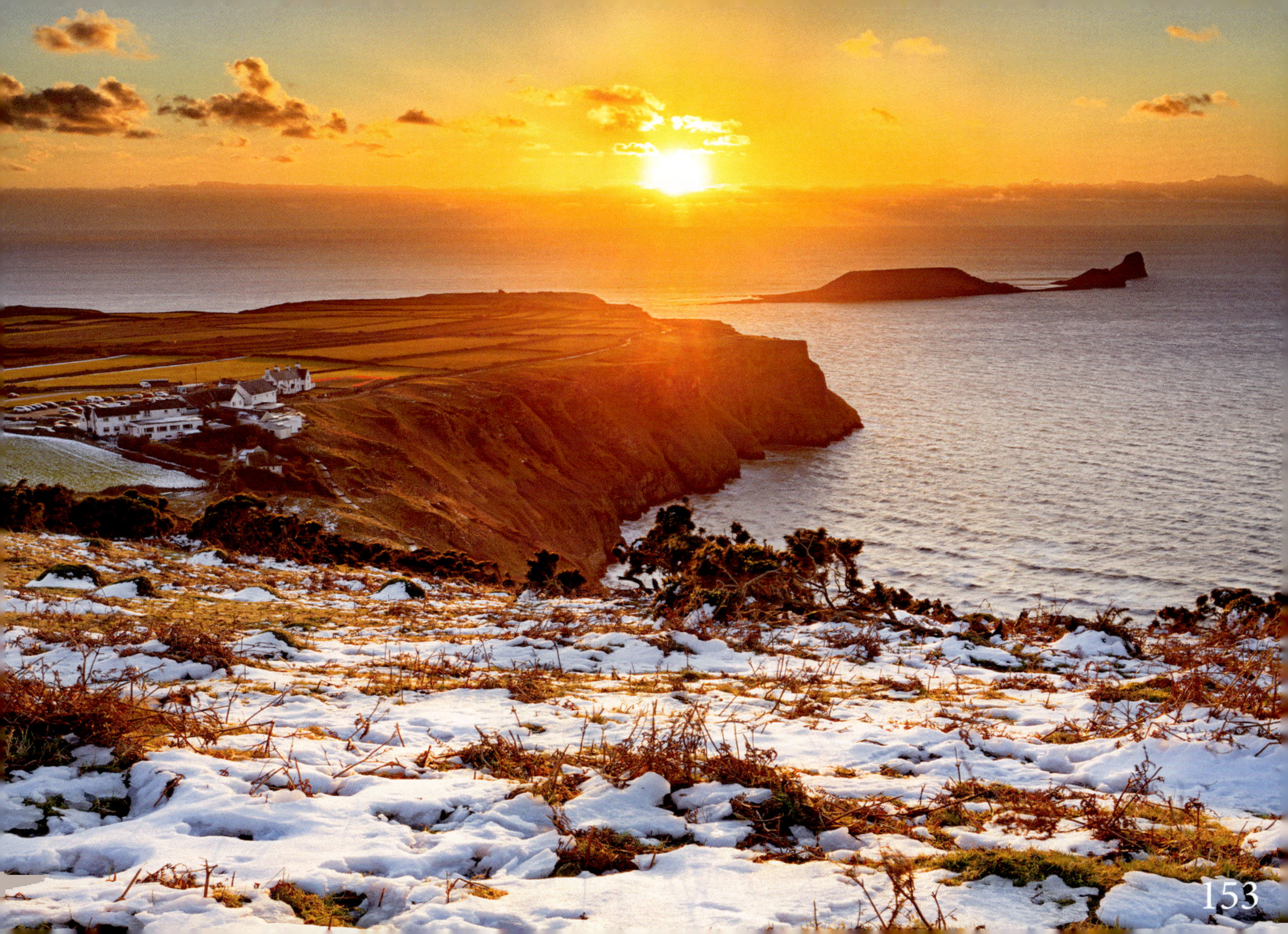

Worms Head and Rhossili Bay

The sky for this particular sunset was very unusual. When I arrived, given the amount of cloud, I didn't really expect to see anything much. I set up with the new ferns in the foreground and the foxgloves to give a splash of purple and waited. After driving all that way, I wasn't going to give up. Suddenly, the sun peaked between a gap in the clouds and the scene was transformed into this. It is the first time I've seen a sun beam going up across the clouds! That combined with the ripples in the water allowed me to take this photo, which I am very happy with.

Rhossili has a claim to fame. Petty Officer Edgar Evans (7 March 1876 – 17 February 1912) was born in Middleton, Rhossili. He went on to join Robert Falcon Scott on the Terra Nova Expedition (also known as the British Antarctic Expedition) to reach the South Pole in 1911-1912. After reaching the South Pole, but being beaten by the Norwegian team, he died along with his team members on the way back before reaching their base. There is a plaque dedicated to him on the church at Rhossili.

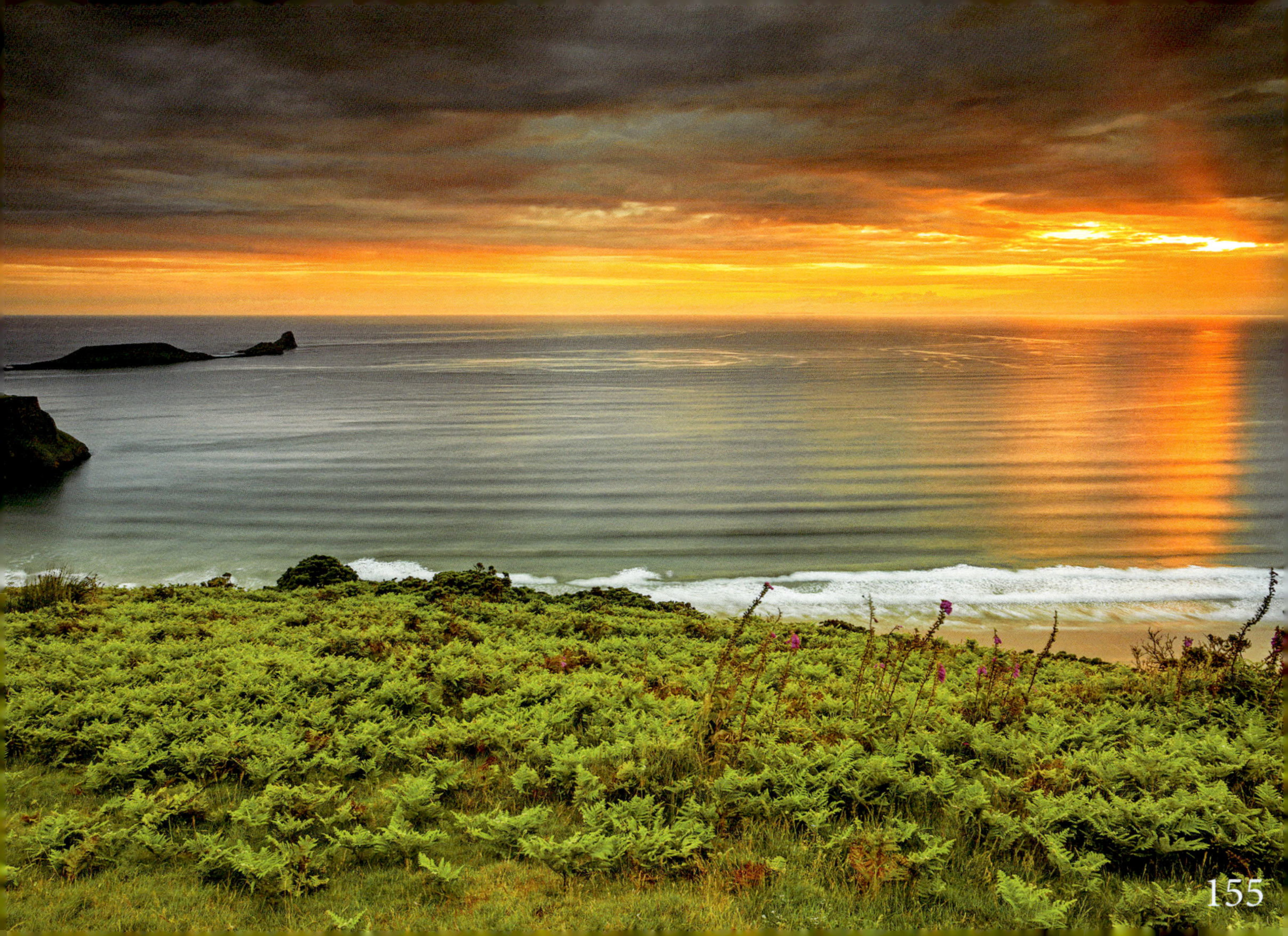

Worms Head and Rhossili Bay

In August, Rhossili Down turns into a swathe of heather and, if you are lucky, the gorse flowers at the same time adding yellow into the mix.

Not far from where this photo was taken are the remains of the World War II Rhossili Radar Station. It was in use from 1942 until 1945 and was one of several radar stations controlled from Milford Haven to cover the Bristol Channel. Manned by the army, it was built to detect shipping and low flying aircraft. Later on it was updated and became part of the Chain Home Low radar network. Chain Home was the codename for the RAF's radar system to protect the UK but it couldn't detect low flying aircraft, so different stations that could, such as Rhossili, became part of the Chain Home Low network. There was also a Chain Home Extra Low which protected the ports.

After the war had ended, during "Operation Eyesore", the site was dismantled and the technical block was blown up to destroy it so the technology couldn't fall into the wrong hands.

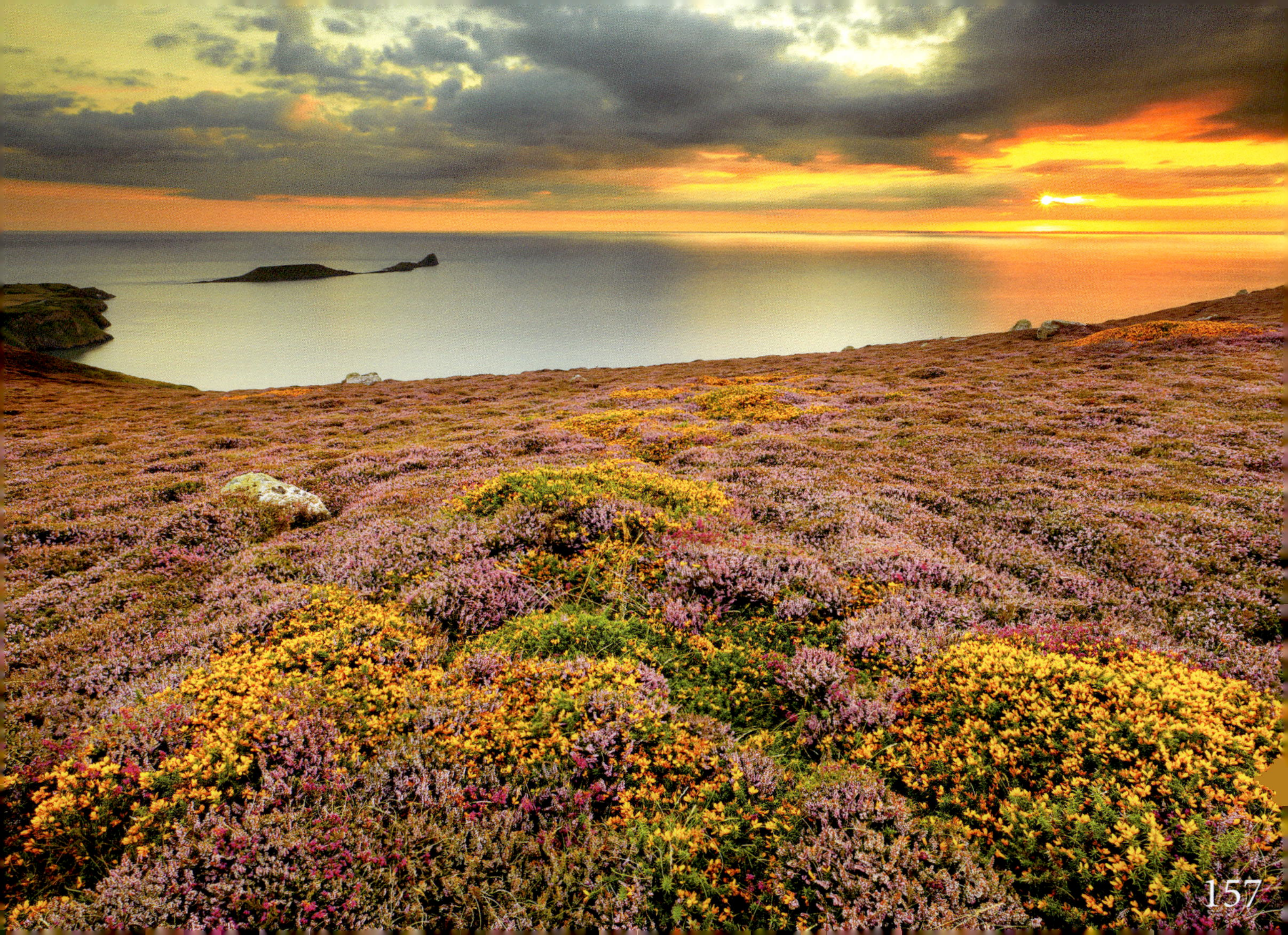

Worms Head and Rhossili Bay

Hidden in plain view on the east side of Rhossili Down is Sweyne's Howes. It is a Neolithic burial chamber around 5000 years old. However, it get its name from an 11th century Viking, Sweyne. Howe is Viking for burial mound. It is possible that Swansea gets its name from this Viking as it might be a derivation that has changed over the years (Sweyn's-ey). It is certainly possible as language changes and morphs all the time (if we met people from a few hundred years ago, we probably wouldn't understand their English – or Welsh!)

I took this photo on a very cold and frosty morning. The frozen air gave an other-worldy colour to the landscape as the sun rose. Winter is one of my favourite seasons for photography, especially when frost, ice and snow are around as it changes the familiar landscape into a different place.

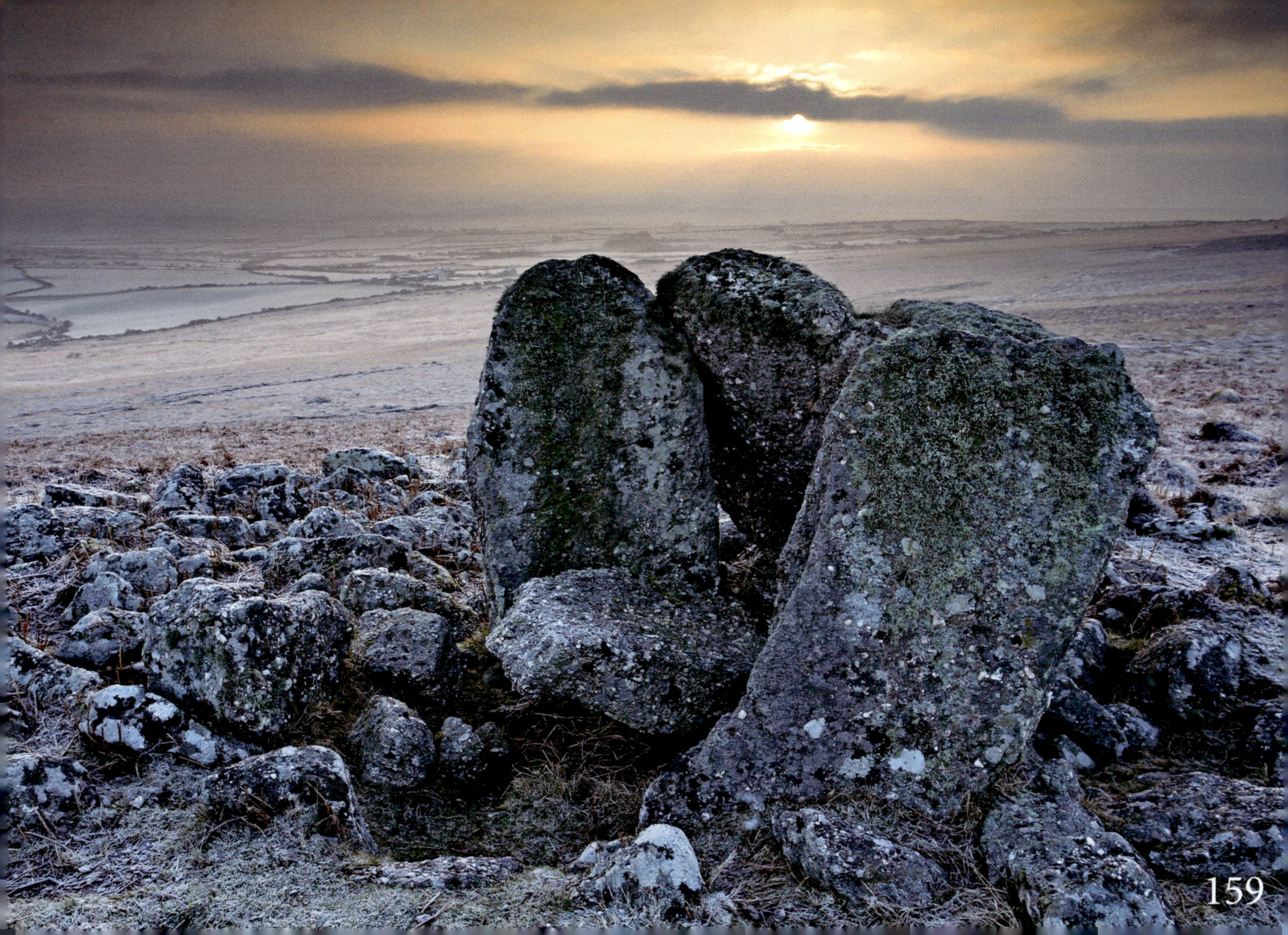

Llangennith and Burry Holms

Rhossili Bay is a huge beach, the north of which is known as Llangennith due to the name of the nearby village. There is a lovely circular walk starting in Rhossili that goes across the top of Rhossili Down and then back again either along the beach or following the footpath along the base of the Down. On the beach is a small stream called Diles Lake that drains Llangennith Marsh. Sometimes storms rearrange the sand and pebbles and dam the river creating a small lake, hence the name.

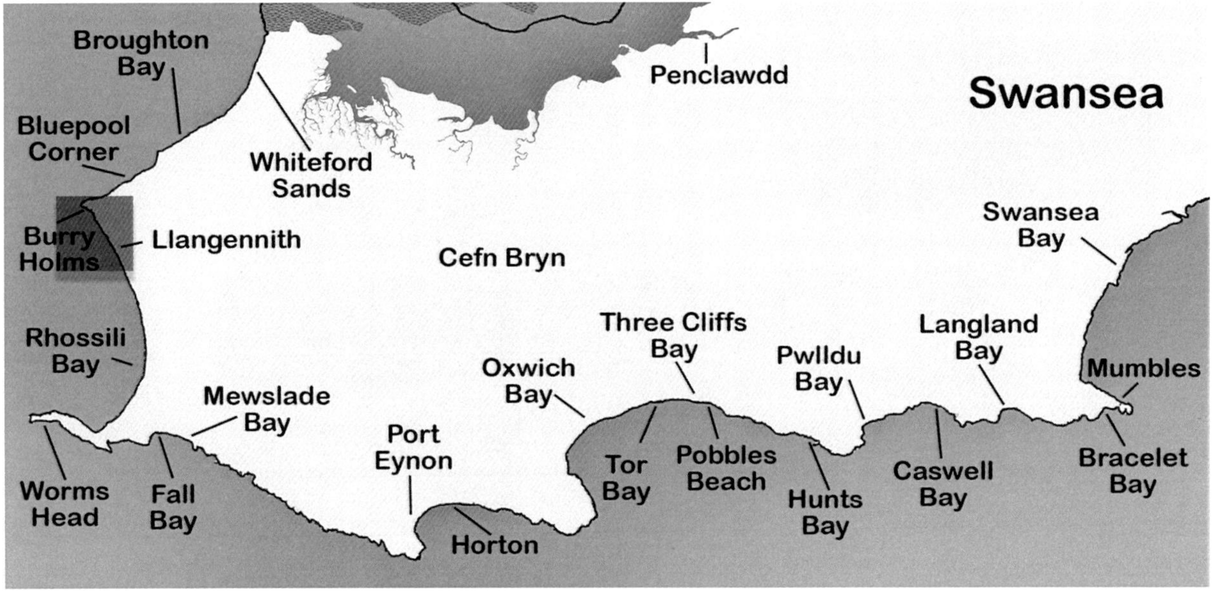

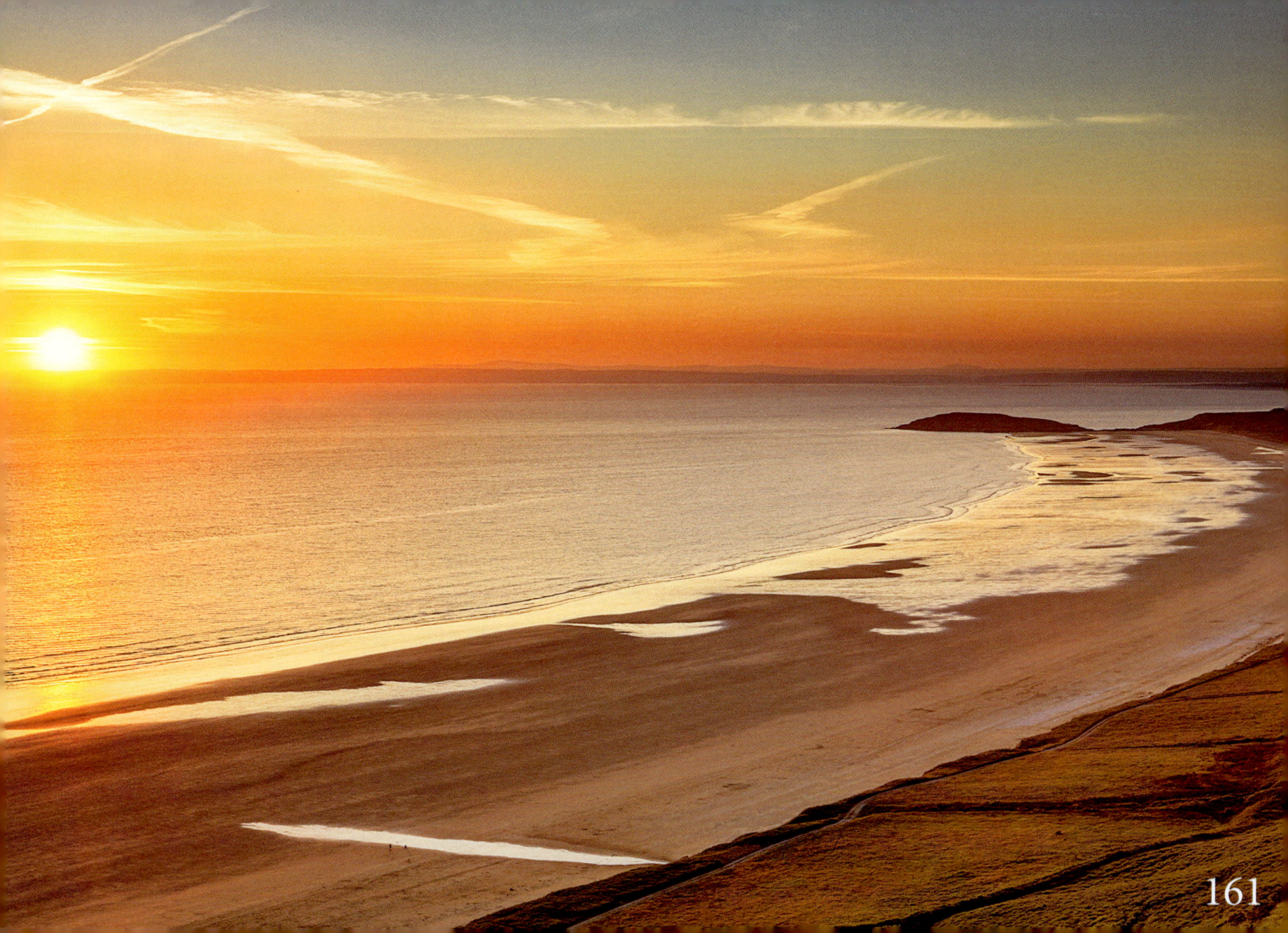

Llangennith and Burry Holms

The house below the cliff is The Old Rectory, which was built in 1850 on the site of an older farmhouse. It is now owned by the National Trust and rented out as a holiday cottage. There is reportedly a waiting list of several years as it is in such a stunning location. The plateau to the south of the rectory is known as the Warren. It is also the site of an ancient village. In 1980, storms exposed bones from the old graveyard and the still standing walls of the church. This lead to an excavation taking place where the remains of a medieval village was found. In the late medieval period great storms caused sand to engulf the village, so it was moved to the top of the cliff where it was safe from the sand. The porch was rescued from the church before the sand covered it and was used in St Mary's Church which can still be seen today.

The late evening light, not long before sunset, turned the whole landscape a lovely golden colour with the clouds making it appear stronger in patches.

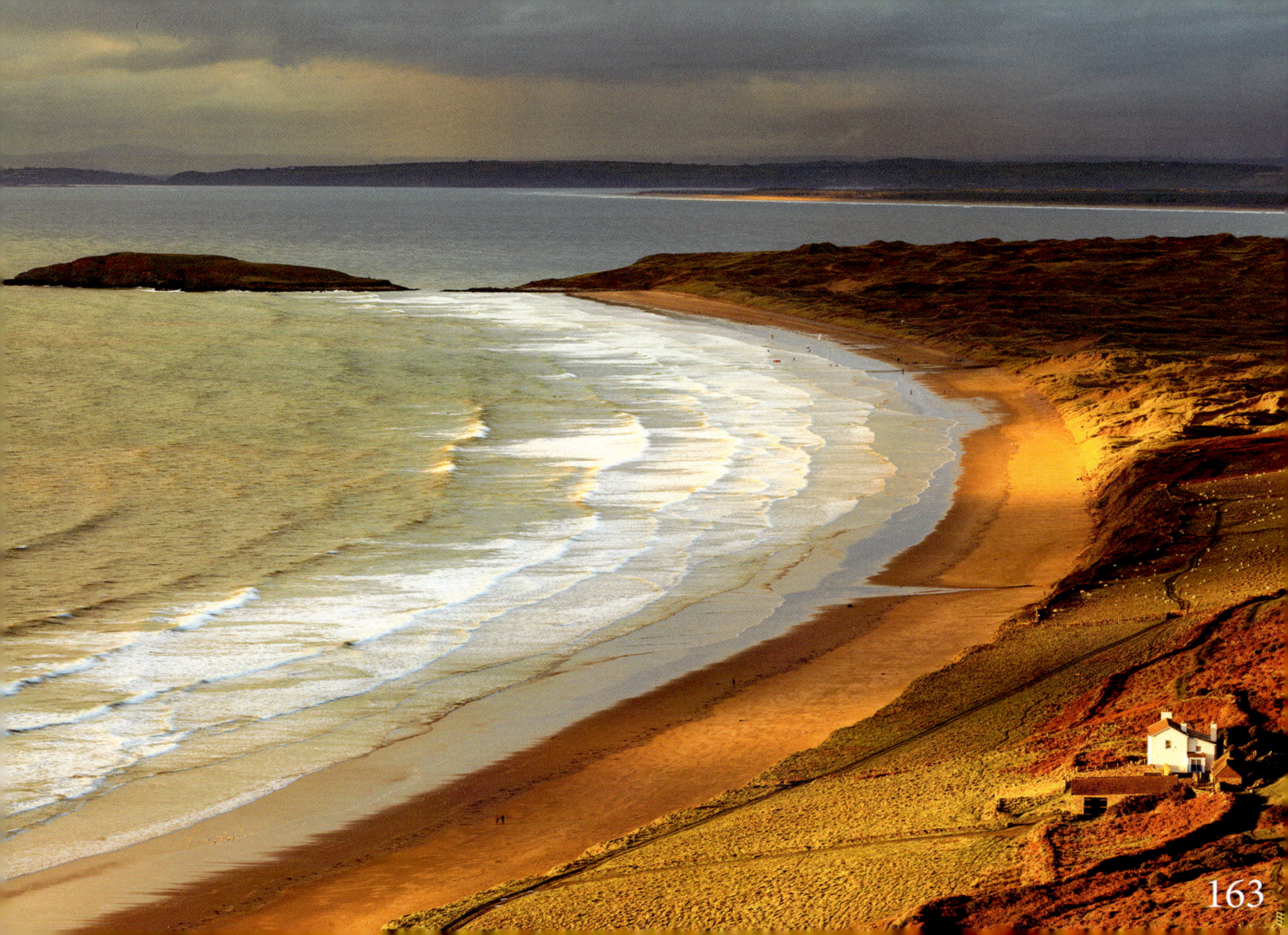

Llangennith and Burry Holms

This is Hillend Camping Park from part way up Rhossili Down. Looking down like this, it is easy to see why camping on Gower is so popular. There are plenty of campsites, some that are right on the beach whilst others have footpaths across their land to 'secret' beaches such as Ramsgrove from Pitton Cross – you might be unlikely to stop there if walking past, but when staying at the campsite an evening walk across fields means you stand a good chance of having it to yourself!

The coast path around Gower is part of the Gower and Swansea Bay Coast Path, which in turn is part of the much longer 870 mile long Wales Coast Path which goes from Chepstow in South Wales to Queensferry in North Wales. Wales was the first country in the world to create a coastal footpath along its coastline, although there are slight deviations away from the sea for military firing areas, etc. The Wales Coast Path was opened on 5th May 2012.

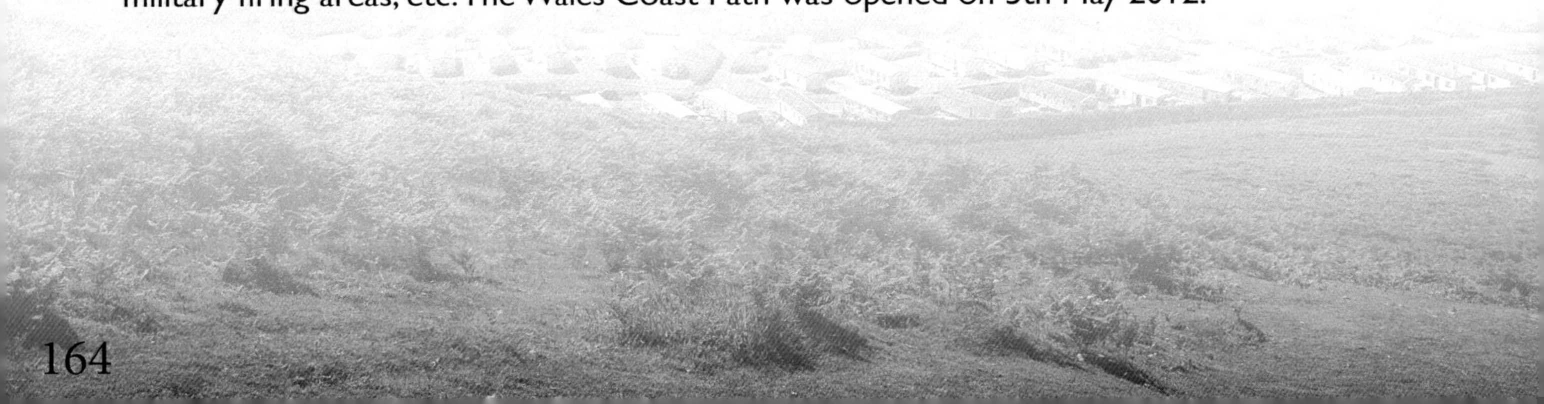

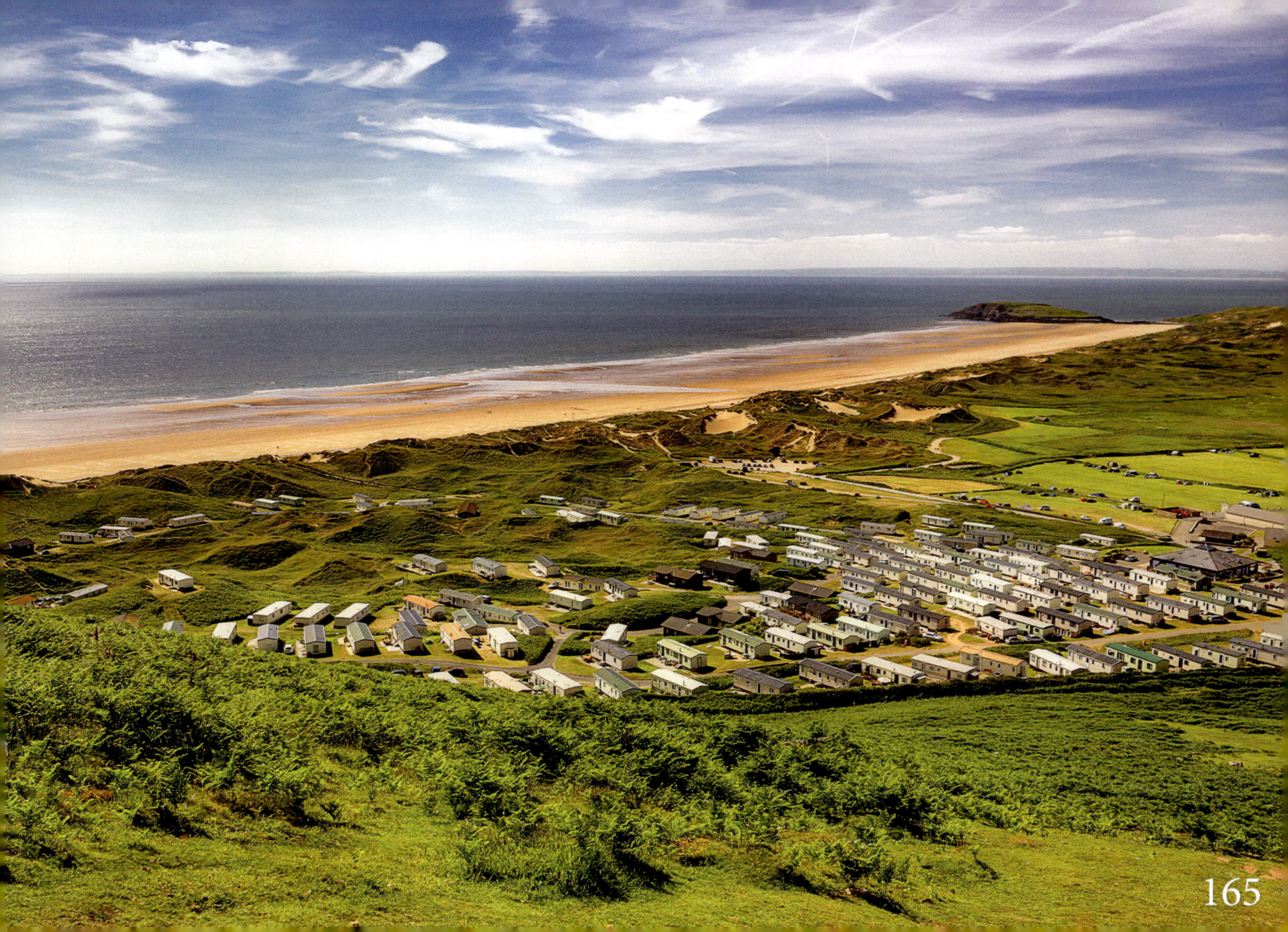

Llangennith and Burry Holms

The walk through the sand dunes leads you to the edge of the beach and this is the view you get! This was a lovely spring evening with little wind and the sound of the sea on the sand as we watched the sun going down. I wanted the golden grasses in the foreground with Worms Head and the sun in the photo.

Llangennith is a great surfing beach with any tide being good and most wind directions too. The main hazards are a strong rip and the shipwreck, the City of Bristol which is exposed at low tide near Diles Lake. The 210 ton wooden paddle steamer went into service in May 1827 and was used on routes from Bristol to Dublin, Cork and Waterford. On Tuesday 17th November 1840, the steamer left Waterford on route to Bristol. Amongst its cargo was 15 bullocks, 280 pigs, 370 barrels of oats and 113 barrels of barley. After leaving port, they got caught in bad weather. The captain decided to seek shelter inside Worms Head, but at 6pm they struck land. The attempts to free themselves failed and they were stuck fast. Heavy seas pounded the wreck eventually claiming the lives of 27 people. Just 2 people managed to get ashore and survived!

Looking at this photo, it seems hard to believe that so many people have died in shipwrecks around Gower.

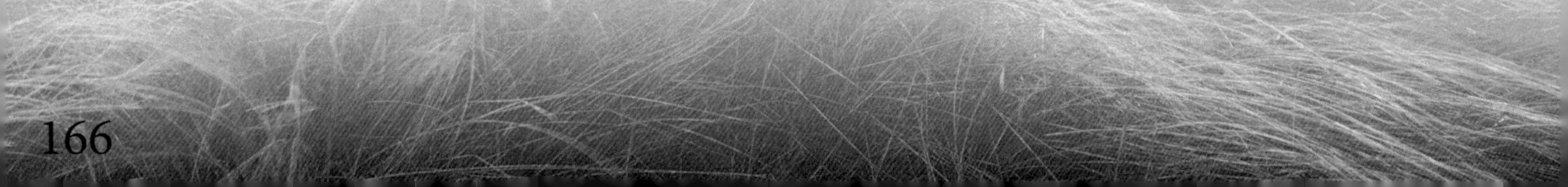

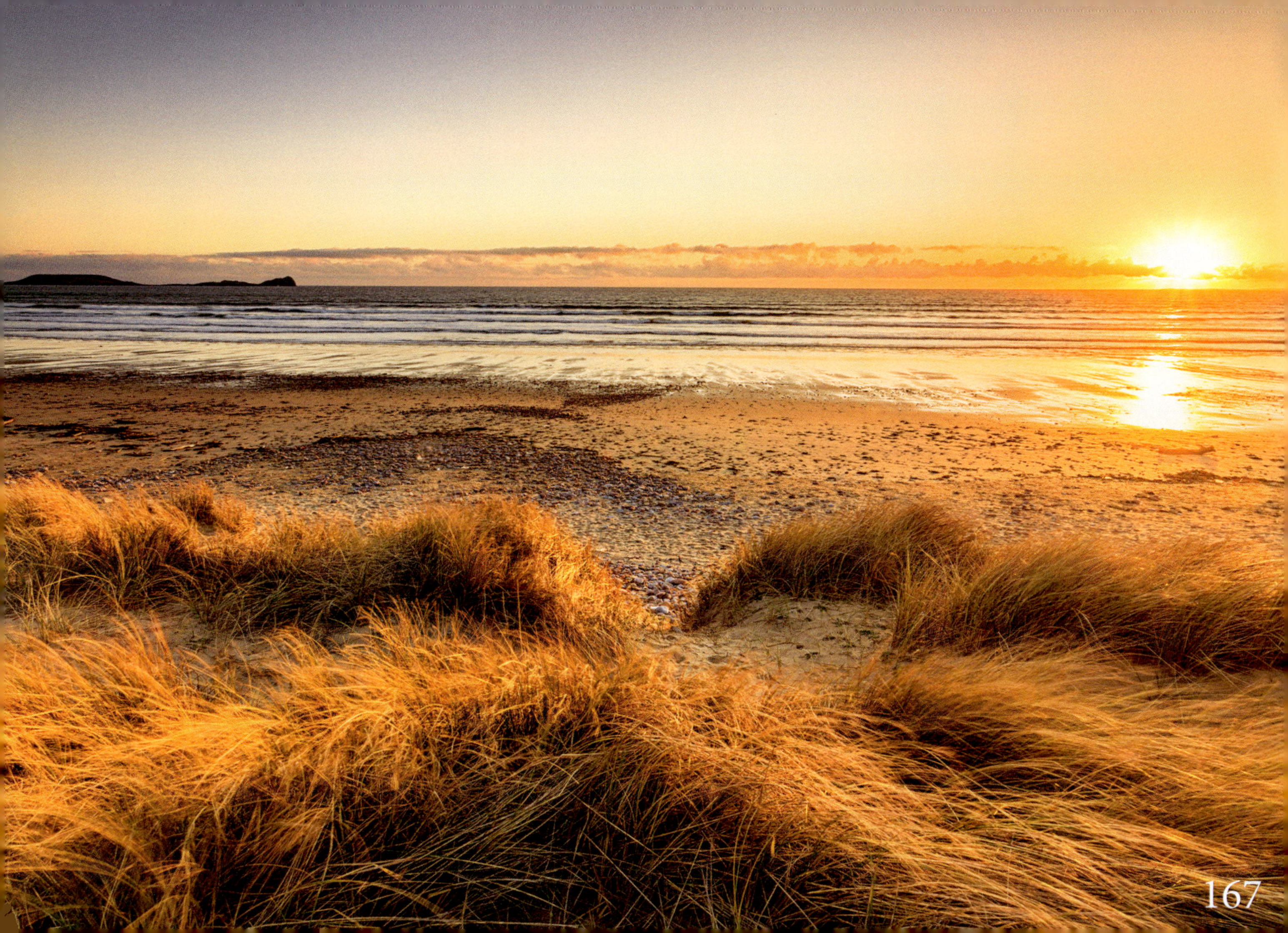

Llangennith and Burry Holms

At the far end of Rhossili Bay lies the tidal island of Burry Holms. At low tide it is easily accessible but take care because the water channel fills quickly meaning you'll either get wet or face a long wait for the tide to recede again. For such a small island, it has a lot of history associated with it. Small flint tools called microliths have been discovered there, suggesting Mesolithic people once camped on what was then just a hill as the sea was a lot further away than it is today. Mesolithic people lived around 15,000 to 5,000 BP (BP means Before Present, which is 1st January 1950, the origin of practical radiocarbon dating).

There is also evidence of Bronze Age occupation with a burial mound and Iron Age occupation with a hill fort on the west side of the island, although perhaps the most influential period in Burry Holms' history was in the Dark Ages. The site, by then an island, would have appealed to Early Christians such as St Cenydd, who is thought to have been associated with the island in the 6th century.

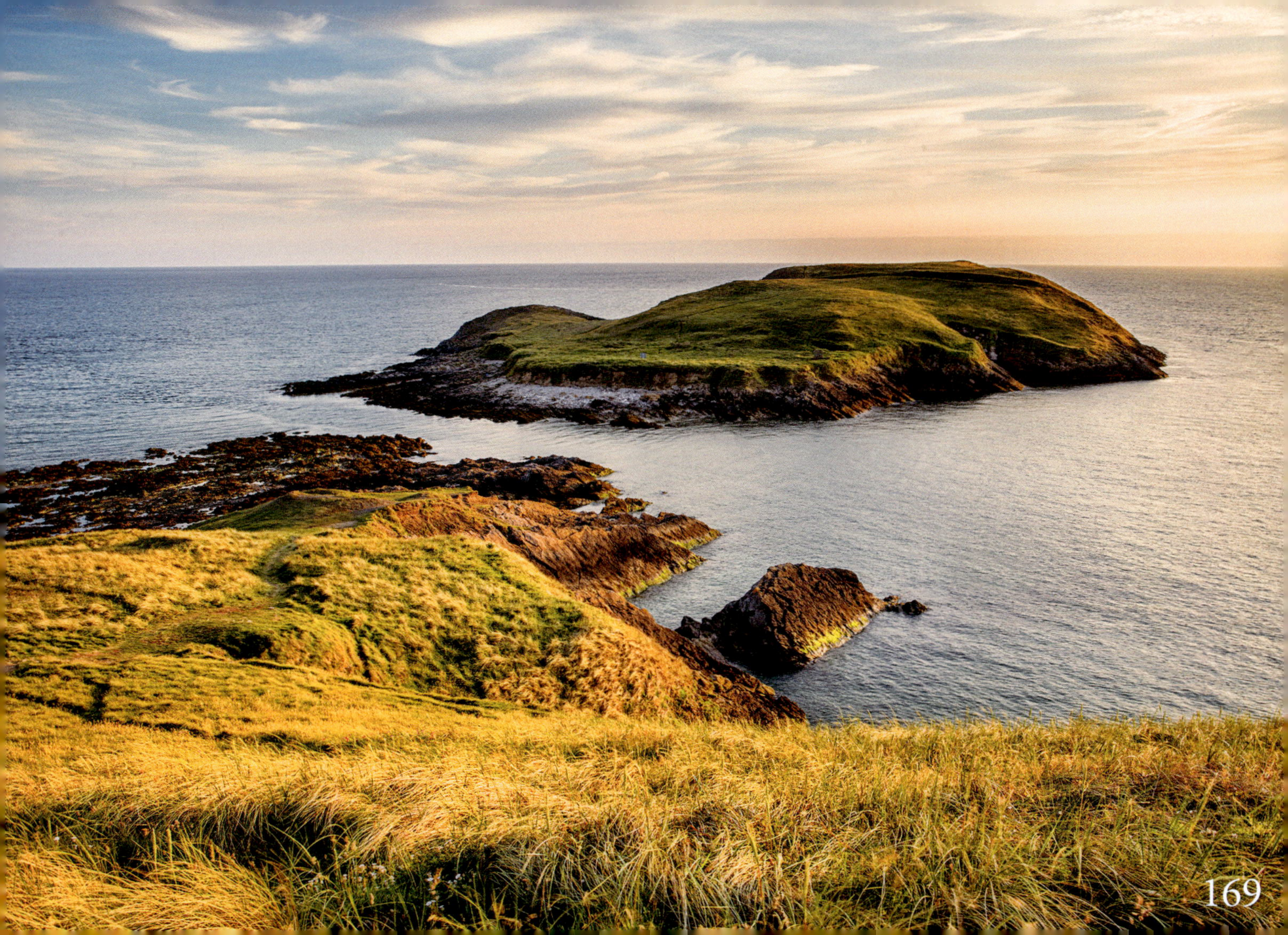

Llangennith and Burry Holms

In the 1960s, the Royal Commission on Ancient and Historical Monuments of Wales excavated the ruins on Burry Holms and discovered various buildings, including an 11th century chapel. The buildings represent 'the hermitage of St Kenydd-atte-Holme'. They also found some Roman pottery which suggests the site has been occupied for a very long time. When you sit on the cliff and look at the island, it's hard to imagine that people lived there for thousands of years, from early hunters who fished the estuary through to people who followed the monastic way of life.

In this photo, you can see a dividing line across the island with the Iron Age promontory fort towards the sea and the monastery buildings towards the land.

The island today is good for bass fishing amongst others and there are three climbing areas accessible two and a half hours either side of low water. There is also a cave about 6 metres above the sand on the north cliff of the island called Cat Hole.

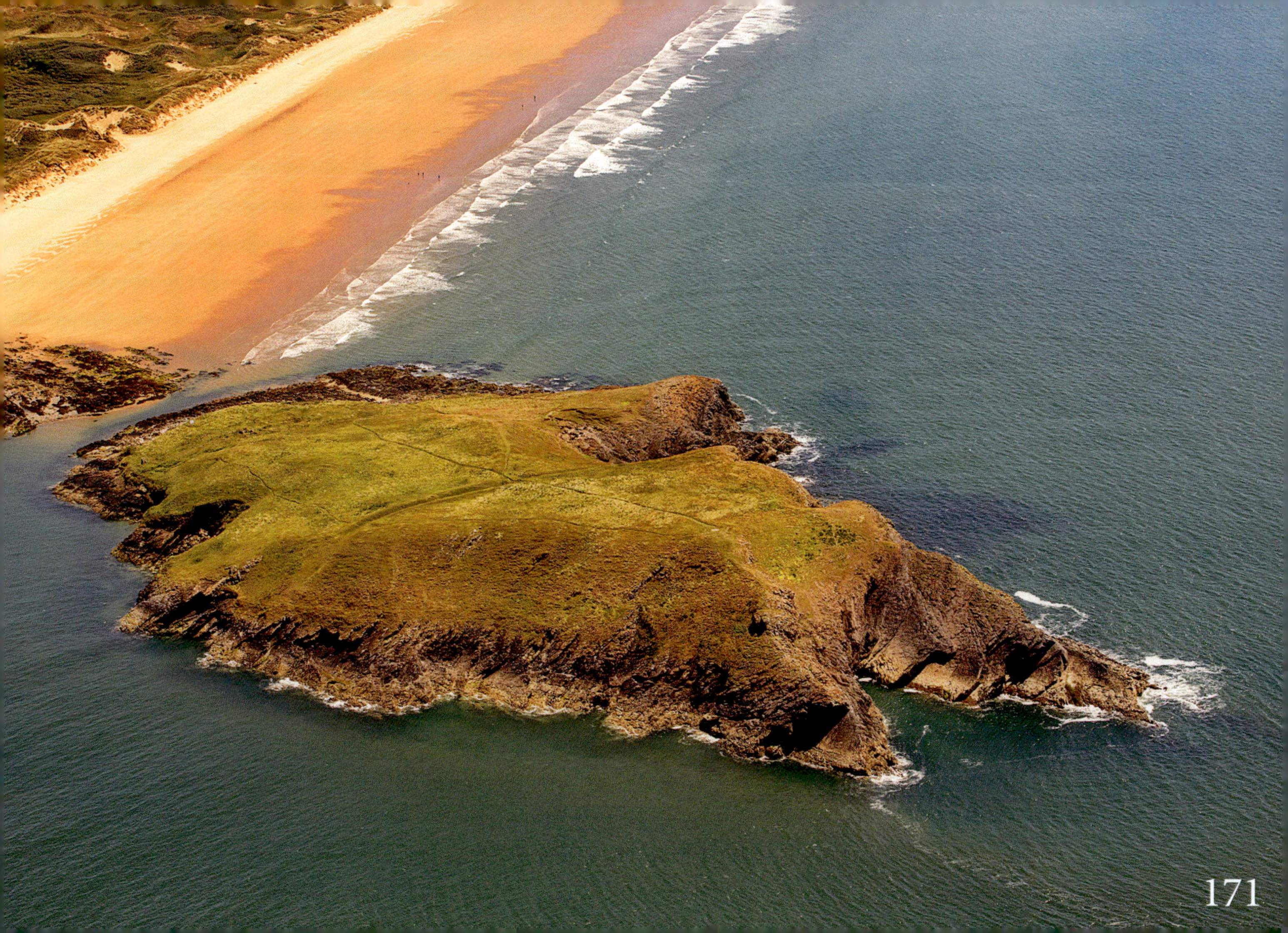

Bluepool Corner

Bluepool Corner is another one of Gower's amazing beaches. After visiting all the beaches along the Gower coast so far, this little gem will surprise you. A relatively quiet beach, until a recent online video brought attention to it, many people will walk past unaware of how special it is. Apart from the unspoilt sand at low tide, there is a deep tidal pool which is rumoured to be bottomless, although in reality it is between 4 and 8 metres deep depending on conditions.

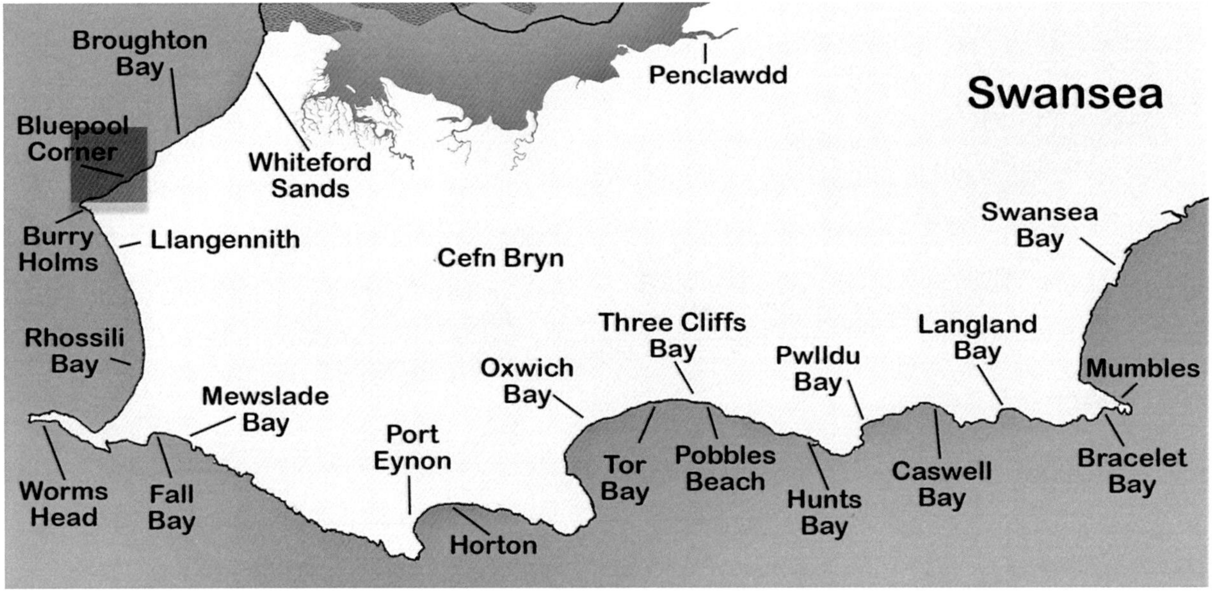

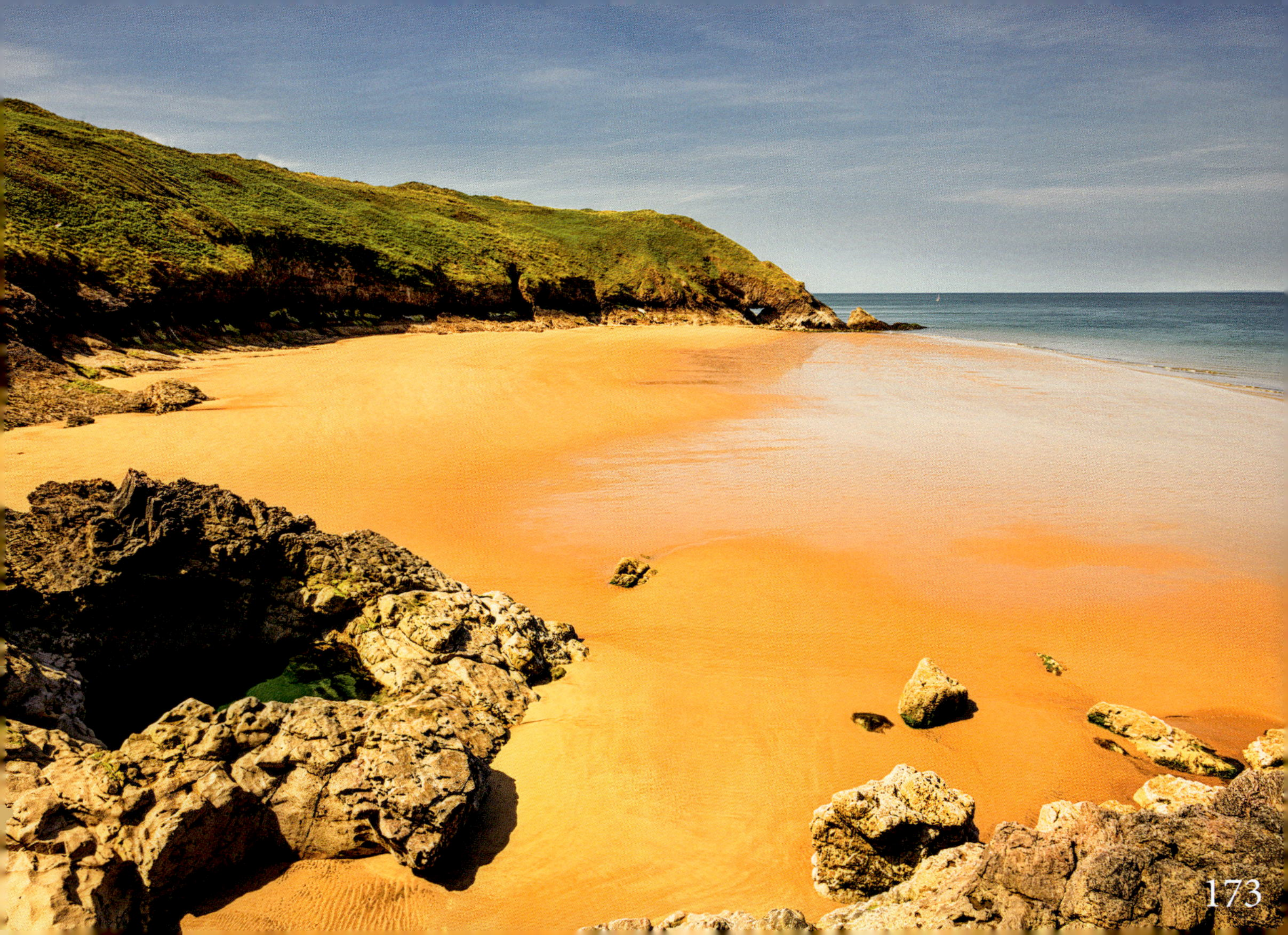

Bluepool Corner

Bluepool is known for diving into, but people should be aware of cold water shock when jumping in. The RNLI get several call outs to Bluepool every year. If it isn't related to the pool itself, it's the sea - swimming isn't recommended here due to strong rip currents. You also shouldn't enter the pool when the sea is close as you can get dragged out of the pool by the waves. Despite the danger associated with this beach, it is well worth carefully clambering down the path onto the sand.

With the tide out, you can walk along the sand to the natural sea arch called Three Chimneys where gold coins were found from a Portuguese shipwreck were discovered in the 18th century.

This photo shows Bluepool with the tide in. Walking past, you would have no idea how much of a special beach this is. The best way to get to the beach is walking along the coast path from Broughton.

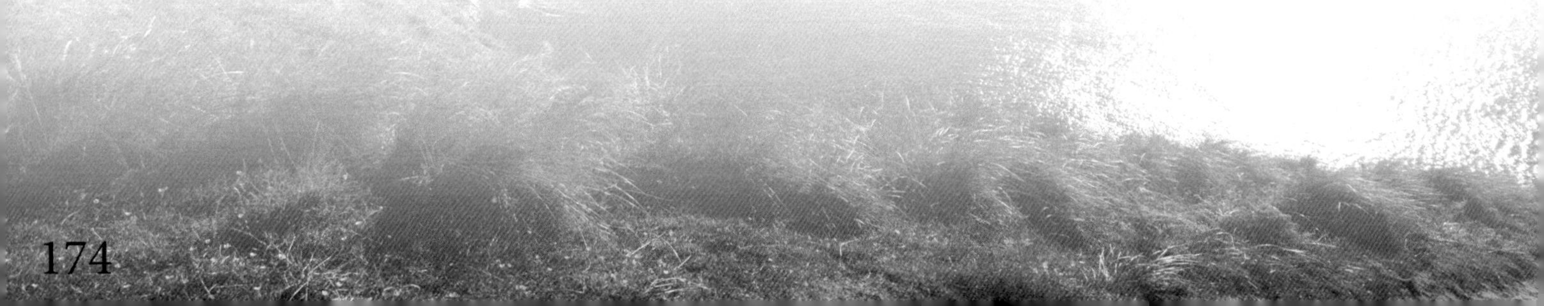

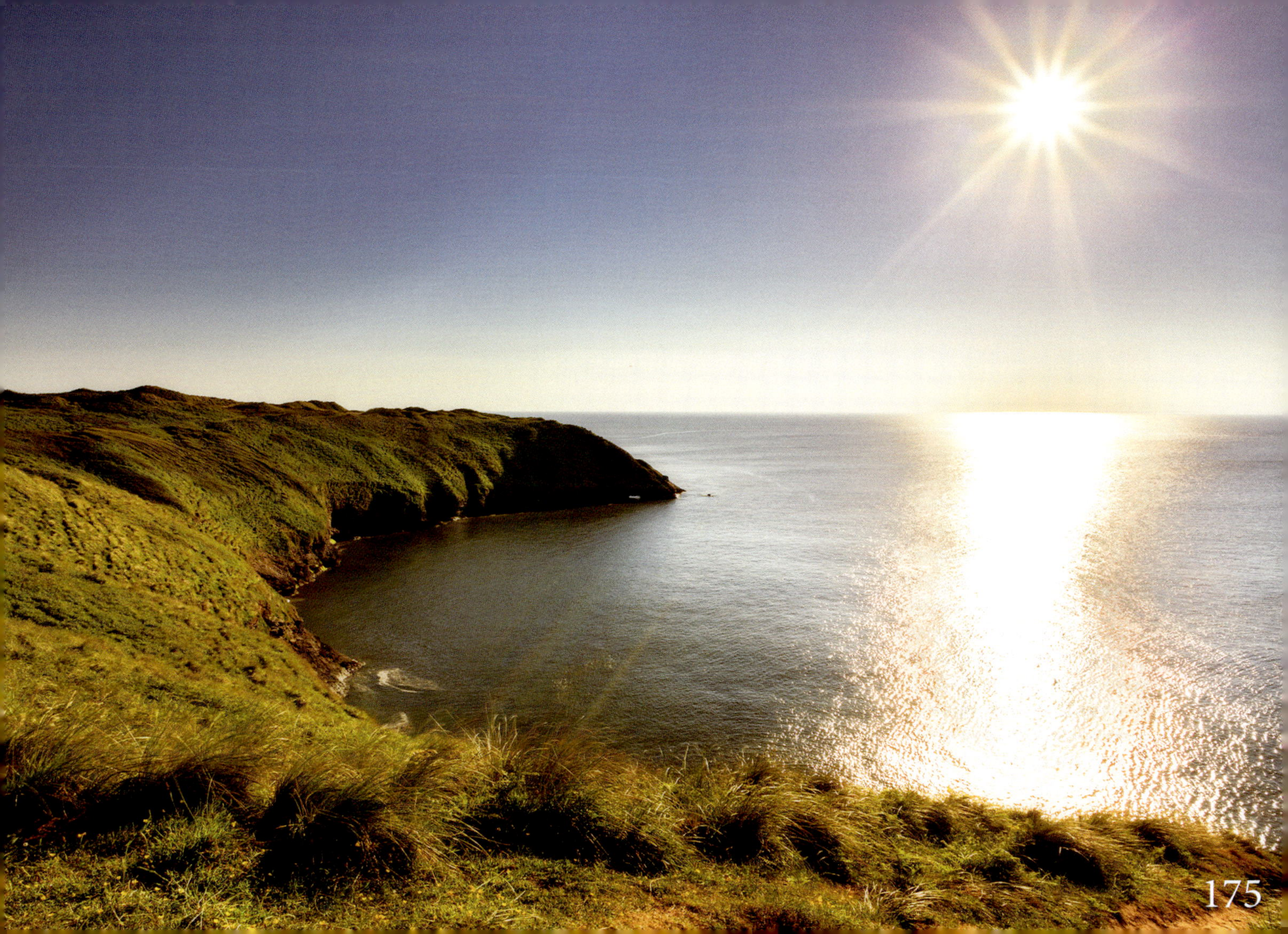

Broughton Bay

"Bruff-ton", "Braw-ton" or "Brow-ton", there is no definite way of saying it and people from the area can't seem to agree. Regardless of how it is said, it is another of the beautiful beaches of Gower that deserves a visit. However, with the Loughour Estuary so close, swimming isn't recommended due to strong currents and rip tides. The easiest way to access the beach is from the caravan site. This photo was taken just before the sun disappeared for the day. I love the texture in the golden grass and the way the rocks on the right point towards the sun.

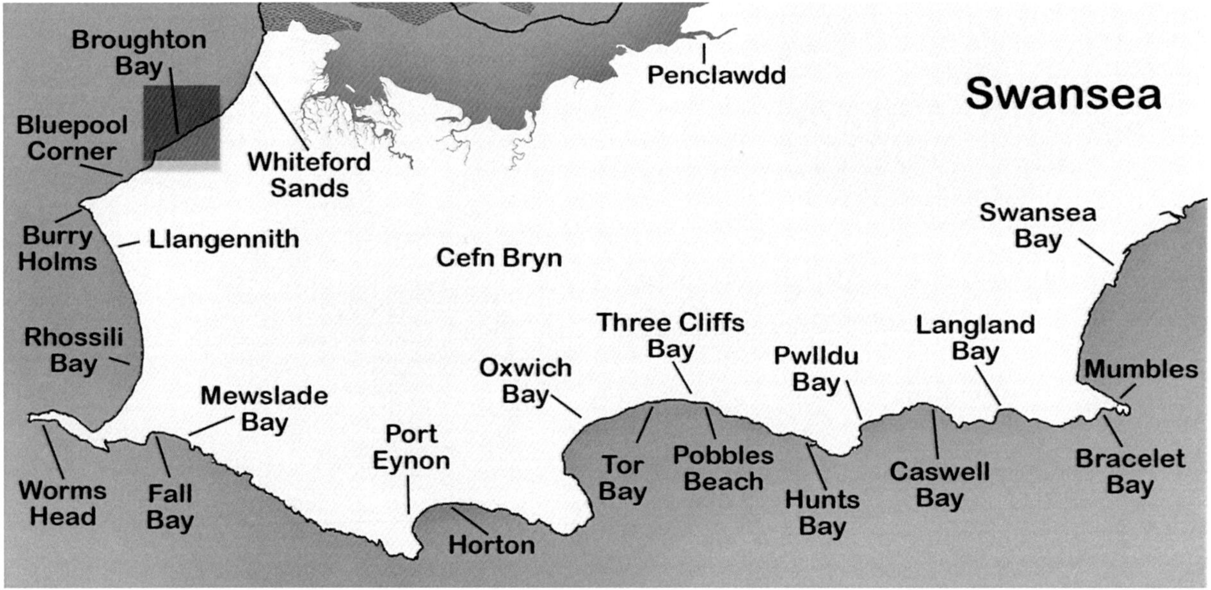

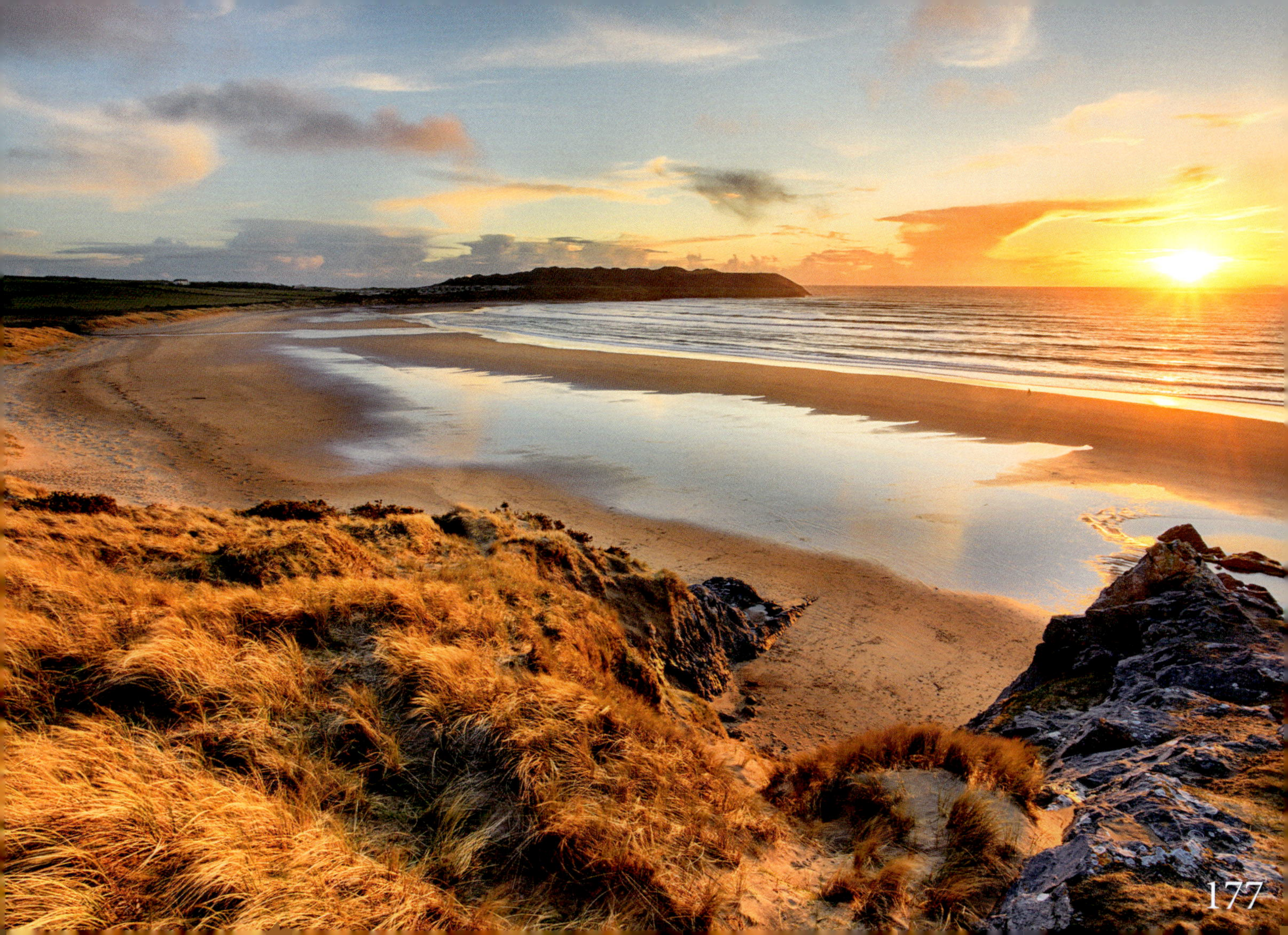

Broughton Bay

The constantly shifting sands occasionally expose old land surfaces and in 1931, ancient tree stumps were visible. Peat and clay have also been exposed from time to time. Red deer bones have been recorded and a 17th century sword found. This area has had its fair share of shipwrecks, mostly because of the proximity to the Loughor Estuary. On 7th August 1880, strong winds caused Tidy, a 105 ton brigantine, to be driven ashore.

It was these pools that caught my eye whilst walking around the beach, some were still and others were catching the wind causing ripples to form. I crouched down low to emphasise one of the pools whilst keeping the sun and the headland in the photo.

At the east end of the bay is Spritsail Tor, also known as Prissen's Tor. On the north side of the tor is Spritsail Tor Cave above the high water mark. First excavated in 1839 and subsequently in 1849 and 1945, artefacts from the early Bronze Age through to Roman times have been found.

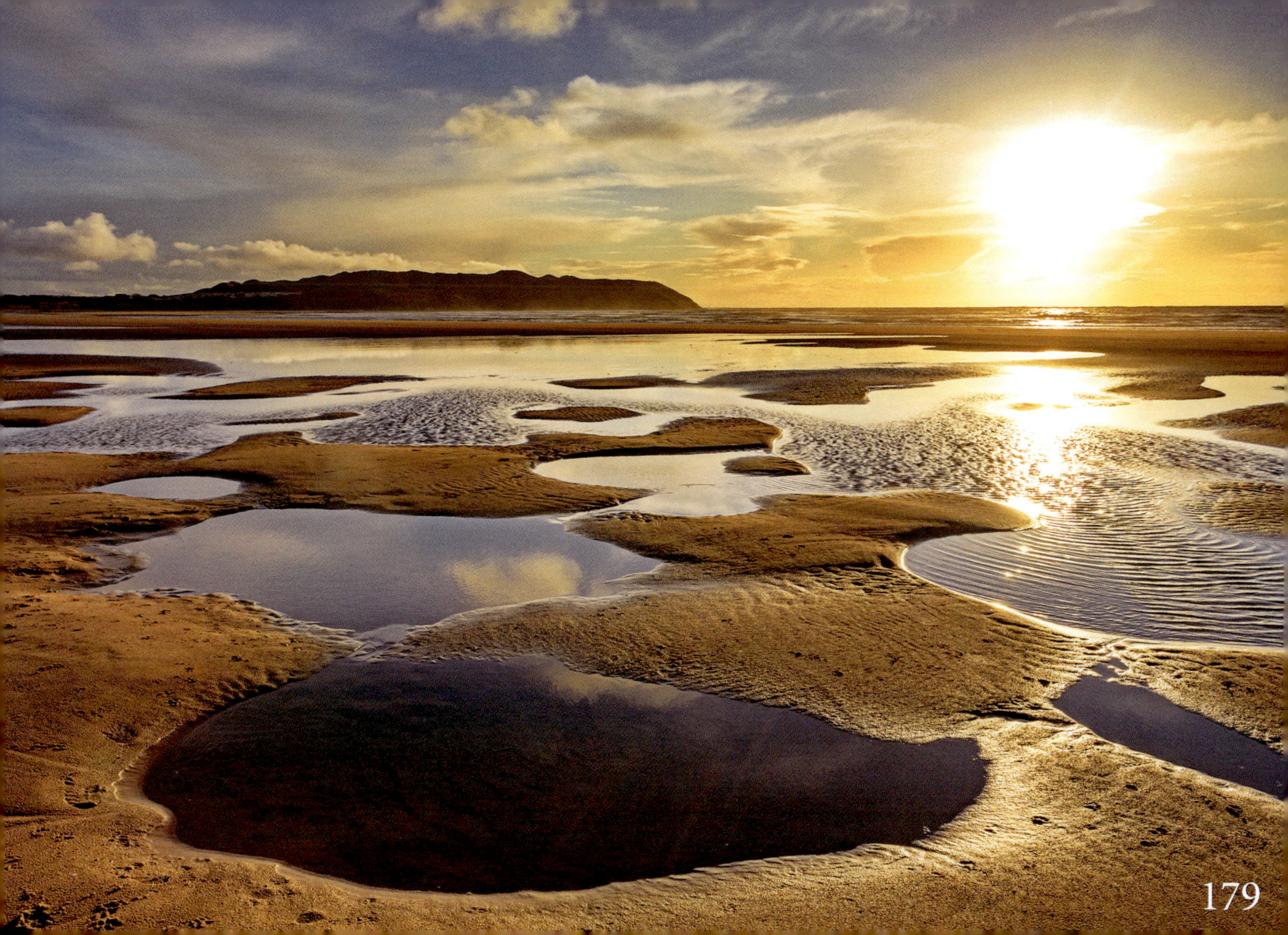

Whiteford Sands

Just on from Broughton is Whiteford Sands (pronounced Whitford), a long beach whose two mile expanse seems to go on for ever when you walk along it. With the closeness of the Loughor Estuary and the strong currents, flotsam and jetsam is often present in large quantities ranging from fishing nets to plastic bottles to whole tree trunks and even the occasional unexploded World War II bomb! As it isn't suitable for bathing or water sports, it is one of the quieter beaches to go to although you might see the occasional naturist!

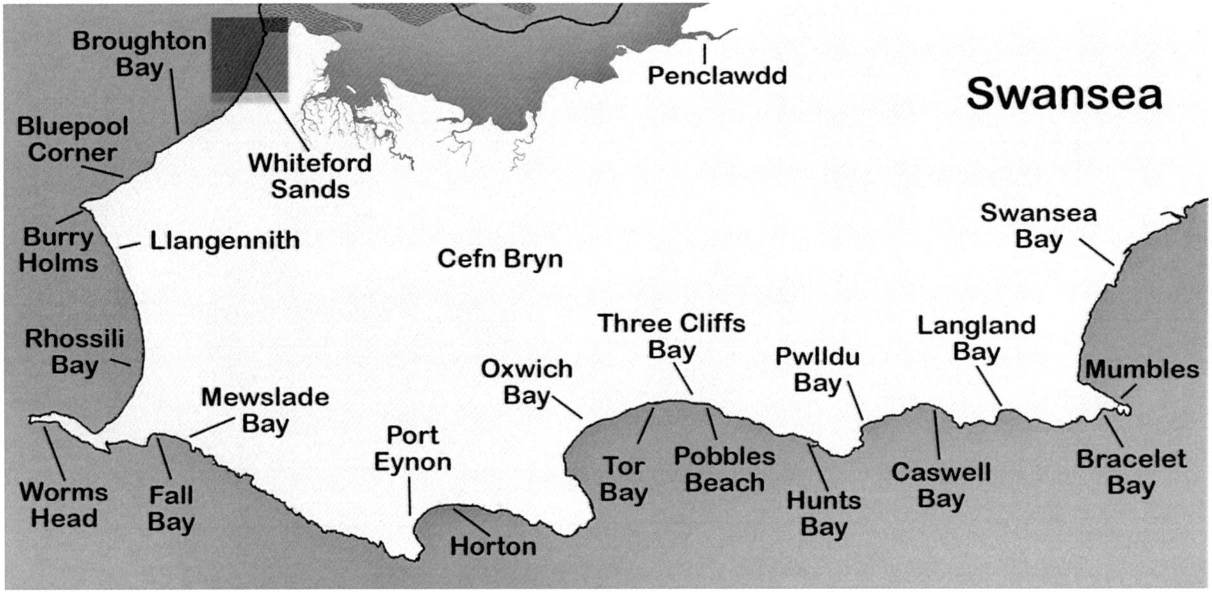

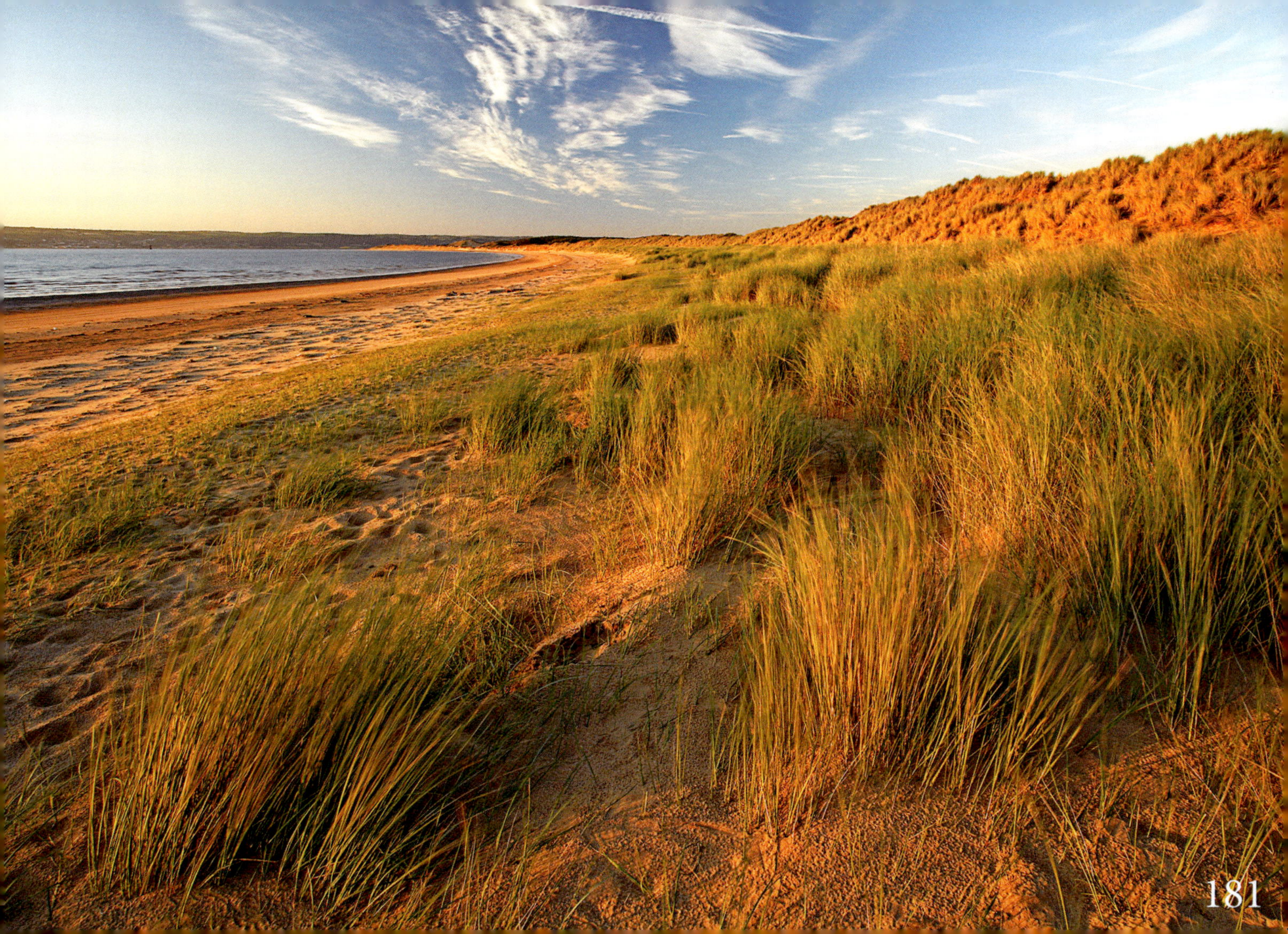

Whiteford Sands

The beach is a lovely place for a long walk, but the tide can come in faster than you can walk, so be wary. A decent way along the beach, you will see wreckage from ships, in particular a rusty capstan and chain. With sand banks and strong currents, it is hardly surprising. On 22 January 1868, a series of ships heavily laden with coal heading from Llanelli were caught out by a huge swell. 16 of the ships sunk that night and the beach was littered with bodies and wreckage the following morning!

Cockle pickers can often be seen on Whiteford as it is part of the Burry Inlet Cockle Fishery. Cockle picking in the area dates back to the Mesolithic period with evidence gathered from middens in the area, which ties in nicely with the Mesolithic finds on Burry Holms. The cockle picking changed to a commercial scale in the Roman times. To control the picking of the cockles, the Burry Inlet Cockle Fishery Order was established in 1965 to ensure the cockles aren't over picked. The cockles are an important part of the diet of several bird species too.

As you walk along the beach, you will come across an incongruous twisted mess of reinforced concrete sticking out of the otherwise unbroken sands. There is little information about this structure, except that it was a Coastal Observation Post. The flat beach would probably have been viewed during World War II as a potential invasion force landing point.

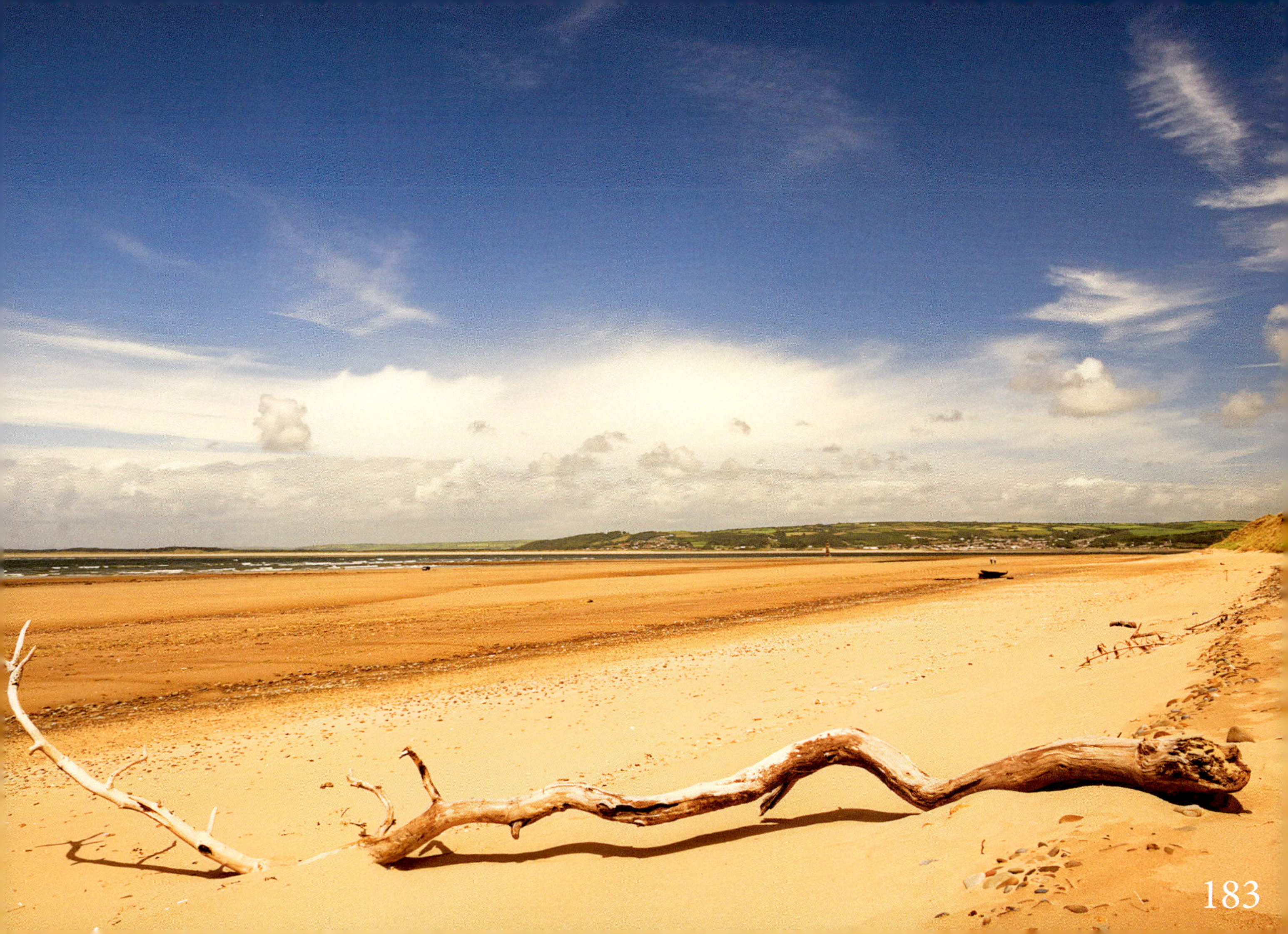

Whiteford Sands

At the end of Whiteford Sands lies Whiteford Lighthouse. It was originally built in 1854, just north of the present day lighthouse, but was damaged when debris was caught in the supports and a ship later collided with it. The lamp was lit in the newly built lighthouse in 1866, designed by local engineer John Bowen. In 1919, upgrading the light to a more powerful gas lamp was considered, but the decision was taken to instead decommission it and build a new lighthouse at Burry Port, which would better serve the estuary.

In 1921, the light was extinguished for the last time and the structure left to the sea. The lighthouse, the only cast iron lighthouse in Britain to be washed by the sea, became a scheduled ancient monument in 1981. In 2000, it was put up for sale for the sum of £1, but under the proviso that the new owner spent a potential £100,000 to repair it!

It is well worth the walk to Whiteford Point to see the lighthouse and at low tide, you can carefully walk out to it!

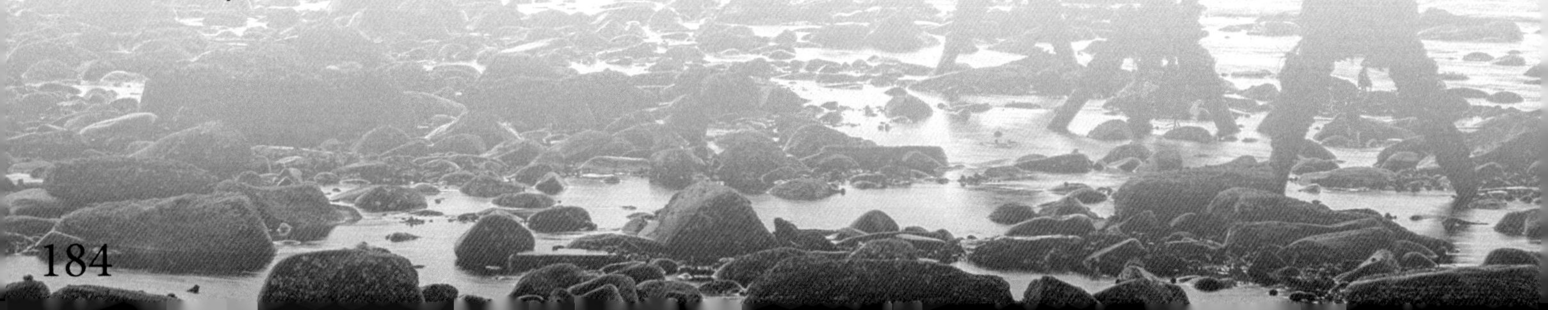

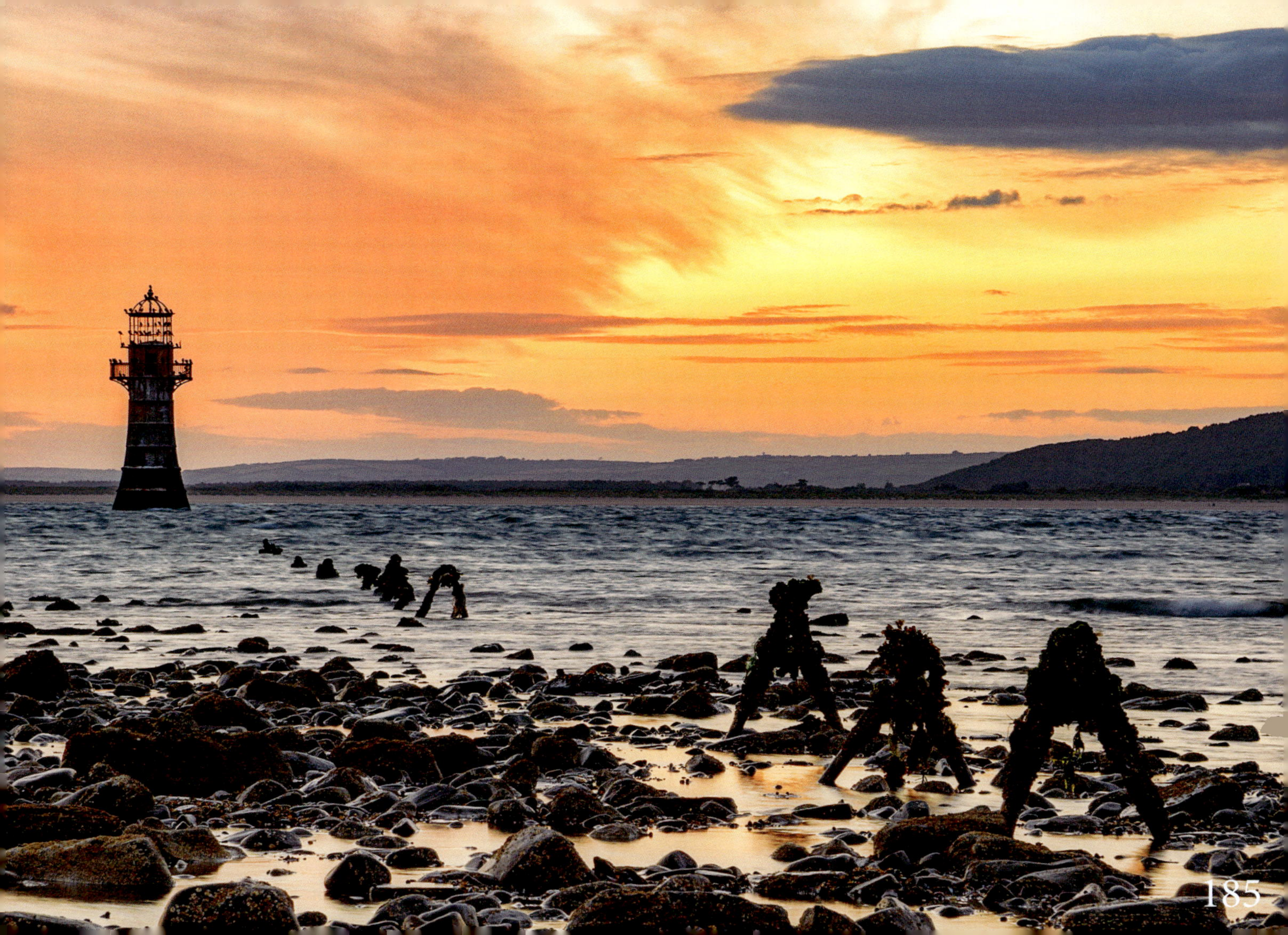

Penclawdd

This photo was taken from a 4 seater plane that we flew around Gower to see it from a different perspective. Near Penclawdd, the salt marsh looks spectacular with little water channels looking like veins feeding the larger river. The green on the mud made this look very much like a tree! Much of the north Gower coast is salt marsh, from Landimore Marsh east of Whiteford Point to Llanrhidian Marsh which runs all the way along the Loughor Estuary to Gowerton. The salt marshes are very important habitats for a wide range of plants and animals.

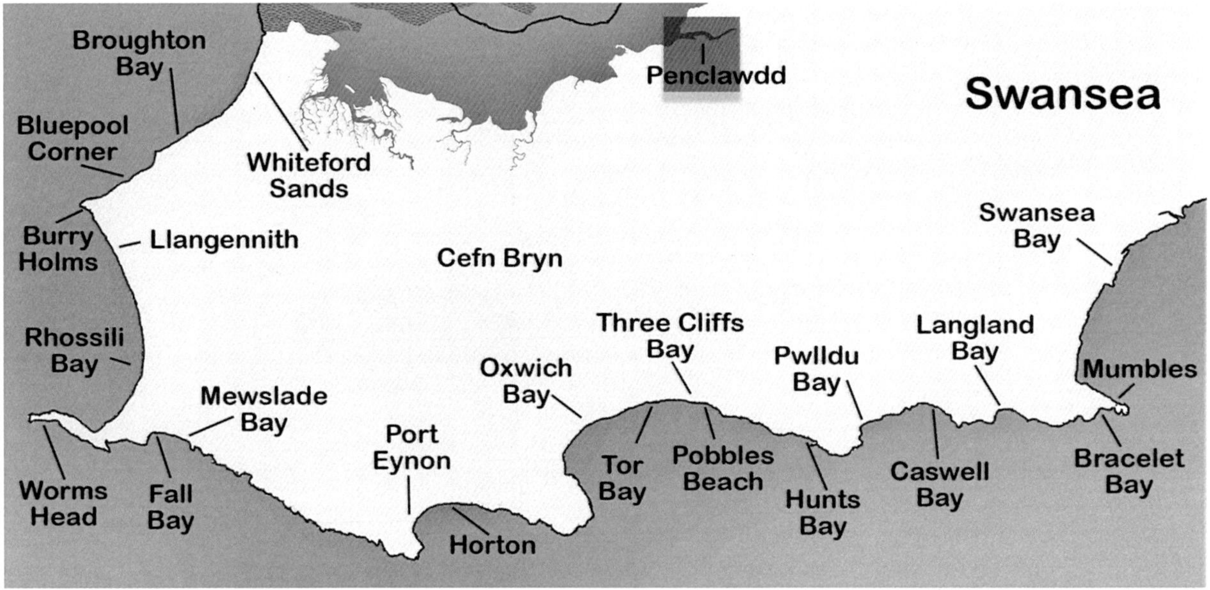

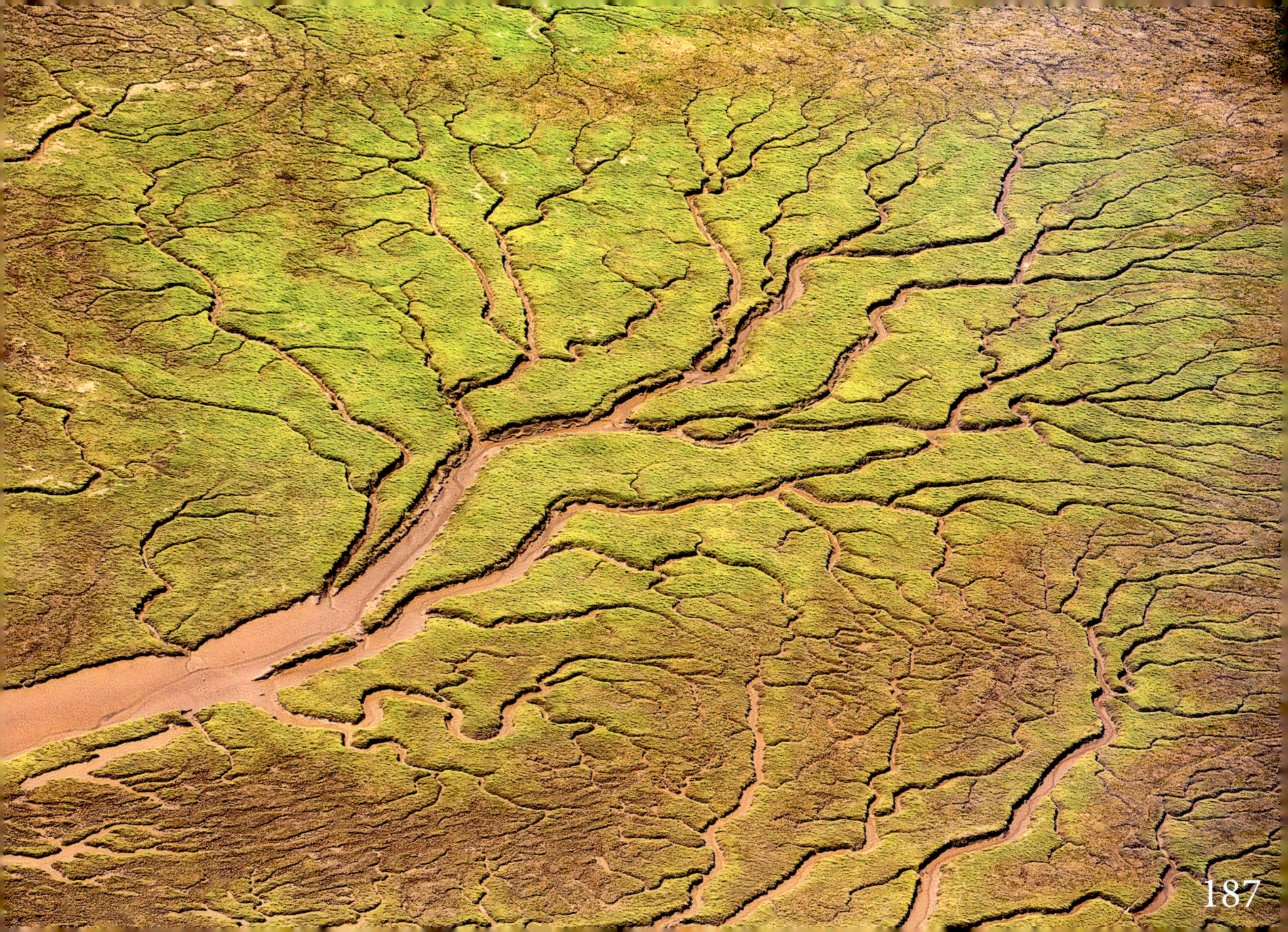

Penclawdd

The marshes are also important as a natural 'soft' flood defence, but unfortunately in the past, large proportions of Britain's salt marshes have been drained and reclaimed for agriculture. The marshes on Gower have been kept and are used for grazing. Gower Salt Marsh Lamb is said to be sweet and tender.

Penclawdd was once a busy port exporting copper, coal and seafood. Although the copper and coal exports have long since stopped, the cockle industry is still thriving with Penclawdd cockles exported all over the world! In the 19th century Penclawdd had hundreds of cockle pickers daily waiting for the tide so they could go out and rake the sands to find the small marine bivalves that would provide the all important income for their family.

This photo was taken during a rising tide; by the time I had set up the photo on dry ground and pressed the shutter, an inch of water covered my shoes – proof of how fast the tide can rise here!

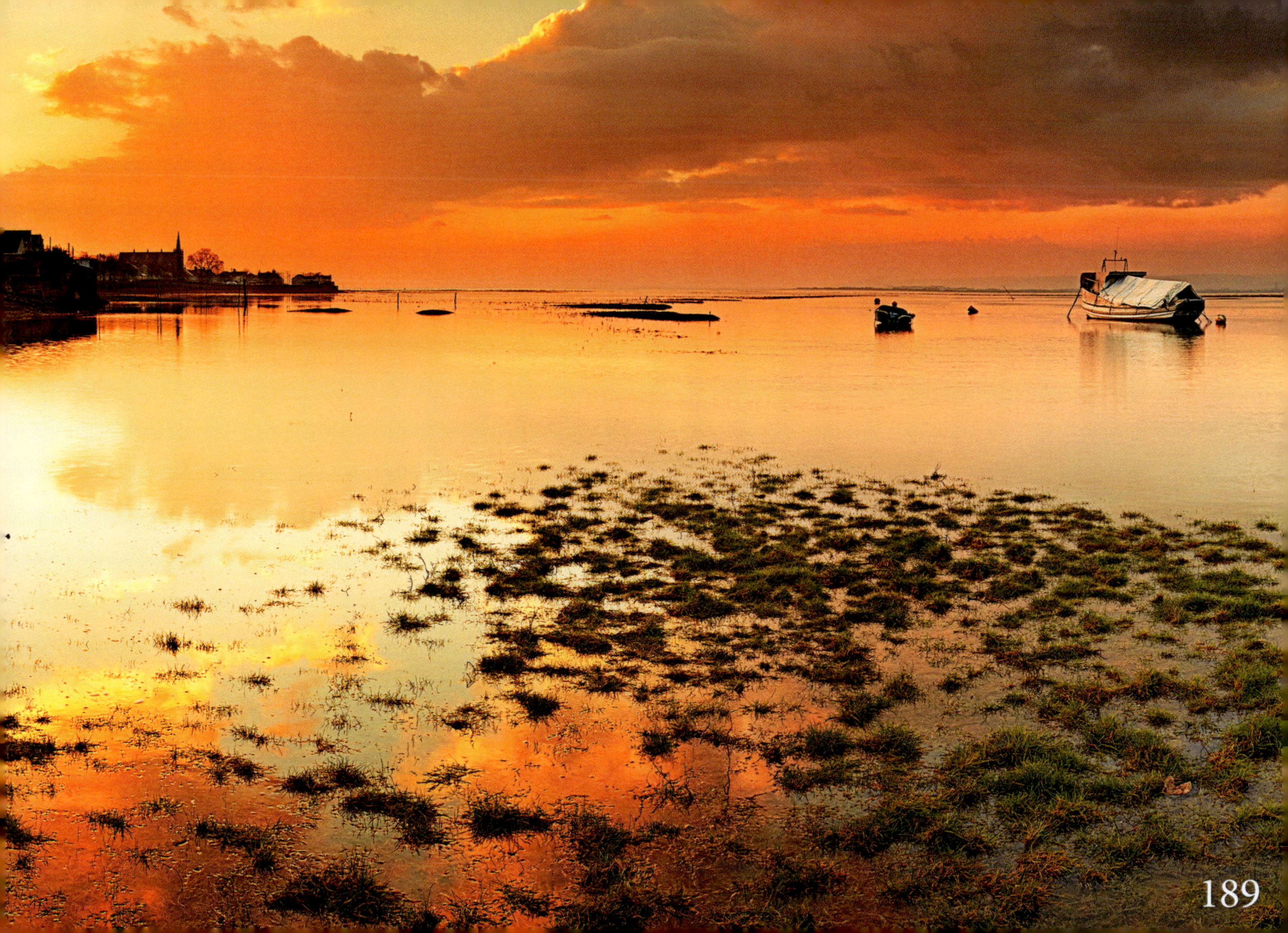

Parc-le-Breos

Park Wood, or Parc-le-Breos, was once a medieval deer park of the Lords of Gower (de Breos). In the park is Cathole Cave which was once used by hunter gatherers between 10,000 and 20,000 years ago. Bones from mammoths, woolly rhinoceroses, bears and hyenas have been found in the cave. In 2010, an archaeologist discovered the oldest known rock art in Britain. Uranium dating showed it was at least 14,000 years old! Shortly after the discovery was made, the ancient artwork was vandalised so a substantial metal grille now stops access into the cave.

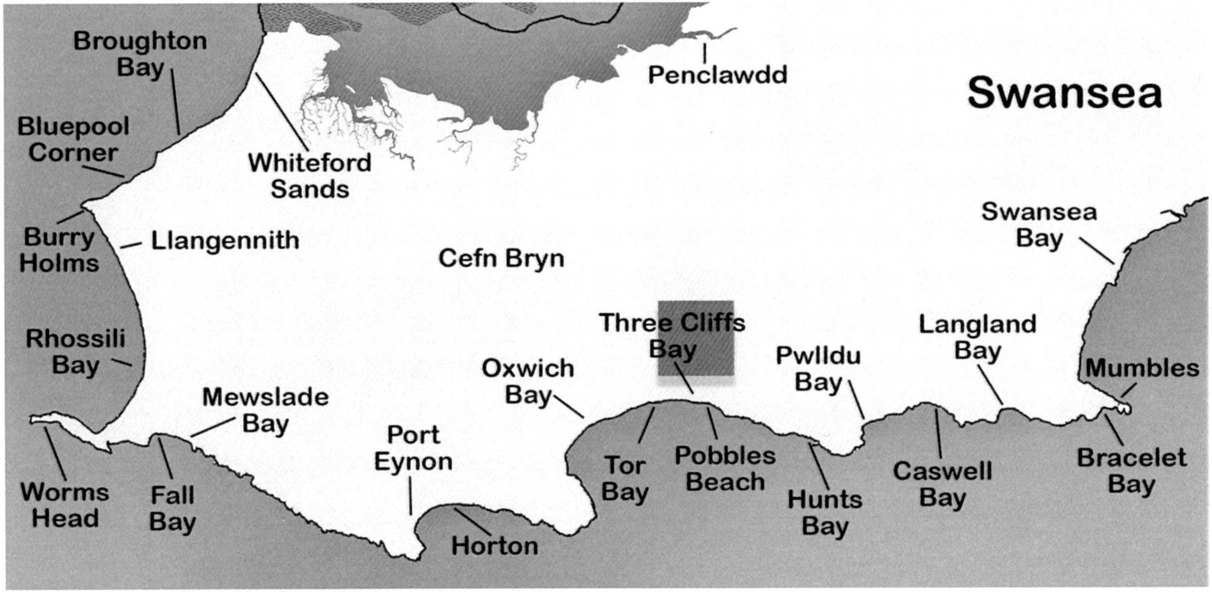

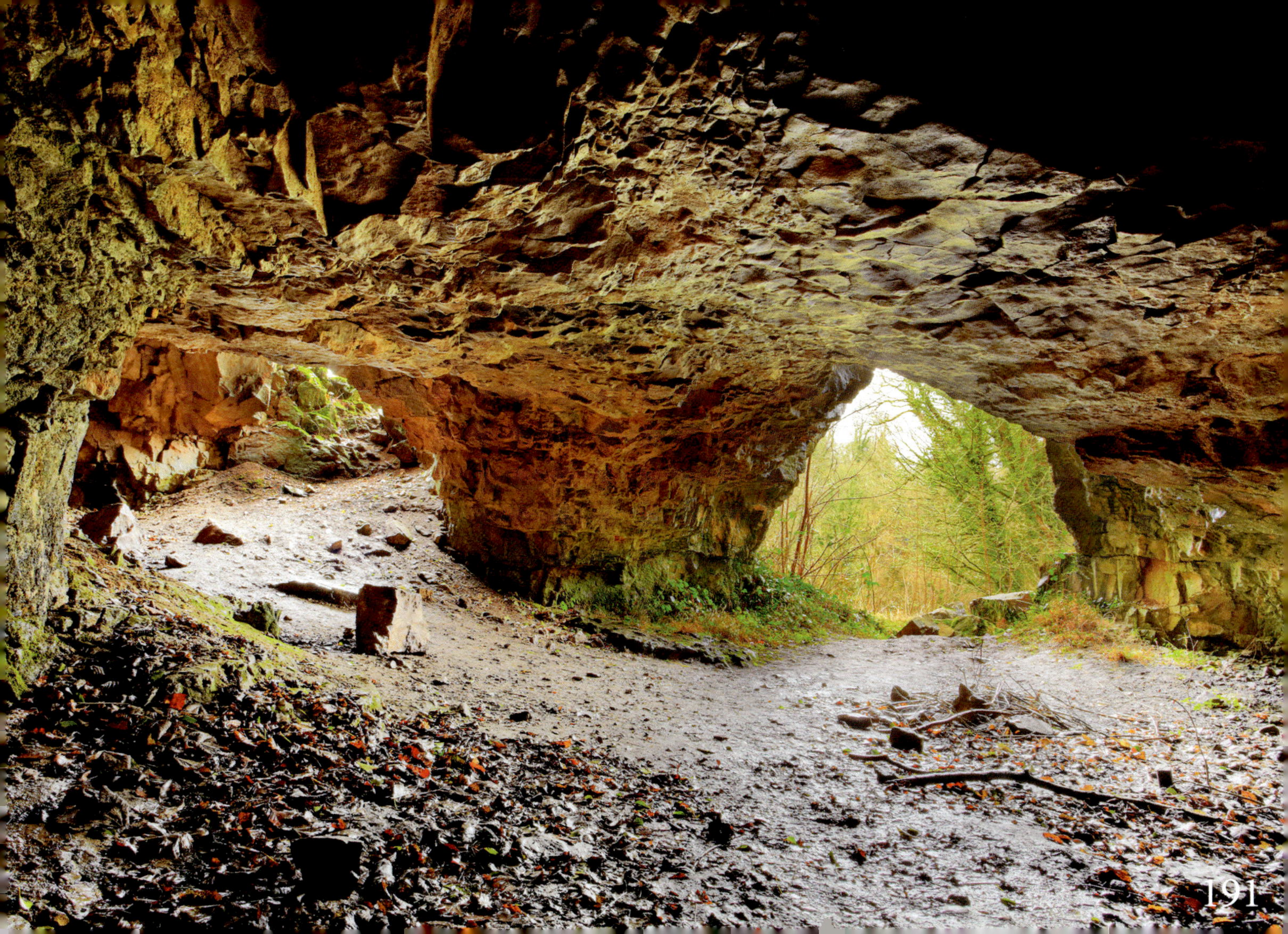

Cefn Bryn

There are many SSSIs on Gower, one being Broad Pool which is a large circular pool on common land below Cefn Bryn. It is a natural shallow basin which is filled with water, thanks to glacial boulder clay which subsided into a sinkhole in the limestone below, sealing it and making it watertight. It is known to have existed since 1645 and has only dried out a few times despite only being around a meter deep. There is evidence that it has been managed with removal of sediment and vegetation since the 18th century. Some rare plants can be found here.

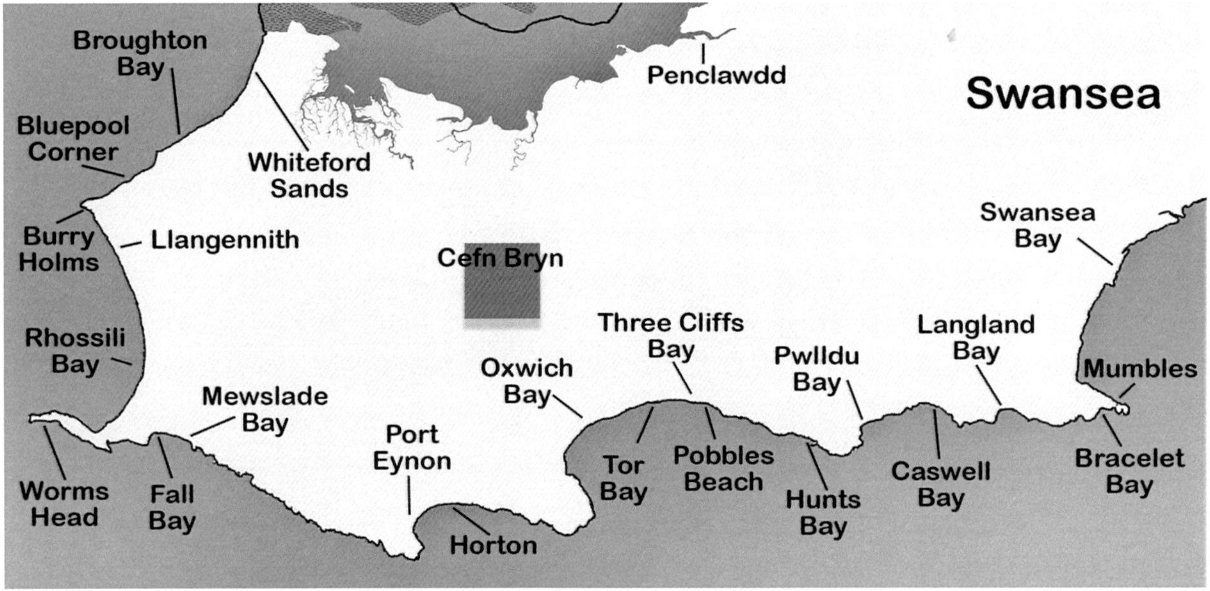

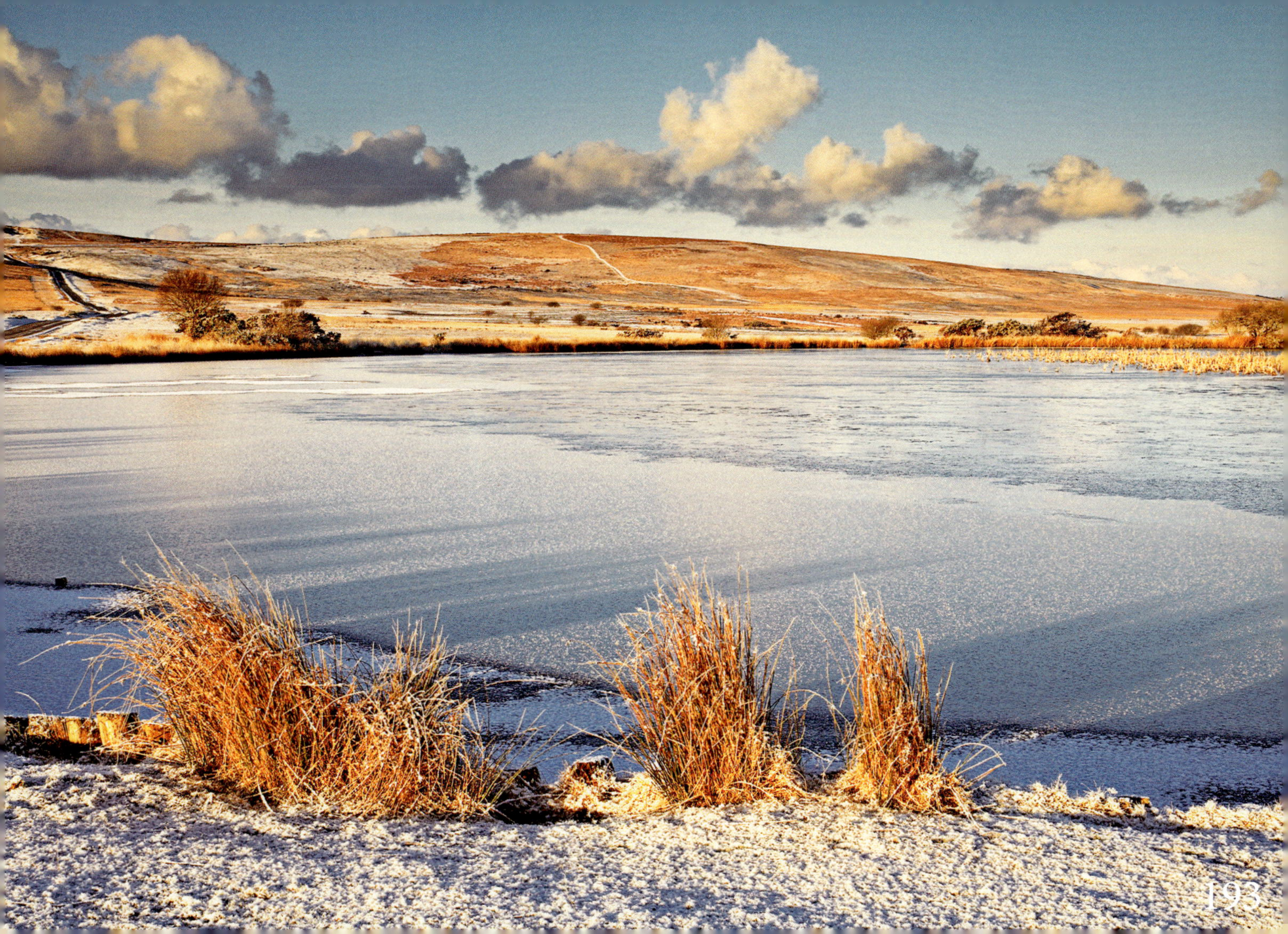

Cefn Bryn

Cefn Bryn, Gower's second highest hill at 188 metres above sea level, is a large upland area in the centre of Gower. Cefn Bryn bears scars of the industrial past with several quarries. It also boasts numerous springs, several cairns and a holy well. There are many tracks and paths over the area and it is now open access land, thanks to the Countryside and Rights of Way Act 2000.

Gower covers just 73 square miles, but is home to 83 scheduled ancient monuments! One of the most well known is Arthur's Stone (Maen Ceti) on Cefn Bryn. It is a Neolithic Burial Chamber that dates to around 2500BC and takes its name from the legend of King Arthur, although no bones have ever been found. It was one of the first sites to be protected by the Ancient Monuments Act of 1882. There are several legends connected with Arthur's Stone, one being that it was a pebble found in King Arthur's shoe. However, the capstone, which weighs in excess of 25 tonnes, is an erratic deposited by a glacier in the Ice Age. An erratic is a rock different in size and type of the local area. The Neolithic tomb was dug under it and propped up with slabs to form the burial chamber.

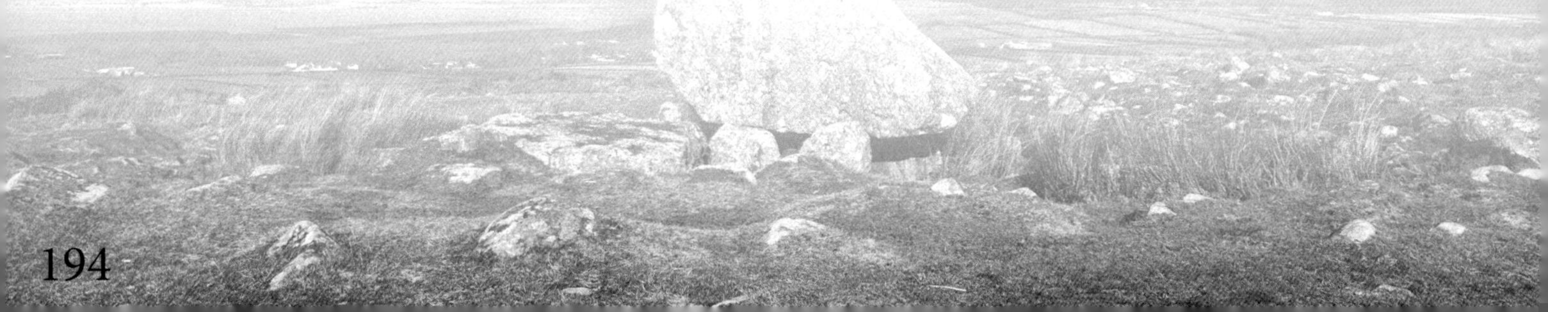

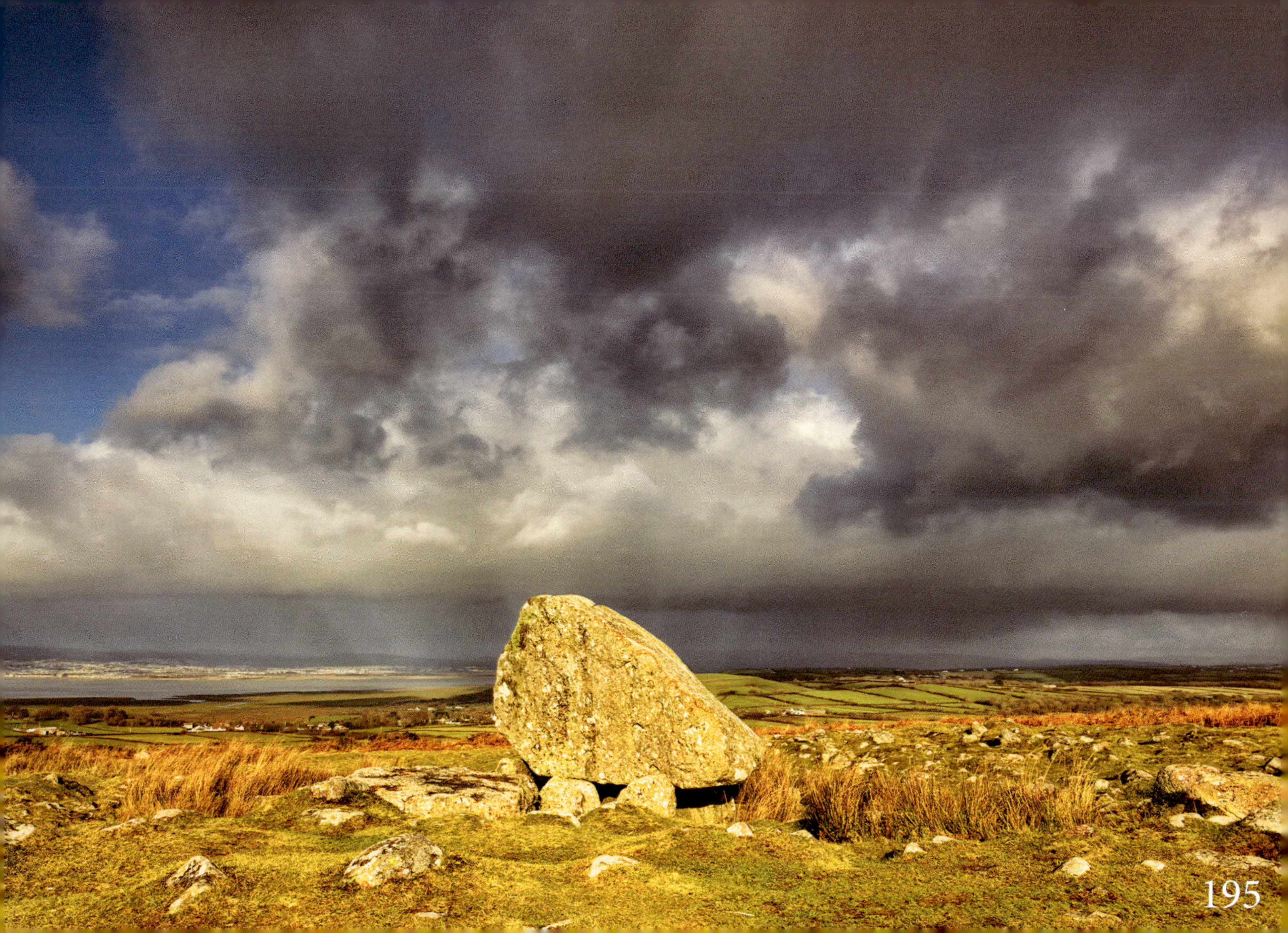

Cefn Bryn

When I moved to the Swansea area in 2005, the very little research I had made into the area paid off as it meant I saw it with completely fresh eyes. When I arrived I had no idea it was there, didn't know how many beaches it had and had no inclination into how it would shape my photography. Discovering Gower was a fantastic journey, each beach unique and each hill with different views. When I started to looking into the history of Gower, I was amazed at how much there is packed into such a small peninsular. The journey of discovery isn't over and I have a feeling it never will be – I've barely scraped the surface here with what I have learnt and photographed.

I hope you have enjoyed my photographic journey around Gower as much as I have enjoyed taking the photos and writing about it. You can keep up to date with my new photos on Facebook and also my website at www.DanSantillo.com.

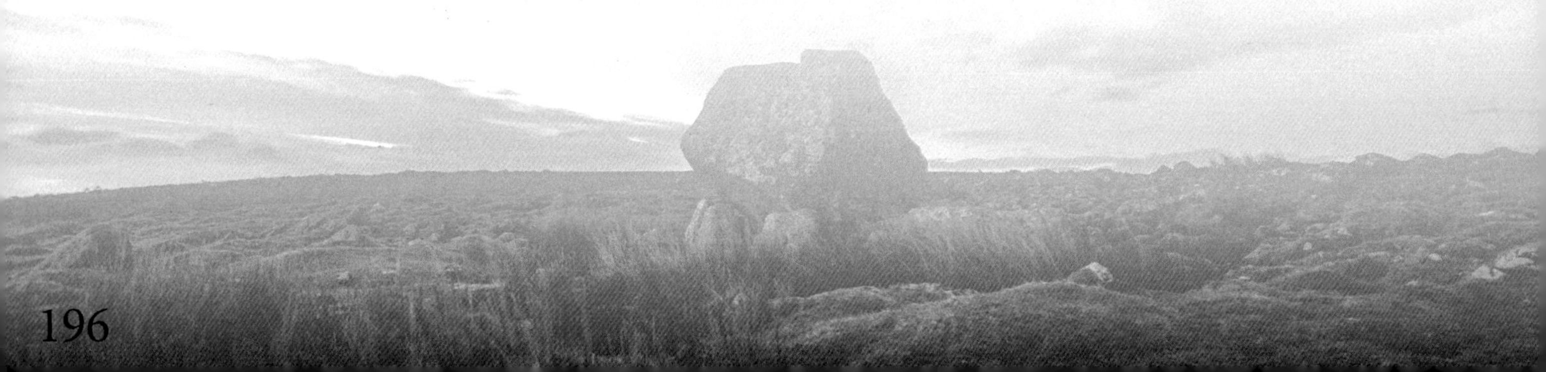

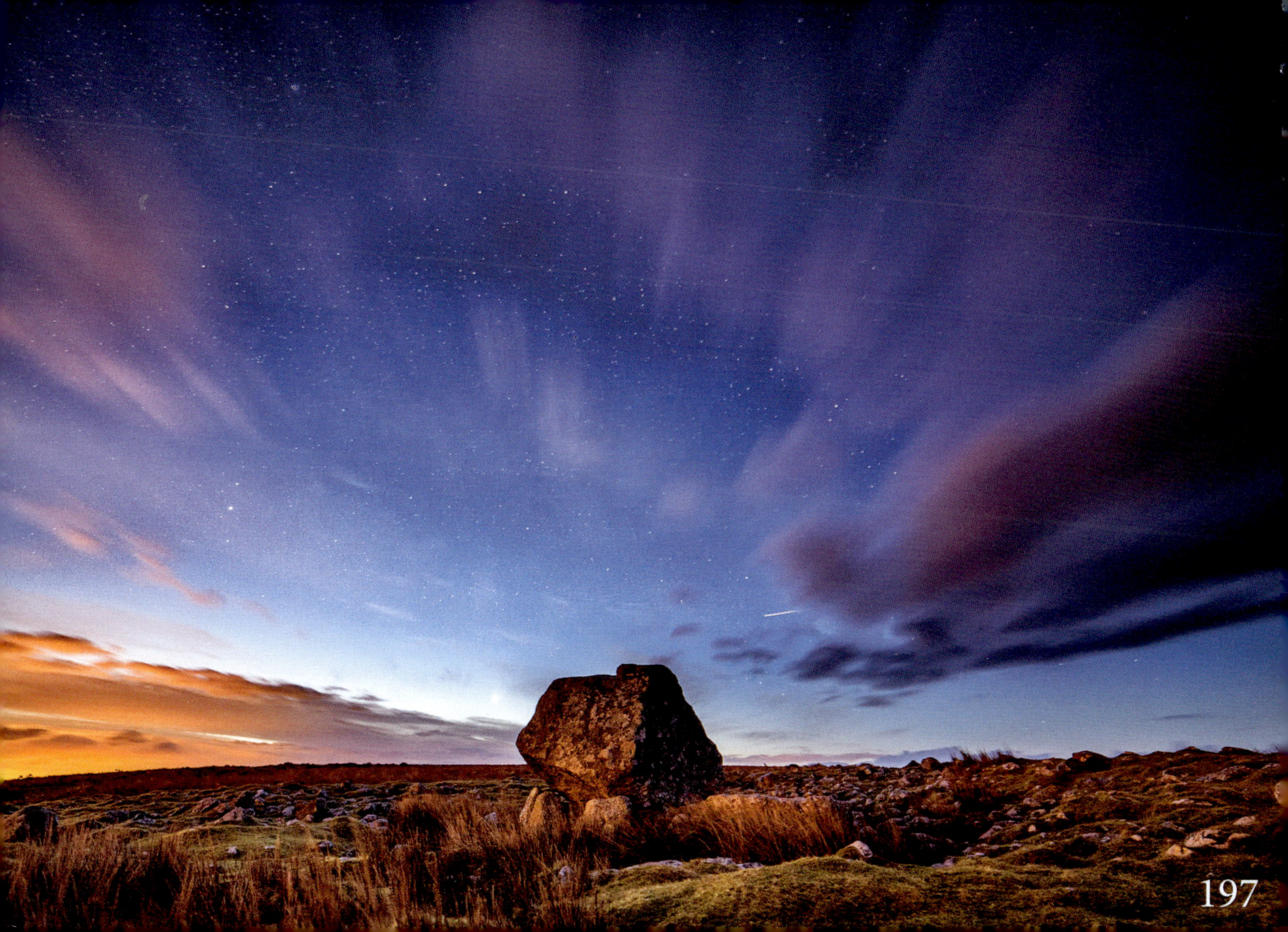

Useful Information

Recommended Reading:

A Guide to Gower; The Gower Society; ISBN 0902767232
Historic Gower; Paul Davis; ISBN 0715407325
Gower Coast Shipwrecks; Carl Smith; ISBN 0951528149
Mumbles Lifeboat; Carl Smith; ISBN 0951528106
The Story of Gower; Wendy Hughes; ISBN 0863812171
Pwlldu Remembered; Heather Holt; ISBN 0952916505
Ordnance Survey Map Explorer 164 Gower/Gŵyr

Websites with useful information:

https://www.telegraph.co.uk, http://www.nciwormshead.org.uk, https://www.nci.org.uk, https://www.facebook.com, https://www.coflein.gov.uk, https://www.walescoastpath.gov.uk, http://beachguide.wales, https://swmc.org.uk, http://caveburial.ubss.org.uk, http://www.shellfish.org.uk, https://www.gov.uk, https://www.geolsoc.org.uk, https://wp.lancs.ac.uk, https://www.walesonline.co.uk, https://en.wikipedia.org, https://naturalresources.wales, http://www.wirefresh.com, https://www.leisurepro.com, https://www.woodlandtrust.org.uk, https://www.nationaltrust.org.uk

Maps:

The maps are based on maps created on Inkatlas. © OpenStreetMap contributors (openstreetmap.org), Inkatlas. Map data Feb 17, 2019. 1:125000

Little Book Company.org
from The Calendar Company

Published and printed in the UK by Little Book Company,
part of The Calendar Printing Company Ltd.